The Algiers Motel Incident

THE
ALGIERS
MOTEL
INCIDENT

John Hersey

WITH A NEW INTRODUCTION BY

Thomas J. Sugrue

The Johns Hopkins University Press

Baltimore and London

To the students of Pierson College

Copyright © 1968 by John Hersey. Copyright renewed 1996 by Brook Hersey.
Originally published by Alfred A. Knopf
Introduction copyright © 1998 by The Johns Hopkins University Press
All rights reserved
Printed in the United States of America on acid-free paper

Johns Hopkins Paperbacks edition, 1998
9 8 7 6 5 4 3 2 1

The Johns Hopkins University Press
2715 North Charles Street
Baltimore, Maryland 21218-4319
The Johns Hopkins Press Ltd., London

Library of Congress Cataloging-in-Publication Data
Hersey, John, 1914–
  The Algiers Motel Incident / John Hersey : with a new introduction by
Thomas J. Sugrue.
    p.   cm.
  Originally published : New York : Knopf, 1968. With new introd.
  Includes bibliographical references.
  ISBN 0-8018-5777-5 (alk. paper)
   1. Riots—Michigan—Detroit.   2. Detroit (Mich.)—History.   I. Title.
F574.D4H4   1997
977.4´34—dc21
                                                   97-29469
                                                    CIP

A catalog record for this book is available from the British Library.

Contents

I   The Odor of a Case
July 26–31

II   Three Cops and Three Days
July 23–5

III   Auburey and His Circle

IV   Confession
July 31

V   The Algiers Motel Incident
July 25–6

VI   Aftermath
July 31 and after

Introduction
John Hersey and the Tragedy of Race

Thomas J. Sugrue

In August 1967, John Hersey, then master of Pierson College at Yale and an accomplished novelist, rushed to Detroit to examine firsthand the aftermath of the city's bloody riot. In nearly a week of violence in the Motor City, forty-three people had died. Seventeen thousand armed officials, including the city and state police, the National Guard, and the 103rd Airborne, patrolled the city and arrested more than seven thousand people, disproportionately young African American men. In the aftermath of the uprising, President Lyndon Johnson created the National Advisory Commission on Civil Disorders to investigate the causes of the urban riots during the "long hot summers" of the mid-1960s. Hersey had been invited to write part of the commission's report, but declined, preferring the freedom to conduct his own inquiry.[1]

Hersey had long since established himself as one of America's leading fiction writers, though he was most famous for his book *Hiroshima* (1946), a passionate journalistic account of the dropping of the first atomic bomb on Japan. Born in 1914 to a family of American missionaries in China, Hersey began his career as a writer for *Time* magazine in the late 1930s, after a brief stint as secretary to novelist Sinclair Lewis. During World War II, Hersey quickly established himself as a writer of great talent. He won the Pulitzer Prize at age 30 for his novel about the American occupation of Sicily, *A Bell for Adano* (1944). Both in fiction and nonfiction, Hersey passionately engaged some of the most controversial issues of his era, including Jewish resistance to Nazism, racial prejudice, educational reform, student radicalism, and the brutality of war. A political liberal committed to civil rights and a staunch supporter of the Democratic Party, Hersey was drawn toward the troubled streets of Detroit.²

Detroit in the mid-1960s was a place of paradox. Nationally celebrated as a "model city" of race relations, it had been a major beneficiary of government largesse during the Great Society. Under the leadership of liberal Democratic Mayor Jerome Cavanagh (1962–69), Detroit garnered more federal redevelopment and antipoverty money than any other city but New York. But mid-twentieth-century Detroit was also a troubled place, economically and racially. The nation's "Arsenal of Democracy" during World War II and the international capital of automobile production, the city went through a period of wrenching economic change and racial conflict beginning in the late 1940s and accelerating through the 1950s and '60s.³

Amidst the superficially prosperous post–World War II years, Detroit's economy began a steady decline. Between 1948 and 1967, Detroit lost nearly 130,000 manufacturing jobs. Many of the city's companies picked up and relocated to suburban and rural areas, and replaced thousands of unskilled workers with new "automated" manufacturing technology. This economic restructuring affected all Detroiters, but hit African Americans particularly hard. During and after World War II, Detroit had been a magnet for black migrants seeking steady and secure blue-collar jobs. But the city's economy promised more than it could deliver. Though a large number of blacks found work in the city's automobile factories and, increasingly, in city government, whole sectors of the city's labor market remained lily white throughout the 1940s, '50s, and '60s. In addition, black workers tended to hold the city's "meanest and dirt-

iest jobs," precisely the unskilled jobs that were beginning to disappear as companies downsized. By 1960, black unemployment
rates were more than double those of whites. Young blacks were hit
especially hard. Thirty-five percent of nineteen-year-old black
men, but only 8.9 percent of nineteen-year-old white males, were
out of work. Many underemployed youths hung out on street corners unable to find work; others were drawn into the city's expand-
ing underground economy.

Detroit also simmered with racial tension. As the city's black
population expanded between World War II and the 1967 riot,
white Detroiters joined in an enormous grassroots movement to
protect their segregated communities from black "invasions."
Angry white residents greeted black newcomers to their neighborhoods with pickets and protests, window breaking, and arson.
Often police officers stood silently by during the sieges; blacks
who happened to pass through white neighborhoods were regularly subjected to police stops and harrassment. In the early and
mid-1960s, white attacks on blacks were still alarmingly frequent,
making clear the high costs of breaching the invisible color lines
that divided the city. The consequence was that Detroit, like other
northern cities, remained strictly segregated by race. The only familiar white faces in African American neighborhoods belonged to
shopkeepers and police officers.

In the divided city, conflicts between blacks and the police became flashpoints of racial resentment. Before the riot, whites had a
nearly complete monopoly over law enforcement jobs. In 1953,
Detroit had only 117 black officers on its police force, all of whom
served in a few predominantly black precincts. The situation had
barely changed in the 1960s. The city's black population had more
than doubled between 1950 and 1970, but by the time of the riot,
the number of black police officers had not kept pace. In a city that
was more than one-third black, 95 percent of police officers were
white.[4]

The racial isolation of the Detroit police force fostered intense
racial antagonism and distrust. A federal survey taken just before
the 1967 riot found that racial prejudice was endemic among white

police officers. Investigators found that 45 percent of police working in black neighborhoods were "extremely anti-Negro" and another 34 percent were "prejudiced." On the streets, the police
often acted on racist impulses. The files of civil rights organizations are full of accounts of petty police brutality. From the 1940s
through the 1960s, hundreds of blacks, prosperous and poor, men
and women, complained to the Detroit branch of the National Association for the Advancement of Colored People (NAACP) that
they had been handled roughly, called names, or mocked by white
police officers.[5] As a consequence, surveys found that a sizeable
segment of Detroit's black population distrusted the police. One
survey of Detroiters taken in 1967 found that 25 percent of black
respondents, but only 11 percent of whites, had complaints against
the police. A follow-up survey, conducted by University of Michigan political scientists Joel Aberbach and Jack Walker, found that
50 percent of blacks were dissatisfied with the city's police, compared to only 20 percent of whites. More than one-third of black
respondents believed that "policemen lack respect or use insulting
language" in their neighborhoods, that "policemen search and frisk
people without good reason," and that "policemen use unnecessary
force in making arrests." Only about 10 percent of whites agreed
with each statement.[6]

When the riot exploded in 1967, it surprised only those who
were utterly unfamiliar with Detroit's troubled past. Decades of
racial conflict and economic inequality provided the tinder for the
1967 riot; a police action provided the spark. In this respect Detroit was not unusual. "Almost invariably," wrote the National Advisory Commission on Civil Disorders, "the incident that ignites
disorder arises from police action." In Chicago, rioting began on a
hot summer day when police attempted to disperse youths cooling
themselves off in the spray of fire hydrants. In Philadelphia, several
days of looting and arson had been sparked by an altercation between police and the black owner of a stalled car; in Watts, violence began after a routine traffic stop led to squabbles between
police and bystanders. In Detroit, the riot began when police
raided a "blind pig"—an illegal after-hours bar. Most of these po-

lice incidents were, on the surface, minor events. But to many African Americans, the police came to "symbolize white power, white racism, and white repression."[7]

Riot-torn Detroit was full of potential subjects for an engaged writer like Hersey: the broken dreams of the thousands of shopkeepers who lost their life investments; the tragedies of the forty-three people who died violent deaths during the riot (thirty-four of whom had been killed by armed officials); the shattered hopes of politicians and community leaders who tried in vain to stop the looting; the seething anger of black power advocates who believed that the uprising was the first stage of a black revolution; the bitterness and glee of youths who smashed store windows and carried away clothes, food, and appliances. Any of these stories would have provided rich material for a book.

As Hersey began interviewing Detroiters, however, he found himself drawn to the disturbing events that occurred in the early hours of July 26, 1967, at the Algiers Motel and Manor House, a seedy establishment a few miles north of downtown. Amidst reports of sniper attacks, police and national guardsmen raided the motel. Inside, armed officials lined up seven black men and two white women guests along the wall of the lobby, tortured them (beating one so forcefully with a rifle that the gun broke in two), stripped the women, and took the guests one by one into a nearby room for brutal interrogation sessions. At the end of the rampage, three black men had been shot dead. All three, ruled a medical investigator, were in "nonaggressive postures" when they had been killed. And in the final indignity, investigators found no evidence of wrongdoing at the motel. Despite rumors of sniping, the police did not find a single gun on the premises.

Hersey quickly began sifting through the muddled accounts of what had happened that night at the Algiers Motel. He conducted his own investigation of the case, poring through police and court records, combing newspaper accounts, and, most importantly, interviewing witnesses, the survivors, the victims' families, and the three police officers suspected of wrongdoing. Using an approach characteristic of his earlier nonfiction writing, Hersey focused on a handful of characters: in this case, the three police officers accused of masterminding the massacre—Ronald August, Robert Paille, and David Senak—and one of the three murder victims, eighteen-year-old Auburey Pollard.

The result of Hersey's investigation was a collage of facts, opinions, evidence, and hearsay, rather than a straightforward chronological narrative. Hersey's unconventional methodology was to tell the story through fragments of interviews, public records, news reports, and testimony, most often presented verbatim. Lacing the manuscript are snippets of minute details, some of them freighted with import, others seemingly inconsequential. Hersey attempted to present all sides of an extraordinarily complicated case. "This account," he wrote, "is too urgent, too complex, too dangerous to too many people to be told in a way that might leave doubts strewn along its path" (30). In occasional asides, Hersey highlighted what he believed to be the most revealing pieces of evidence.

Many of Hersey's reviewers were frustrated by the fragmented style of the book. One called it "a profusion of details, surmise, hearsay, and murky recollection." Another chided Hersey for writing "one of the more disorganized books of the last few years."[8] But Hersey's assemblage of details and facts was deliberate, not disorganized.

The fractured structure of Hersey's narrative served two purposes. One was to convey the intense state of confusion that surrounded the entire event. July 26 was, he wrote, a "night of hallucination" (160). What happened at the Algiers Motel could never fully be ascertained. Many witnesses in the case proved to be wholly unreliable. The Detroit police officers, national guardsmen, and state policemen who were on the scene offered different versions of who entered and left the motel and when. An unidentified man had been found lurking in the alley behind the hotel. At one of the trials, a surprise witness reported seeing a black man with a rifle at the hotel earlier that evening. The motel guests, beaten and traumatized by the police, had spent most of their ordeal lined up facing a wall, unable to see what was happening behind them. Many gunshots were fired, but it was not clear who shot whom and when. And after the fact, the crime scene was tainted by police oversights: detectives had not adequately secured the building, the county coroner had refused to take away the bodies for fear of entering the riot zone, and maids had begun cleaning the building before police detectives had completed their investigation. In a reflective moment, Hersey recalled "the thesis of Leo Tolstoy in *War and Peace* . . . that after a battle there are as many versions as there were participants in it" (229).[9]

Second, the book's anecdotal and scattershot style conveys Hersey's sense of urgency. Passionately, angrily written, *The Algiers Motel Incident* was, perhaps, compiled too hastily. The book was published less than a year after the incident, and Hersey's publisher rushed the book to print only five weeks from the time that Hersey submitted the final manuscript. In addition, much of the book's material was raw. Hersey gathered so much material so quickly that he was unable to consider fully its possible significance. Rather than distilling and reordering his evidence as a lawyer would do for a legal case or as a historian for a monograph, Hersey simply transcribed lengthy, undigested quotations right from his tape recorder.

To view *The Algiers Motel Incident* as merely a compendium of raw data would, however, be misreading the author's careful control of the material. Hersey believed that the task of the author was to exhort and provoke. His story was unabashedly moralistic. Optimistic about the redemptive role of journalism, Hersey targeted a white readership who, he hoped, would take action to heal America's racial divide. An advocate of racial justice, Hersey drew inspiration from the works of mid-twentieth-century racial liberals, most notably Gunnar Myrdal's *American Dilemma*. "The Negro problem," wrote Myrdal, "is a problem in the heart of the American. It is there that the interracial tension has its focus. It is there that the decisive struggle goes on." Like Myrdal, Hersey saw the problem of race as a personal one. Racism was at root an individual pathology that needed to be solved at the individual level through reasoned debate and education. "If real progress is to be made," Hersey argued, "it cannot be made simply by expenditures of funds, even in great sums, on 'programs'; racism must be educated or coaxed or wrenched or stamped out of the centers of injustice and grievance. . . . The remedy is in the minds of men" (36). Above all, Hersey saw his writing as didactic—he hoped to inform, appeal, and persuade.[10]

Although he was clearly sympathetic to the black victims and hoped that his story would provoke outrage at racial injustice, Hersey drew complicated portraits of the three police officers as well as the victims, carefully avoiding the temptation to demonize the white police and lionize the black victims. Officers August, Paille, and particularly Senak were portrayed as racially prejudiced and quick to judge, but also tragically limited by circumstances beyond their control. Each had been hardened by regular encounters with seemingly incorrigible criminals. Their frustration mounted during the riot. Officer Robert Paille told Hersey bitterly: "I saw more crime transpire (the first day of the riot) than I saw all two years I been on the force. And there was nothing I could do about it, because I didn't have the orders" (73–74). After three days of near sleeplessness and almost constant seige, the three officers were nervous, angry, and jumpy. They began taking the law into their own hands. Their combination of adrenaline and racism, particularly in the case of Senak, proved deadly (Senak had been involved in two other fatal shootings during the week of the riot).[11]

Auburey Pollard was likewise a complicated character, his life options constrained by his poor education and economic hardship. A teenager at "the fork in the road," he faced an unhappy choice between the hardscrabble, insecure, working-class world of his childhood and the dangerously appealing underground life of crime and drugs that seemingly provided the only way out of poverty. A sensitive artist and a ruthless fighter, Pollard was torn between the steady life of his clean-living friend Fred Temple (also murdered at the motel) and the violent life of his fellow victim Carl Cooper, who was in constant brushes with the law before his death at the Algiers. By sympathetically recounting the troubled life of Auburey Pollard, Hersey hoped that his book would "narrow that distance" between black and white, appealing to his readers' consciences.

By the late 1960s, however, Hersey's racial liberalism was fading in fashion. Blacks grew increasingly pessimistic about the possibility of racial harmony. Whites professed to be more open to the idea of racial integration, but racial divisions remained deep, particularly in housing and education. Impatient with the slow pace of change, a vocal minority of black activists and their white allies demanded that blacks take power into their own hands. True racial justice, argued one left-wing critic of Hersey, would not come through the conversion of whites to notions of racial equality but "through the massed political power of blacks."[12] At the same time, the white majority, who had never been particularly sympathetic to calls for racial equality, lurched rightward. A growing segment of the electorate demanded "law and order" politics and repudiated what they believed were the excesses of the civil rights movement. Only a few months after the publication of *The Algiers Motel Incident*, nearly 60 percent of American voters supported conservative Richard Nixon or segregationist George Wallace; many blamed Democrats for capitulating to the demands of "angry" African Americans.[13]

In the tense, racially charged atmosphere of the late 1960s and early 1970s, the victims of the gruesome events at the Algiers Motel found little vindication in the courts. In August 1967, murder charges against Officer Robert Paille were dismissed because he had not been properly informed of his *Miranda* rights—a particularly ironic twist, since only a few years earlier, police officers had fiercely opposed the Supreme Court's *Miranda* decision. Shortly after Hersey's book came out, Officer Ronald August was charged with murder. Detroit Recorders Court Judge Thomas Poindexter (a former anti–civil rights activist) ruled that the publicity surrounding Hersey's book made a fair trial in Detroit impossible and sent the case to a notoriously conservative suburban judge, William Beer, who promptly moved the trial to rural lily-white Mason, Michigan (the town in which Malcolm X's father had been murdered in 1931). Beer allowed the defense to show televised footage of the riot that was unrelated to the events at the Algiers Motel. Although the prosecution asked that the charges include manslaughter, Beer instructed jurors to consider an "all or nothing" charge—either August had committed first degree murder or was not guilty. After a brief deliberation, the jury acquitted August.

After the murder charges had been dismissed, federal prosecutors filed charges against the three police officers and a security guard under an 1871 federal law for conspiring to violate the civil rights of the three slain men and the other members of the infamous line-up. In the federal trial, held in Flint, Michigan, another all-white jury also acquitted the defendants, after days of inconsistent and contradictory testimony from prosecution witnesses. In the end, Officers August, Paille, and Senak were never convicted for their role in the sordid events at the Algiers Motel.[14]

Ultimately, the most important contribution of Hersey's book was that it chronicled the enormous gap between blacks and whites regarding issues of law and order. For many black observers, the events at the Algiers Motel offered a particularly graphic example of the random, regular brutality that black people had been facing at the hands of the police for decades. That the deaths of three African American men and the torture of several others went unpunished fueled the black community's conviction that the criminal justice system was deeply corrupt. White advocates of "law and order," on the other hand, hailed the decisions. Carl Parsell, president of the Detroit Police Officers Association, discounted "charges of police brutality" as "part of a nefarious plot by those who would like our form of government overthrown. The blueprint for anarchy calls for the destruction of the effectiveness of the police. Certainly, it must be obvious that every incident is magnified and exploited with only one purpose."[15] The Algiers Motel incident was a graphic reminder of two versions of justice that had prevailed in the American past, separate and unequal.

From the infamous 1930s-era trials of the Scottsboro Boys to the hasty acquittal of the murderers of Emmett Till and civil rights activist Medgar Evars, African Americans have chafed against the injustices of the American judicial system. The profound distrust that many blacks continue to feel toward the police and toward the court system—reflected in the cases of Rodney King and O.J. Simpson and in the angry, antipolice lyrics of gangsta rap—is a legacy of the unresolved issues that John Hersey so powerfully documented. In the end, Hersey's story of three white police officers and three dead black men is an American tragedy of power, inequality, and injustice, a tragedy whose consequences continue to poison race relations in America today.

Notes

1. See below, 30–31.

2. For overviews of Hersey's career, see David Sanders, *John Hersey* (New York: Twayne Publishers, 1967); Sanders, *John Hersey Revisited* (Boston: Twayne Publishers, 1991); and Nancy L. Huse, *The Survival Tales of John Hersey* (Troy, N.Y.: Whitston Publishing Co., 1983).

3. The material in this and the following two paragraphs draws from Thomas J. Sugrue, *The Origins of the Urban Crisis: Race and Inequality in Postwar Detroit* (Princeton: Princeton University Press, 1996). See also Sidney Fine, *Violence in the Model City: The Cavanagh Administration, Race Relations, and the Detroit Riot of 1967* (Ann Arbor: University of Michigan Press, 1988) and Robert Conot, *American Odyssey* (New York: William Morrow, 1974).

4. Detroit Police Department, Office of Director of Personnel, "Tabulation of Non-White Personnel," March 24, 1953, in the Donald S. Leonard Papers, Michigan Historical Collection, Bentley Library, University of Michigan, Ann Arbor, Box 21. For 1967 figures, see Fine, *Violence in the Model City*, 104, 109.

5. U.S. Commission on Civil Rights, *Hearings Held in Detroit, Michigan, December 14–15, 1960* (Washington, D.C.: U.S. Government Printing Office, 1961), 302–21. For examples of police brutality complaints, see Detroit Branch, National Association for the Advancement of Colored People Papers, Part II, Box 31, Archives of Labor and Urban Affairs, Walter P. Reuther Library, Detroit, Michigan.

6. Joel D. Aberbach and Jack L. Walker, *Race in the City: Political Trust and Public Policy in the New Urban System* (Boston: Little, Brown and Co., 1973), 49, 52.

7. *Report of the National Advisory Commission on Civil Disorders* (New York: Bantam Books, 1968), 37, 38–39, 206; see also Robert Fogelson, *Violence as Protest: A Study of Riots and Ghettoes* (Garden City, N.Y.: Doubleday, 1971), 53–78.

8. Stephen Schlesinger, "Shoot-up in Detroit," *Atlantic Monthly*, September 1968, 124; Robert Conot, "One Night in Detroit," *New York Times Book Review*, July 7, 1968, 3.

9. The most comprehensive and persuasive account of the details of the case can be found in Fine, *Violence in the Model City*, 271–90.

10. Gunnar Myrdal, *An American Dilemma* (New York: Harper Brothers, 1944), 60–61. For a superb discussion of Myrdal and the course of racial liberalism in mid-twentieth-century America, see Walter A. Jackson, *Gunnar Myrdal and America's Conscience: Social Engineering and Racial Liberalism, 1938–1987* (Chapel Hill: University of North Carolina Press, 1990). For a discussion of Hersey's didactic approach, see Huse, *Survival Tales*, 153–60.

11. If Senak was indeed involved in the three murders at the Algiers Motel, he was present at a total of five violent deaths during the week of the riot (one considered to be a non-riot-related death). Sidney Fine suggests—drawing from a close reading of evidence presented in the three court cases and other accounts—that one of the dead men at the Algiers Motel, Carl Cooper, had died before police arrived, possibly murdered by an intruder. See Fine, *Violence in the Model City*, 273–77.

12. Nat Hentoff, "Waking Up the White Folks Again," *New Republic*, July 20, 1968, 37–39.

13. Jonathan Rieder, "The Rise of the 'Silent Majority,'" in *The Rise and Fall of the New Deal Order*, eds. Steve Fraser and Gary Gerstle (Princeton: Princeton University Press, 1989), 243–68; Thomas J. Sugrue, "Crabgrass-Roots Politics: Race, Rights, and the Reaction against Liberalism in the Urban North, 1940–1964," *Journal of American History* 82 (1995): 551–78.

14. Yale Kasimar, "Was Justice Done in the Algiers Motel Incident?" *New York Times*, March 1, 1970; Fine, *Violence in the Model City*, 285–90. On Poindexter's earlier career, see Sugrue, *Origins of the Urban Crisis*, 209–10, 227–28.

15. Quoted in Dan Georgakas and Marvin Surkin, *Detroit: I Do Mind Dying: A Study in Urban Revolution* (New York: St. Martin's Press, 1975), 191.

The Algiers Motel Incident

Persons Involved in the Incident

THE DEAD
Carl Cooper
Auburey Pollard
Fred Temple

POLICEMEN
Ronald August
Robert Paille
David Senak

WITNESSES
Carl's and Auburey's friends
Michael Clark
Lee Forsythe
James Sortor

Fred's friends, "the Dramatics"
Roderick Davis
Cleveland Larry Reed
and three others

STATE POLICEMEN
Corporal Hubert C. Rosema
Trooper John M. Fonger
Trooper Stan Lutz
Trooper P. A. Martin
Trooper Robert Michelson
and several others

NATIONAL GUARDSMEN
Warrant Officer Theodore Thomas
Sergeant Paul Gerard
Specialist Five Thomas Kelly
Private First Class Wayne Henson
Private First Class Robert Seaglan
and others

FAMILIES
Carl Cooper's
Margaret Gill (mother)
Omar Gill (stepfather)
six surviving children

Fred Temple's
Mr. and Mrs. John Temple
Eddie Temple (brother)
five other children

OFFICIALS
Congressman John Conyers, Jr.
Mayor Jerome P. Cavanagh
Police Commissioner Ray Girardin

Wayne County Prosecutor William L. Cahalan
Assistant Prosecutor Avery Weiswasser
Assistant Prosecutor James Garber

OTHERS
Leon Atchison, Administrative Assistant to Congressman Conyers
S. Allen Early, Jr., attorney who took the girls to the authorities
Clara Gilmore, night clerk at the Algiers Motel

The veteran	*The girls*	*The older man*
Robert Greene	Juli Hysell	Charles Moore
	Karen Malloy	

PRIVATE GUARDS
Melvin Dismukes
Charles Hendrix
Fletcher Williams
and two others

Auburey Pollard's
Rebecca Pollard (mother)   Mrs. Lucy Pollard
Auburey Pollard, Sr.   Robert Pollard
Lance Corporal Chaney Pollard   Thelma Pollard
Tanner Pollard

Judges of Recorder's Court   *Defense Attorneys*
Robert E. DeMascio   Norman L. Lippitt
Frank G. Schemanske   Konrad D. Kohl
Geraldine Bledsoe Ford   Nicholas Smith
Gerald W. Groat
Robert J. Colombo

Glenda Tucker, Larry Reed's girl
Lawanda J. Schettler, a volunteer witness
Dr. Clara Raven, Deputy Medical Examiner, Wayne County Morgue
Eli ("Bubba") Carter, resident of the Algiers Motel

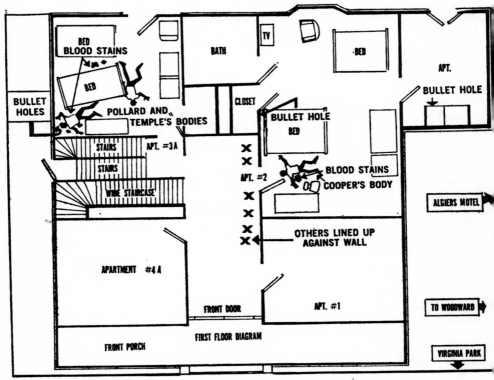

Diagram of ground floor of the Algiers Motel Annex used in court.

I

The Odor of a Case

1

Do You Hate the Police?

1 | We'll Be Following You All the Way

The ordeal seemed to be drawing to a close.

One of the officers went into room A-4 and told Michael Clark and Roderick Davis to get off the floor and go out in the hall.

There were still seven people, five black men and two white girls, spread-eagled against the wall of the hallway. One of the girls had nothing on but her panties; the other was half undressed.

The big officer had come in from outside, and he stood behind one of the young men in the line and asked, "Do you hate the police?"

"No."

"What have you seen here?"

"Nothing."

The police said the blacks should go out the back way and go on home. One of the officers said, "Start walking in the direction you're going with your hands above your heads. If you look back, we'll kill you, because we'll be following you all the way home."

Roderick started out on stockinged feet, and he was sharply surprised when, passing into room A-2 on his way to a back door, he came on the body of Carl Cooper prone in a stain of blood on the carpet; he had not seen the body earlier, as most of the others had, and he had not believed, even after all the shooting he had heard, that the uniformed men were actually killing people. He had to step over the body, for it blocked the passage through the room between one of the beds and the dresser.

Seven men moved, in relays of twos and threes, past Cooper's body and through the connecting door to room A-5 and out through its French doors onto the back porch and down the steps to the parking lot. The girls stayed behind. The older black man and the black paratrooper just back from Vietnam doubled around into the main part of the motel; the others walked across the parking lot and through the alley by the carwash out to Euclid and Woodward.

There, on the far corner, in front of the Great Lakes Mutual Life Insurance Building, National Guardsmen, seeing them coming, cocked their rifles and halted them and made them lie down in a row on the plot of grass in front of the building.

The Guardsmen stood the boys up one at a time. They searched each one. "What you been doing?" "Why you walking home?" The boys tried to answer, and the Guardsmen let them go at intervals with instructions to walk with their hands on their heads. One said to Roderick, when Roderick blurted out some of what had been happening, "Too bad. Keep walking. You niggers are always starting some kind of trouble."

Roderick was next to last to be let go. His friend Larry Reed was about a block and a half ahead of him. After a couple of blocks Roderick peeked around behind to see if another friend was following them. He ran and caught up with Larry.

"Did you see Fred?"

"No," Larry said. "Fred's still in there."

Lee Forsythe and James Sortor, two others who had been in the line, joined up and ran together toward Carl Cooper's house, a mile and a half away. Carl's stepfather, Omar Gill, told me later of Lee's account of the flight. "He said he run and he crawled. He say he went down Clairmount, he say he come down cutting through yards and things down to Clairmount. They was stopped at Twelfth and Clairmount and beat again. They were hit again." Sortor told me later that somewhere during the evening, probably here on the street, his wrist watch was pulled off over his hand and twenty dollars were taken from his pocket. They were sent on with hands up. "He said he was so weak," Mr. Gill told me, "he say he started to kick a porch out, you know, with them slats in it, he say he started to kick a porch out and crawl up under there. He'd have probably laid there and bled to death. He said, 'Something just kept telling me I had to get to you and Miss Margaret.' " Lee and Sortor kept running.

Michael Clark went to the Mount Royal, a transients' hotel a half-dozen blocks north of the Algiers, with a soot-streaked façade of stone arches supporting three dark-brick upper stories, in its lobby a load of the past—potted palms, antiques, a weighing machine, an open-cage elevator with a folding iron gate. Michael checked in, and as soon as he was alone in a room he got on the phone.

"Michael called me," Carl's mother, Mrs. Margaret Gill, told me, "and I thought it was Carl calling me back, because I had laid down, and when he called me—this must have been about two o'clock when he called me and told me—I thought he was kidding, you know. I said, 'Look, you all quit playing with me, it's too late at night, I'm in the bed sleeping, or trying to go to sleep. Where's Carl at?' He said, 'Miss Margaret, I'm not at the hotel, I'm down at another hotel.' Said, 'They killed Carl.' He kept telling me that, you know. I said, 'Aw, Michael, don't play with me.' He said, 'I'm not kidding.' He said, 'They made Lee and them run and told them don't quit running.' He said, 'They said they'd kill them out there running,' you know."

"After my wife woke me up and told me that Clark had called and said that Carl was dead," Omar Gill told me, "I got up, and I went to the phone. His call was right after they turned Clark and them loose; it must have been like three o'clock in the morning, something like that. I didn't notice the time, I wasn't thinking about no time. Because I got mad with her, I told her, 'I won't play this, now don't tell me this has happened.' But then I looked at the expression on her face, and I could tell that this had happened, after I looked up at her, you know. So that's when I went to the phone and called the hotel, and so when I called, a policeman answered the phone, the switchboard operator didn't answer, a police answered. So I told him, I said, 'Look, a guy just called me and told me that my son was dead, and I'd like to come over there and see if he's dead, you know?' I said that, and so he told me, he said, 'You know you can't come over here.' I said, 'What do you mean I can't come over there? My son is dead, and I can't come over?' He said, 'If you bring your goddam ass over here you'll be dead just like him.' And then I asked him, I said, 'Well, why are you talking to me like this, and you killed my son?' He said, 'I don't want to talk to you.' And he hung up the phone. Didn't ask my name, or who I was, or anything."

"Lee got back here about a quarter after three," Mr. Gill told me. "He didn't ring the bell or anything, him and Sortor just came in, and when he came he fell and crawled and he was crying and he said, 'Miss Margaret, they killed Carl.' That's all he was saying, 'They killed him, they killed him, they killed Carl.' And I said, 'What did they kill him for?' He said, 'Nothing.' He said, 'I think they killed Auburey, too,' he said, 'they took Auburey in a room and I heard them shoot and Auburey didn't come out.' I said, 'Well, how do you *know* Auburey's dead?' He said, 'Because everybody that was living left there, because they made them get out and run.'

"When Lee crawled in he was so bloody that he would have scared you. I wondered how he made it. I really did, and when I went to fix his head, I thought maybe I could just wipe the blood off, but the gashes in it was so big I just couldn't. I told him, 'Man, I can't do nothing with this.' Because you could see the *bone*."

"You could see down in the white part of this boy's head," Mrs. Gill said. "There was two—one place was busted wider, that was along his head, then right off it was a lick, sort of. And other knots was in his head."

"Sortor couldn't talk," Mr. Gill said. "Yeah, Sortor couldn't talk. He had big knots on his head, almost big as my fist, just all *over* his head."

Having walked forty-two blocks on stockinged feet, Roderick and Larry made their way across open lots and were about to cross some railroad tracks, near Dequindre, and a train came, and the light of the locomotive shone on them, and they waited. After the train had passed they crossed the tracks, and some police and Guardsmen stopped them. "Why are you all bloody?" The boys tried to tell them. "It's a good thing," the men said, "the light from the train was on you, because we were about to shoot." Hamtramck policemen took the boys to St. Francis Hospital, where the worst cuts on Rod's head were stitched. Then the officers drove Roderick and Larry to a police station in Hamtramck. "Where do you live?" "Where do you work?" "What have you been doing?" The two tried to tell. At last an officer drove them home.

Mrs. Gill, who was becoming hysterical, called her mother, and Lee got on the phone. "Grandma B," he said, "Carl is dead. I looked at him, Grandma B, they beat me because I wanted to see if Carl was dead, but I know he's dead." And he said, "They took Auburey in the room, and I heard them shoot. Grandma B, if they hadn't have shot him, the way they had beat Auburey up, the way he looked, I doubt if he could live anyway."

"Sortor called," Thelma Pollard, Auburey's sixteen-year-old sister, told me. "He didn't know what to say, he hung up. He says, 'Auburey there?' I was mad, because this was about four o'clock in the morning. I said, 'Just a minute! Auburey's not here. He didn't come home last night.' So he says, 'Okay. Bye.' "

Sortor gave me a different version of this call. "I was at Carl's house," he said, "I called soon as I got to Carl's house. I called and I said, 'Well, may I speak to Mrs. Pollard?' She said she was in bed. And so I said, 'Well, you know, Auburey done got killed.' So she hung up the phone. Then she called back and say, 'He dead for real?' I said, 'Yeah, he got killed over there.' "

2 | Auburey Pollard, Jr.

Auburey's father sat square-shouldered and stiff with defiance on the edge of a sofa, weeks later, in the house to which, after the collapse of his family, he had moved to live alone, and, speaking in explosive and emphatic cadences, he talked to me, while he toyed with a knuckle of pork on a plate on a coffee table before him—his lonely supper—more or less about his dead son:

"He was a hell of a character. This is a fact; most people wouldn't want to say this: He was a hell of a character. He always wanted to live up to par. But what I always told him: You got to give something to get something. He wanted to go a long ways. He loved to paint. He was a good artist, a beautiful artist. He was smart in some ways. Everybody's dumb in some ways. He was young. Every father loves his own son, he loves his own because he's older. I don't have nothing to lose in life, but I don't intend to give it away for nothing. You understand what I mean? Now, understand me thoroughly: I've got nothing to lose in life, but I'm not intending to give it away for nothing. Any time I give my life away it's to save me.

"He was fast-minded. Everything he did he wanted to do it real quick. If it couldn't be done real quick, he'd say, 'Oh, well, it takes too long.' Because he was young! And when I was young I was the same way, I'd figure if I wanted to go to the store I'd walk fast. I'm forty-three now, I can move pretty good, I can move pretty daggone good if I have to. But the boy, he was just a normal American boy. He didn't know nothing about no discrimination, about no hate, because I never taught him. I always taught him one thing: to treat people as you want to be treated. If you should step on my foot and I happen to glance over my shoulder and see that you're not mentally balanced, why should I turn myself around and get myself in trouble over you? Well, that's just one foot stepped on, I can bypass that one. If I'm not shoved in a corner, why should I have to come out fighting? I always told him that. I don't give a kitty, if you're going east and I want to go due north, I'm going due north, it's my prerogative. Your prerogative is to go where you want to go, and my prerogative is to go where I want to go. You must have a mind of your own! Without something of your own you have nothing. And any time you got to follow somebody else you're stone weak in the beginning. You just a stone weakling. I'd rather be dead on my own than to have to follow the crowd to say I'm right, just to be seen or heard. I don't want to be seen or heard, I want to be happy within myself.

"The Negro always wants to make the Joneses look good, and the grays do the same, they want to make the Smiths look good, and I don't care anything about what the Smiths or the Joneses or the Beedles or the Doodles do, I want to be happy. I don't care if I'm loading manure, if I'm happy and loading manure that's my business. But most people, they follow one pattern. 'Well, the Joneses, they got two cars,' and 'Oh, she's got new bedroom slippers.' I don't know what they're doing when their doors are closed, they don't know what I'm doing when my doors are closed. So I'm not worried about what they're doing, as long as I am happy and at peace, I am satisfied.

"It's too many nice jobs for Negro kids today for them to

make the same mistakes I made. He can go to school, he can work in a bank, he can be a computer, a teacher, he can work in a scientific laboratory, it's a million things he can do—work for the government! Auburey started, he was a pretty good welder. Now, I'm going to tell you something else. Now, most fathers would say he'd been a champ. You know what I'm going to say? It's this: He had to find himself. Within himself, when he'd have found himself, then he'd have been as great as he wanted. I'm not going to build him one teeny little bit to say he'd have been the best welder in the world. The boy wasn't old enough to find himself. I'm forty-three years old, and I haven't fully found *my*self.

"I'll tell you what this have done to me. I lost a son. That's all that matters to me. The rest of the world, I'm not worried over it; I've lost a son. I have lost a son. I have lost something that with the world at the rate it's going now, with automation going as it's going now, he could have lived and prospered with a good life, maybe. What I mean, he was only a baby. I went in the service when I was sixteen years old—lied about my age—and *I* was only a baby. That's the only way I learnt life, that's where I learnt my life. I wouldn't be hard like I am now if I hadn't have been. I learnt the hard way. But the poor little thing, he never knew what hardness was, he had to crawl through a bucket of blood. The poor little fellow, he didn't even know what life was really all about. Auburey was a beautiful kid, but he was just a baby, that's all. Just a baby."

3 | A Pleasure-Loving Clientele

The Algiers Motel was one of many transients' hostelries on Woodward Avenue, a rod-straight street, the city's spine, that divides eastern Detroit from western Detroit. A couple of miles north of the cluster of massive buildings called "downtown," and only a few blocks from the section of Twelfth Street where the black uprising of those July days and nights had started, the Algiers stood at the corner of Woodward and Virginia Park, an elm-lined street elegantly brick-paved in the old days but

potholed now and patched with asphalt, a street of once prosperous wooden and brick houses with boastful porches and
back-yard carriage houses recently declined into rooming houses
and fraternity houses and blind pigs, as Detroit calls its illegal
after-hours drinking spots. The section had evolved from proper
WASP to up-and-coming second- and third-generation immigrant
to, recently and more and more, middle-class black.

Detroit is a vast flat sprawl of houses planlessly intermixed
with schools and colleges and great automobile factories and
little works and warehouses and stores and public buildings, and
in this sprawl the resident nations of black and white had for
years been encroaching and elbowing and giving way to each
other; there was no great ghetto; there were pockets of pros-
perity, of ethnic identity, of miserable poverty, of labor, of seedy
entertainment and sometime joy. The Algiers had had a habit
of reaching into several of these pockets; its management had
changed a few years back, and it was now run by Negroes
mainly for a pleasure-loving black clientele.

Facing Woodward, the main part of the motel was announced by a massive sign on two fieldstone posts, with a neon-
fronded palm tree drooping over a chrome frame enclosing the
legend of its Africa-whispering name. Behind the bold advertise-
ment stood a complex that would have been admirably suited to
a Florida beachfront—a discreet glass-fronted office off to the
left, straight ahead a large pool with tables and beach umbrellas
around it and cabana-like rooms beyond, and to the right a
two-story wing of rooms with pink-painted concrete-block
walls.

The Algiers Manor House, where most of the action of this
narrative hid itself, was an annex to the motel proper, originally
one of the big bourgeois houses of Virginia Park, a three-story
brick bulk trimmed in white wood. From under the odd curving
eyebrows of enormous dormers on the third floor jutted air
conditioners; big bay windows on the ground floor were primly
curtained in white; a high, wide, and unhandsome porch was
supported by too-heavy white pillars.

Behind the motel and the manor was a blacktop parking lot

which could be reached from Virginia Park by a driveway running between the motel proper and the annex, and which also gave onto an alleyway that ran through to the next street to the north, Euclid Avenue.

ʻNorth of the motel on Woodward, between the Algiers and Euclid, were Max's 25-Cent Car Wash and a Standard Oil gasoline station.

4 | It Was Not Safe

Detective Thayer and Warrant Officer Thomas testified to parts of this in court; Detective Hay reported some of it in his Detective Bureau write-up of the night's mission; Charles Hendrix told part of it to a Free Press *reporter; Clara Gilmore told some of it to Homicide; and the Wayne County Morgue forms for Autopsy No. A67-1011 confirm certain essential facts:*

Not long after the task forces drove away from the Algiers, Charles Hendrix, Negro owner of the private-guard firm known as Hendrix Patrol, himself in the uniform of his enterprise, came to the motel office and found his employee Fletcher Williams, who was also in uniform and was supposed to be on duty guarding the Algiers, and Clara Gilmore, the young black receptionist at the motel desk and switchboard operator, huddled in the office, chatting and looking scared. He "got kind of mad," as he put it later; he wanted to know why Williams was not doing his job. When Williams and Miss Gilmore began to talk about some gunfire, Hendrix asked why Williams had not checked on it, and Williams said there had been so much shooting he was afraid to go out.

Clara Gilmore was able to say that she had heard several shots out back in the direction of the annex, the Algiers Manor, and that a few minutes later she had seen an Army jeep and three or four police cars park on the west side of Woodward, right in front of the office. Several men in uniform took cover behind trees and behind the several sections of turreted, stone-capped brick walls that formed an annunciatory two-lane gateway to the faded gentility of Virginia Park, the elm-lined street to the south of the Algiers, onto which the manor's front door gave. She heard several shots. A little later, the switchboard buzzed; a girl was calling, and she said she had been talking a few minutes before to her boyfriend, Larry Reed, in room A-3 in the annex, and she'd heard shots in the background, and Larry had just gone off the phone without hanging up, and she was worried about him. Miss Gilmore cut into A-3 and found the line open. She heard someone yell, "Get your hands up." Someone else shouted, "Watch out!"—and something about grabbing a gun. Then, hearing several shots, she panicked and pulled the plug. She and Williams then sat talking fearfully about what was going on.

Hendrix, having heard her story, hurried to the manor, and he came on three bodies, one in A-2 and two in A-3, and he felt them and found them still warm. He went back to the office and called the Wayne County Morgue to report the deaths and to ask that the cadavers be taken away.

Marvin Szpotek, a clerk at the morgue, telephoned the Homicide Bureau of the Detroit Police Department and told Detective Joseph Zisler, who picked up the phone in the Homicide bullpen on the fourth floor of Police Headquarters, that a party had called him from the Algiers Motel and told him there were corpses over there.

Detective Zisler set in motion a radio command, which was picked up at about two o'clock in the morning by Scout Cars One, Two, and Seven from the Thirteenth Precinct: "8301 Woodward. At the Algiers Motel check for dead persons."

Half a dozen policemen soon descended on Clara Gilmore. She told the men where to look, and after a search of the annex Patrolman Edward Gardocki returned to the motel office and called Homicide and spoke to Detective Edward Hay, telling what he had seen.

Detectives Hay and Lyle Thayer and a police photographer, Patrolman Dale Tiderington, arrived at the scene at a few minutes after three. Besides Patrolman Gardocki and his fellow officers from Thirteenth, there were now on hand, Detective Thayer later testified, "several people that purported to be newspaper people in front of the place." The detectives took down Miss Gilmore's story, to which she now added the embellishment of a U-turn of scout cars on Woodward before the assault began, and then Hay and Thayer proceeded to the annex, where they conducted what Detective Thayer called "a preliminary search" for weapons. They found a knife near the body in room A-2, but no firearms. Though by Thayer's account the detectives stayed for nearly two hours, they did not pick up any of the many cartridges and shell casings that were strewn on the floors; they removed no slugs from woodwork; they took no firearms evidence.

Everyone was jumpy. When the detectives checked an exit giving out from a dormer in room A-15 on the third floor to the top of a white-railed wooden fire escape which ran down the back of the building, a private guard out on Euclid Avenue, who had seen their dim figures climbing around, apparently on the roof, for all the world like a pair of snipers, gave a new alarm to National Guard Warrant Officer Theodore Thomas, stationed at the Great Lakes Building on the next corner north, and Thomas shouted a challenge. The detectives withdrew. As Thayer put it in court, "We had been taking photographs, the flash of the bulb, and some of the rooms had no lights, the flashlights and us moving around the different floors—we felt that it was not safe."

The detectives called Assistant Wayne County Medical Examiner Dr. Edward Treisman, and according to Thayer's testimony he "refused to come to the scene. He didn't feel it was safe." Dr. Treisman ordered the bodies, unpronounced dead on the spot by him, to be removed to the morgue. The detectives called for transportation, and eventually, shortly before five in the morning, a morgue wagon and a General Hospital wagon arrived, and the detectives ordered the manor doors sealed with paper warnings from the Medical Examiner's office; in their haste the morgue people put a seal only on the front door, the glass of which, in any case, was broken out. The corpses were carted off. "And we," testified Detective Thayer, "left the premises to be searched at a more safe time."

The crucial issue here was how word of the killings reached the authorities. Under cross examination in court, Detective Thayer said that he did not know for a fact that the central communication office of the Police Department had not received a report on the killings from police officers who had been present; but had such a call actually been received, it would have been reported at once, as a matter of iron routine, to Homicide. There is no record of such a call; no one has come forward, in court or out, to say that such a call was received. Indeed, this was the first-noticed and finally fatal flaw in the theory that three snipers had been killed in an open firefight at the Algiers that night: the evident failure of the patrolmen who had been present during the shootings to follow the dictates of prudence, of humanity, and of standard operating procedure even during the confusion of the riot, by reporting the deaths to headquarters.

5 | Carl Cooper

In her parlor, which was strewn with her older children's long-playing records and her younger children's toys, Mrs. Omar Gill, Carl Cooper's mother, a plump woman of thirty-six with a broad face and wide-set eyes, sitting on a hassock, dragged-down and weary-looking, in a dressing-gown, with her four-year-old Julius and a mongrel puppy playing around her feet distracting her, told me about her dead son:

"In a way of speaking, he was kind of a mean kid. In other words, he didn't take no stuff off of anybody, didn't like no one to mess with him.

"He liked school. He was no trouble in school. His teachers spoke well of him. He went to Sherrill, then Pattengill, and Angell, and Sampson, and Lessenger. He tried to play baseball a little while, took up wrestling at the Training School and got a few awards for it there. Course he liked music and dancing.

"See, he was very likable. You never seen him without a

smile. You'd be walking along the street and he'd go to smile at you. He had a lot of friends.

"He was funny about food. He didn't eat anything with onions, didn't like boiled foods. You could give him French fries and chicken every day of the week and he'd eat it, that's all he really liked. If you had rice with the chicken he didn't like gravy, he wanted butter.

"Carl was kind of spoiled. He was the first boy on our side. My father was the only boy my grandmother had, and Carl was named after him. He was the oldest, he was seventeen when he died. Then comes Theresa, she's fifteen, and Tamara, she's thirteen. They're Coopers. The four little ones, they're Gills: there's Della, she's eight, Omar Junior, he's seven, Michael, he's six, and Julius here, he's four.

"Carl, he liked nice things, and he liked to have money for them. He'd help people take their groceries out to get extra money. He liked to go to a show, and while he was seventeen he'd go to the show two, three times a week. I never had no trouble out of him at home. He always if he got money he'd give me some.

"He lied about his age to get these jobs, then they'd find out he lied and they'd let him go. He worked for the Housing Commission, and he worked in shipping for Wrigley's Cap and Gown, and he worked at Chrysler's. Before he was sent to Lansing, he worked in a drug store as a stock boy. In Lansing he was sent out to various jobs; worked for a car wash for a while.

"I work at Walker Crouse Enterprises, power sewing, I went to school for that. Carl wanted to go into tailoring. He liked clothes quite a bit, and he talked to my instructor out there a couple of times, you know, he went to the school with me and talked to him, and I think he gave Carl momentum to want to do this. After he got laid off from Chrysler's, that's when he went in and put in for this. He was supposed to start classes August the seventh.

"All the police knew Carl. Beginning when he was thirteen,

fourteen, they began to pick Carl up, they'd take him to the police station and keep him overnight or maybe two days, there was never any charge, just suspicion, they never put a finger on anything he actually did, you know. One of the detectives told me once, 'Carl isn't a bad guy, he just doesn't like people to talk nasty to him, call him "nigger," "punk," all like that.' Once he come home with a black eye, they'd picked him up and drove him round in their car and took him in a dark street and just beat him up. I wanted to get a lawyer, but Carl said, 'No, Momma, it would just be their word against mine, and you know how that would end up.' One time he come home and said they grabbed his arm and bent it up his back, and they're saying, 'Come on, now, where you been? What you been up to?'

"When he began to get in trouble, going in people's houses and like that, I'd ask him, 'What you doing out there where white peoples live?' And he'd say, 'They the ones got the nice things, Momma.' I'd get to crying and he'd say, 'Don't you cry, no use to cry, I did this to myself.' We were pretty close, me and Carl, you know. Whenever he earned money or got ahold of some money, he would always give me some, to help out with the kids. And he *would* help out, you know, he was a big help. I used to scuffle so hard for them, and looked like he was trying to pay me back."

6 | As Though the Viet Cong . . .

"Negro snipers," it said on the front page of the Detroit *News* the next morning, Wednesday, July 26, 1967, "turned 140 square blocks north of West Grand Boulevard into a bloody battlefield for three hours last night, temporarily routing police and national guardsmen. . . .

"It was as though the Viet Cong had infiltrated the riot-blackened streets. . . .

"Tanks thundered through the streets and heavy machine guns chattered. . . ."

Then, still on the front page:

"Three unidentified Negro youths were killed in a gunfight behind the Algiers Motel, Woodward and Virginia Park.

"Their bodies were found on the ground floor of the Algiers Manor, a three-story annex to the motel.

"Police and Guardsmen were called to the scene about midnight when sniping began from the Manor.

"Homicide Detective Edward Hay said shots were coming from the roof and windows on all floors.

"Police and Guardsmen were pinned down for several minutes before the firing stopped. . . ."

7 | A Hurt Feeling

"Carl Cooper's auntie called," Auburey's sister Thelma told me. "Sortor was over there that night. She said, 'Is your mother there?' I said, 'She's asleep,' you know. So she says, 'It's about your brother.' So I thought he was in jail, because the riot was still going on."

"So when I got to the phone," Mrs. Pollard told me, "she said, 'Mrs. Pollard, you don't know me and I don't know you, but I've heard about you, but I'm sorry to tell you,' she says, 'but Auburey was killed this morning.' I said, '*What?*' And she said, 'Yeah, he was killed this morning. He was cooking hot dogs and the police walked in there and killed him.' She said, 'I can't describe to you how they killed him. They killed him like a dog.' She went to tell me how he was begging for his life. And when that woman told me that I had to let down the phone. I couldn't talk to her. I was sick. My daughter had to finish taking the message. Then I called the morgue, because to verify it. They wouldn't even give no information. Then I called my husband off his job . . ."

"I was on a job," Mr. Pollard told me, "at Outer Drive and Sherwood. I works for DPW. I loads a truck; I do not pull any punches. I'm a laborer aide. I do not mind it. So Pete was the foreman, the gentleman's name is Pete, very nice guy, he came up to me, he says, 'You've got a phone call from home, there's something happened, one of your boys in trouble or one of your boys got hurt, one.' Which do you know who I thought it was? I thought it was my third boy, because he's always googy-googy. So I said, 'Gee whiz,' I was just shaking, 'I hope it's not Tanner.' So therefore I goes in a telephone booth and I calls up. When I calls up between the operator was nice enough to let me listen to two conversations at one time, which when I picked up the family was already talking, she was saying, 'Well, Auburey, they found Auburey dead this morning in the Algier Hotel.' I said, 'Oh, *no,*' because he was supposed to be at home. I works two jobs, I was working right there on Sherwood right off of Outer Drive, that's where I work at night. I work for a stainless-steel place, you know, where they put the rolls of stainless steel in, fix them up, but I was a janitor, not like a lot of people, I wasn't no stainless-steel helper, I was working as a janitor. So I went home from there, you know. On the way I said to myself, 'How in the world could all this be?'—you know. I said, 'Maybe it's a mistake.' That's the way I wanted to feel. So, my maw was there. My maw said, 'Well, Baby, I tell you. We'll go see.' I said, 'Maw, what's this? A mistake?' I said, 'It couldn't be Auburey, I know Auburey got more sense than that.' Maw said, 'Well,' she said, 'Baby,' she said, 'you never know. So let's go see.' So we goes down to the morgue. So the lady at the morgue, she was very nice, she was beautiful, she was a stone champ. She was a very beautiful lady. She's a ageable lady, she's within knowledge of the world, she's no fifteen, sixteen, twenty, or twenty-two years, she's in her late forties or early fifties, right along there someplace. So we talked. We sit there and I bet you we talked for about thirty-five minutes, and we talked about youngsters, you know, how they communicate, how they do not if they want to be slick, you know—it's life, we talked about everyday life. And then she says, 'You know,' she says, 'I've been living in this place so long, just take out my trash I pay so much, just do little odds-and-end different things I have to pay so *much.*' So we sit there and talk, and she said, 'Well, I see you want to see him.' I said, 'Sure.' So I walked up. There he was. She take me over and showed me Auburey. I said, 'That's my son.' "

"And when he went to that morgue and identified Auburey," Mrs. Pollard told me, "he ain't been right since. He ain't been right since. I don't know what kind of shape they had him in, but they had him buck-naked down there, and those bloody clothes we got back, yessir, they give me his clothes back. I got the clothes and wallet. I got his clothes back. I got them for evidence, I got them bloody clothes. I can't look at them. It makes me sick, just makes me sick to even look at them clothes."

Lee had passed out, and Mrs. Gill was near collapse. Carl's step-great-grandfather, James Young, brought his car to the Gills' house. Mrs. Gill washed Lee up, took his bloody shirt off, and put a clean one on him. With the help of two men named Johnny and Bob who were living on the upper floor of the Gills' house, they carried Lee out to Mr. Young's car, and Mr. Young drove both Lee and Mrs. Gill to Northwest General Hospital. In the emergency room there Mrs. Gill was given something for her nerves, and a doctor took twelve stiches in the cut on the back of Lee's head. Two policemen came into the emergency room, and Mr. Young told me that the following exchange took place.

Policeman: "Who brought him here?"

Mr. Young: "I brought him in."

"You know him?"

"Yeah, I see him nearly every day."

"How does that happen?"

"He's a friend of my grandson. I see him at his house."

"How do you happen to be there?"

"I'm the grandfather, why shouldn't I be there?"

"Why'd you bring him in here?"

"I'd bring *you* here if I found you in his condition."

Lee was now conscious, and the policeman questioned him. Lee said he had been beaten on the head by cops. "They told him he was lying," Mrs. Gill said to me, "hadn't no police beat him up, he'd jumped through some kind of plate glass, looting. Got the doctor kind of mad. The doctor said, 'Why would he be lying? He's under sedation.' "

The doctors sent Lee on to Detroit General Hospital, where he was given a bed.

Sortor testified that he went that morning to Dr. Thomas R. Carey, on Joy Road, who gave him some pills. Then he went to the morgue with Mr. Gill. They identified Carl's remains and got his clothes. Missing from the trouser pockets was a roll of bills that Sortor estimated should have been about four hundred dollars; missing from the wrist of the body was a watch that had diamonds on it; missing from one of Carl's fingers was a ring that Julie Hysell believed was worth more than a thousand dollars.

Lance Corporal Chaney Pollard, Company A, 7th Engineer Battalion, United States Marine Corps, Auburey's twenty-one-year-old brother—Chaney happens to have been the surname of the black civil rights worker who was murdered in Mississippi in 1964 with two white colleagues—had been in Vietnam for nearly twelve months when Auburey was killed. "He could have been home," Mrs. Pollard told me, "but see, he re-signed up to stay over there for another five months. After he could have come home. I felt pretty bad all the time about his being in Vietnam, I figured something was going to happen to him all the time, I wasn't never thinking about something going to happen to Auburey. I was always thinking Chaney was going to get killed because he was over there in action, you know. He was going around building roads, digging booby traps, and stuff like that. I read there in the paper where some of the stuff he was doing, you know, it kind of scared me, you know. So I never thought it would be nothing ever happen to Auburey. I called the Red Cross, to Mrs. Hudson, and told them that my second son was killed, I had to have Chaney home. I had to verify it at the morgue to make sure before they sent for him, so my husband went down to the morgue and verified it, and I called them back . . ."

Robert Jewel Pollard, Auburey's seventeen-year-old brother, was imprisoned in the Michigan Reformatory at Ionia, serving a three-to-ten-year sentence for having stolen seven dollars from a newsboy. "My counselor, Mr. Jackson," Robert told me, "was the first one who told me about it. He told me one of my brothers had got killed. He couldn't pronounce the name too good, he said, 'Aub, Aub, Aub.' I didn't say nothing. Wasn't nothing for me to say. I called up, they let me call home. I called home that same day, and my mother and my brother and father told me. They didn't know too much about it. They told me most of it. I learned about how the police beat on him and all that when I read it in the paper later. One of the police kept on telling my brother to stab him, that one that killed him—to stab him."

Larry Reed's father called the Temples very early that morning to say that someone had called to tell him that Fred Temple had been killed at the Algiers Motel. Mrs. Temple, who always got up at five in the morning to fix lunch for her husband to take to work, called at that hour to ask her sister to drive Mr. Temple to the motel. At the Algiers Miss Gilmore told Mr. Temple that the bodies had been taken away. A policeman took him to the annex, and Mr. Temple found Fred's glasses on the floor of room A-3. From the Algiers Mr. Temple went to the morgue, which was closed; from there he went to police headquarters at 1300 Beaubien, where he could not learn anything; he went back to the morgue, but it was still closed. He went then to his job.

Later Eddie Temple, Fred's oldest brother, went to the morgue and identified Fred's body. There Eddie encountered Mr. Gill and Sortor, and they told Eddie what they knew. "This," Eddie told me, "was the first I'd heard of the nature of the incident."

No official person ever notified any of the families of the deaths of their sons. "They don't tell you nothing," Mrs. Gill said to me. "They won't give you no kind of information. What hurts me so bad is they didn't even notify me that Carl was dead. If it don't be for the boys I wouldn't never have known it."

"The police didn't even notify us," Mrs. Pollard said to me. "That's a hurt feeling."

"My maw and I left the morgue," Mr. Pollard told me. "My maw and I was coming on home, my maw said, 'Baby, I thought you was going by the Algier Hotel.' I said, 'Yes, I'll go.' So when I got to the Algier Hotel, there was people there. Some people talking, some not, some watching, and some isn't, you know how people do." The place, in fact, was swarming. Homicide was back; the seal at the front door had been broken long before they got there. "I'm very funny anyway," Mr. Pollard said to me, "I'm very funny that way, I'll never say anything when I don't know anything, I don't say nothing if I don't know nothing. I'll wait to see what I'm doing. So I told my maw, I say, 'I'm going home and get my camera.' I go back. So I started from the top floor and worked to the bottom. That's when I went to finding deer shots. That's what they killed Auburey with, deer shots. They used double-barreled. I found a 300 high-speed Savage, and deer shots, and shotgun shells. I worked with the detectives. They were very nice to me. Now if I'd been like the most averagest Negro, or the most average human being white *or* Negro, if it had have been *his* son, when he walked up and asked the guy something, he'd have been cussing, swearing; I never got overemotional. I never would have found out what I knew if I'd have got overemotional. And they was beautiful. Each one of those gentlemen was beautiful. I talked to a guy of the Homicide, and he gave me a card to see him. I goes downtown to see him, and when I goes downtown looking for him, he was the same guy I just got through talking to! So I picked up real quick, so I just cooled it, I played it cool. But I never give up what I was doing, I doubled right back around and went back doing what I was doing. I didn't think hard of him, because he had a job, that's why the city pays him, because he got a job to do. He's got a filthy job. Most filthy job in the world. And I've got the next to the filthiest job in the world."

"After I'd heard that Fred had been shot in the Algiers," Eddie Temple told me, "I heard in the news reports that three snipers had been killed at the Algiers. So when I heard the way it happened, I was sure that that *was* the way it happened. I knew Fred would never pick up a gun and shoot anybody, or shoot *at* somebody, or be a party to anything like that, ever. When I got home, Cleveland [Larry] Reed came over, and he told the family what had happened. About the line-up, and how he saw blood running down the back of Fred's head. I talked with him at length. Then I talked with one of his friends, Rod, Roderick Davis. And it was after that that I called Detective Schlachter. I had heard his name at the morgue as the person who was investigating this. I waited down there at the morgue; I wanted to talk to the investigating detective on this. They said it would be Detective Schlachter who would be taking care of this. So it's pretty hard to get through to the police to talk about anything. I went down to the Police Department. They wouldn't let me in. They had it quadroned off, and they wouldn't let you up the steps. So I telephoned, and I got him. He said he'd heard about it, but he hadn't had a chance to get over and start the investigation yet. He said three snipers had been killed. That was when I proceeded to tell him that they were not snipers, that there wasn't any sniping from that particular building, but that they were murdered."

8 | Fred Temple

In an immaculate living room with a carpeted floor and white plaster mirror frames and sconces against dark walls and crinkling, transparent plastic covers over handsomely upholstered

sofa cushions, Mrs. John Temple, a large woman with an aqui-
line nose and a steady, deep gaze, talked to me, her voice
controlled and her words measured, about her dead son:
"He was kind of slow in his books. Anyway, I never had any
trouble out of him, he was always a good boy at home. He liked
to work with photography, that was what he mostly liked. He
was the baby: first Ella, then Eddie, then Eva May, then John,
then the twins Hal and Herbert, and he was the last one, Freddie.

"He was a normal child, that's all. After he got to be seventeen, he wanted to work like his father, wanted to get a good
job in a factory. He slipped out of school and got a job with
the Ford Motor Company. I got on him *so* bad trying to get
him to get back in school, but he'd had a hard time with his
reading, and he said the teacher told him it would be best to
work at a job and go to adult school.

"Let's see, we moved around some. I've been in Detroit for
twenty-six years, and Fred's father, he's had the one job, machine operator, Thompson Products, the same job for twenty-
three, twenty-four years. Let's see, he went, let's see, to Cath-
erine B. White School, Cleveland Junior High, Nolan Junior
High, and in Pershing he reached 11B.

"He had low blood pressure at one time, and his last job at
Ford's they had him working around the fires, and he couldn't
stand the heat. So he quit there, and he started working with
his uncle seven days a week. His uncle's a contractor—Robert
Williams—he said he was going to teach Freddie to lay bricks
to have a trade. Fred just didn't work that one Sunday. Larry
Reed called him, and I just thought he was going over on the
next block, said he was going to do some backstage work. That's
why he got to the Algiers at all.

"I just feel it didn't have to come to this. If they'd been *any*
kind of police. I don't want to feel bitter toward no one, but
when someone can be *that* cold. It looks like after you beat
people for an hour you ought to be able to come to some kind
of sense . . ."

2

A Dangerous Account

At this point in the narrative, enter myself. Reluctantly. I have always, before this, stayed out of my journalism, even as a manipulative pronoun, having believed that it sufficed for a writer to "come through" to the reader—by the nature of his selections from the whole, his filtering of all that had gone through his eyes and ears and mind; by the intensity of feeling that might be read in the lines; by his "voice." But this account is too urgent, too complex, too dangerous to too many people to be told in a way that might leave doubts strewn along its path; I cannot afford, this time, the luxury of invisibility. For the uses of invisibility, as Ralph Ellison has made so vividly and painfully clear—an inability or unwillingness to see the particularity of one's fellow man, and with it a crucial indifference as to whether one is seen truly as oneself—these uses of not-seeing and of not-being-seen are of the essence of racism.

In August 1967, soon after the Detroit riot of that summer, David Ginsburg, who had been appointed executive director of the President's Commission on Civil Disorders, asked me if I would write part of the commission's report. After much thought I declined, on the ground that I did not want to attach my work to a document over which, as a whole, I would have no control at all. In the aftermath of that decision, however, I came to feel that I owed some sort of debt of work to this, the most intransigent and fear-ridden issue in American life, and I broke off the writing of a novel in order to undertake a piece of reportage on one of the summer rebellions. I went to Detroit, with a general intention of writing overall about the devastating uprising there, and I began to interview various officials, starting with Mayor Jerome P. Cavanagh and Police Commissioner Ray Girardin and certain Negro leaders and some young black militants.

As I explored Detroit's riot in those first weeks, the incident at the Algiers Motel kept insisting upon attention, and eventually I determined to focus on it. This episode contained all the mythic themes of racial strife in the United States: the arm of the law taking the law into its own hands; interracial sex; the subtle poison of racist thinking by "decent" men who deny that they are racists; the societal limbo into which, ever since slavery, so many young black men have been driven in our country; ambiguous justice in the courts; and the devastation in both black and white human lives that follows in the wake of violence as surely as ruinous and indiscriminate flood after torrents.

It was not easy to get started. It took weeks to build bridges into the still-seething ghetto. I simply could not barge in on the homes of the bereaved and injured, like a carpetbagging lawyer with cash in hand to purchase witnessings; I needed friendly introductions, and I was fortunate, at last, in finding a young woman who was a close friend, not only of one of the families that had lost a son, but also of the black militant who organized the tribunal about which, if you go on, you will in due course read. She opened doors for me, and then I was on my own.

My own education in the course of the researches that followed was a staggering one. At the outset I learned how little I knew. I learned that experiences that I might have considered as credentials for this task had not given me sufficient insights for all that I was to confront. I had been born in China, had felt as a child the puzzling guilt of being pulled through the streets in a rickshaw by a yellow man; I had witnessed death and pain in war; I had tried to learn something about racism while writing several novels with racial themes; I had lived for part of the anxious summer of 1964 in the home of a black farmer (*I* was anxious; it was truly dangerous for him) in Holmes County, Mississippi; and for the past two years I had lived in intimacy with college students, the most open, most threatened, most serious, most generous people I had ever known. But these were not enough. Now I learned all sorts of new things, both about reality and about myself, and I learned how much more I have to learn about issues of race in my country.

At first, when I moved at night through streets of the scattered ghettos of Detroit, I felt the foreignness I had experienced as a child in China; the sense of apartness, of being alien and in a minority. I was afraid. My fear was indiscriminate. The people I came to know helped me to rid myself of that fear. Like them I am prudent now when I move through the night streets, but I am no longer afraid in that particular way. In dealing with them I was obliged, in order to reach out all the way to their trust, to confront myself with a searing honesty, and at times, I must now confess, I was deeply chagrined to discover that stereotypic thoughts lurked in corners of my own mind, which I had hoped was more or less open, and that some of my own fears had been tinged by the irrational in our history.

I was immeasurably aided in the ventilation of my mind by that surpassingly remarkable document of our time *The Autobiography of Malcolm X*, which every white American with any pretensions to racial understanding simply must read. (If you have not read it, close this book now and read that other and come back to these premises, if you will, later. I also wish, by the way, that some of our black friends who revere Malcolm X would read again with special care the last chapters of his book.) I had, besides, over the years, made it my business and pleasure—sometimes—to read works by Ellison, Richard Wright, James Baldwin, John Williams, LeRoi Jones, John Oliver Killens, William Melvin Kelley, Eldridge Cleaver, and other authors of their race, and I had found, indeed, that life imitated their art, when they achieved it, and that they had prepared me for my work.

In the end my new friends gave me such trust as to tell me secrets I wish I had not heard, for I must, or be a monster, withhold attributions of them from the book, and I had really wanted to avoid all holding back, all distortion; I heard murmurings of incest, of crime-breeding hatreds within families, of urges to kill outside families and across the dreadful color line. But I heard—apart from some ritual salutes from a few young militants I met—no word of hatred of me because of my being white; I was taken into black homes and was made to feel serenely at home; I observed at firsthand manifold examples of courage, loyalty, and family closeness; particularly moving were the sweet consideration of the tough young men for their mothers and their extreme loyalty to each other at all hazard; I had with these families and young men a sense of the importance of every moment of life much like that imparted to me by my student friends.

Eventually I had to face the problem of how to write about what I had learned, and I made certain decisions which I want to share with you, at a risk of being (as is my habit) obvious, before we go any farther. There was a need, above all, for total conviction. This meant that the events could not be described as if witnessed from above by an all-seeing eye opening on an all-knowing novelistic mind; the merest suspicion that anything had been altered, or made up, for art's sake, or for the sake of effect, would be absolutely disastrous. There could be no "creative reconstruction." Doubts about chronology could only be revealed, not resolved. No names could be changed, because when you change a man's name you change the whole man. The story would have to be told as much as possible in the words of the participants; and because I was all too aware that the truth had not always been told me, and indeed had not always been spoken under oath in court, I would have to let you, the reader, know at every step of the way exactly who was speaking, and to whom, and under what circumstances; and I could only use quotation marks when I had actually heard words spoken with my own ears, or was quoting from testimony given in court, or could give a clear attribution of a source which you could evaluate for yourself. An able Detroit newspaperman, Ladd Neuman, helped me run down some details; I will tell you when he quotes others. In a story involving such a large cast of characters and such terrible cross currents of jeopardy and of desire for justice and safety and revenge, I am bound to have made some mistakes, no matter how scrupulous I may have tried to be. I can only hope they will have been small ones.

Let not any of this suggest to you that I have been trying to persuade you, in the fraudulent tradition of American journalism, that I have been, or shall be, "objective." There is no such thing as objective reportage. Human life is far too trembling-swift to be reported in whole; the moment the recorder chooses nine facts out of ten he colors the information with his views. I trust this chapter will have revealed some of my bias for discount.

There were limitations within which I had to work. Trials of this case were being prepared, and some participants could not, and some would not, openly speak to me. I was unable to see three important witnesses. Nevertheless, I think you will find that a great deal was disclosed by those who did talk to me and did testify, for their very speech—the cadences, the images, the texture of their telling, the conscious and unconscious subterfuges they used—was, in my view, profoundly revealing.

Why did I not wait for the trials to be spun out? Was there not a risk of distorting or adulterating the legal process by such exposure as this? There was. I was fearfully aware that jail sentences, reputations, and perhaps even lives were at stake in the trials that were pending from this case. But I was also aware that lives had already been lost in it; that trials and appeals might drag on for several years (one constitutional issue at the first murder hearing might well be destined to go to the Supreme Court of the United States); that time does not stand still in the crisis of black and white in our country; that the families of the slain boys perceive the justice of a Northern city—one that was supposed to have been particularly enlightened—as being barely distinguishable from that of Mississippi. The assassination of Martin Luther King, Jr., which occurred during my writing of this book, demonstrated that white racists had learned nothing from that great preacher of nonviolence and less than nothing, even, from the instructive violence in the summers in the cities; and it gave me, along with a sense of despair, a sense of great urgency about the completion of this book. I am not so foolish as to believe that my telling of these events will change the course of history, or even of justice in this narrow instance; but I do believe that every scrap of understanding, every door-crack glimmer of illumination, every thread that may lead not just to survival of the races but to health—all should be shared as soon as possible. There is so much to be done in so little time.

Perhaps I should say at this point that I will not take any money from any source for the publication of this story.

If this declaration suggests to anyone that part of my motive in writing it may have been guilt, so be it. There is plenty of guilt lying around for the taking. Perhaps the whole point of this book is that every white person in the country is in some degree guilty of the crimes committed at the Algiers.

The report of the President's Commission on Civil Disorders, which was published in March 1968, blamed the explosive conditions in our cities that gave rise to the summer rebellions of recent years upon white racism. In its tone of frankness this was a remarkable document, and the spectacle of President Lyndon B. Johnson, who had not hesitated over the months to suggest, by epithet and inuendo, that anyone who disagreed with his Vietnam policy was a coward—the spectacle of this man running for cover from the conclusions of the commission which he created, and which he charged with the high task of seeking truth, was not only disgusting; it was positively inflammatory, for it denied the very thesis of the report. The Texan seemed to want to deny the charge of white racism. Only with the death of Dr. King did he stir himself to piety, and then his words proposed much too little much too late.

Remarkable as the commission's report was, it did not face up to the implications of its own historic accusation. All of its recommendations were in the nature of palliations, and they did not attack the root problem of racism itself. There was not a whisper in all its pages about sex, which I believe to be at the very core of racism. If real progress is to be made, it cannot be made simply by expenditures of funds, even in great sums, on "programs"; racism must be a educated or coaxed or wrenched or stamped out of the centers of injustice and grievance—namely, out of police forces, courts, legislatures, unions, industry, schools, the civil service, and the bureaucracy of welfare.

There are four main causes of racial violence: unequal justice, unequal employment opportunities, unequal housing, unequal education. This book, to put it in perspective, deals only with the first. I believe that is the one that should be attacked first, because it is at the cutting edge of irritation in the inner cities; because it is the prime cause of the deep anger of those without whom there would be no summer rebellions, the young black males; and because, to be practical about it, its remedy would cost not a cent. The remedy is in the minds of men. Unequal justice is experienced by the black populace at two points: what happens with the cop in the street, and what happens with the prosecutor and lawyer and judge in court.

The men and women involved in the Algiers incident were caught up in processes much larger than themselves. This does not mean that they do not deserve compassion or punishment or, in one or two cases, both. It means rather that their fates— for fate intervenes precisely when the individual is helplessly caught up by cyclonic forces of history and of human nature—their fates, far from being commonplace, are elevated to something close to the tragic. I do not think I am overblowing. Though the principals of the Algiers incident may not be heroic figures and so may not be entitled to the fullest measure of tragedy, I bid you to read on about them and see whether you are not pretty well purged of pity and terror as you follow this tale of humble citizens to its unresolved ending.

3

Too Hot to Handle

Wednesday evening, July 26,
to Monday afternoon, July 31

1 | We Began Yelling

"It was kind of an accident," Leon Atchison, administrative assistant in Detroit to U. S. Representative John Conyers, Jr., told me, "that we took the Algiers case to the Justice Department. Me and Congressman Conyers and Arthur Featherstone and Julius Watson of our staff here and State Senator James DelRio, a friend of ours named Lester Morgan, and Julian Witherspoon, who works for TAP, had volunteered to go out on Wednesday night, take these bullhorns out and try to persuade people to observe the curfew, you know. We went over to the Tenth Precinct. The Police Commissioner had called over there and told this lieutenant that we were coming, and we went in the office there and the lieutenant sat us down and told us what the routine would be, said there were going to be these three squad cars to take us out and the officers who were going to ride in those squad cars were having dinner, and we would just wait for them there in the office.

"So we sat around awhile, and then we got tired of waiting, and we wandered out into the lobby. The police stations in

Detroit were the most guarded place of any place in the city. They had all these National Guard and policemen and Army people standing around at parade rest with their guns, so there were so many of them there that when we got out there in the lobby they didn't even notice us, and we just stood around there and watched what was going on."

This was not the first time Congressman Conyers had been willing to take his chances in the riot. Conyers, a handsome, mustached, impeccably dressed bachelor, one of two Negro U.S. Representatives from the city—Detroit being the only city in the country in 1967 to have two Negro Congressmen—had gone out on Twelfth Street late Sunday morning and had climbed up on the hood of a car with a bullhorn to try to cool the first mob of the riot. "We're with you," he had shouted, according to *The New York Times*. He tried to tell the crowd that he would make an effort to have all white policemen withdrawn from the area. "No, no, no," the rioters chanted. "Uncle Tom!" "Don't want to hear it!" A bottle crashed on the curb by the car. A rock hit a nearby policeman. Someone gave Conyers a hand and he jumped down. "You try to talk to those people," he said to a Detroit newspaper reporter, "and they'll knock you into the middle of next year." Later he said to another newspaperman that he doubted if anyone—except possibly the late Malcolm X—could have stemmed the riot at that point.

Atchison went on: "And they were taking these prisoners out of the garage beside the station one by one past the desk sergeant to another door, where they were having the interrogations. We were just standing around there, and the door from the garage flew open, and here came this cop with no shirt on, with a judo lock around the neck of this fellow, a colored man, and he was shouting, 'You big black motherfucker, you come on now, come on, get in here.' He couldn't move him, so he took two handcuffs and put them around his hand and hit him on the forehead and just split his head open. And then a little bit later the interrogation room door flew open, and this prisoner came out all bloody and with a smashed nose, and they took him out and put him on a bus; they had three buses outside they were putting these prisoners on. And after that the door to the garage opened, and this woman came out just covered with blood.

"So at that point we began yelling, and then all the doors closed, and the police officers began being real circumspect. And this lieutenant came out, and he explained to us how tired the police were, how their buddies had been shot in the riot, and the touchiness of the situation, and all that bullshit.

"So we refused to go out the way we had said we were going to.

"The next day ABC called and said, 'We understand your office has burned down, and we'd like to come and do a filming right on the spot of the office,' and we agreed to that, and we met out there at the office, and they were doing all this filming and interviewing. While it was going on, an armored car backed up to the bank that was next door to take the money from the vault; backed right up on the sidewalk and blocked the view from the next part. There were all these soldiers around guarding it. After the filming we had to go past the armored car and around to get back to our cars, and the Congressman went over to the officer in charge and asked for an escort back to our cars so we wouldn't be molested. And he very willingly said he would give us that, and I came around in front of everybody, around the armored car, and on the other side there were these two policemen talking with another cop, and a cop with a gun ran at me and hit me on the forehead with the gun that he was holding up to bar my way. So I shoved him back at the wall, and he stumbled over some bricks and fell over. He took his safety off his gun, and he was going to blast at me, and just then all these cameras came around the corner of the armored car. That saved my life. We asked him his name, but he refused to give it to us. The police weren't wearing badges during the riot, so we couldn't report him.

"So then we went straight down to Vance, Secretary Vance"
—Cyrus L. Vance, President Johnson's personal emissary to

Detroit during the riots—"and we demanded that the Justice Department be brought in on this thing.

"So the next day Murphy"—Deputy Assistant U.S. Attorney General Robert A. Murphy—"came over to Congressman Conyers's house. While he was standing there ringing the doorbell, I was on the phone getting a report about this woman who'd been raped in the Tenth Precinct. Murphy went to the house of the woman, and it turned out that what had happened was that the cops had been propositioning the women in the police station. One of them did submit, and they just shoved her back in the enclosure with the rest of them. What they were doing, they were stripping these women and feeling them up and taking pictures of them with a Polaroid in indecent positions with them."

(In a summary of seventy-three complaints of police brutality issued by Conyers's office, there is no mention of the alleged rape, but this item—the name, address, and telephone number of the woman are given—appears: " . . . dragged into station and searched ripping off upper clothing, photographed while officer held breasts, given sweater and that taken away so still naked. Told to pull off lower clothing, officers pulled them down. Subject has pajama top that was torn to shreds.")

"One of the officers," Atchison said to me, "they did kick one of the officers off the force, that's one thing they did do something about. The next day the complainants were found on that and all these other things. They began to find out where the Congressman had moved his new office to; that was the Retail Store Employees Union Hall, at 2550 West Grand Boulevard. They have these sort of modern offices there, and they came streaming through there, among them Omar Gill and Eddie Temple and some of the witnesses to the things that had happened at the Algiers.

"Then at the end of the day, they couldn't afford to keep the Union Hall open, so we went down to Nathan Conyers's office" —Nathan Conyers is an attorney, brother of the Congressman —"and that evening it was down there that these witnesses of the Algiers incident gave their testimony to Murphy. They took all our notes on it, and they won't give them back to us."

2 | A State of Shock

"So I talked with Mr. Gill again," Eddie Temple told me, "it would have been Thursday. I came back down to the morgue to see the wounds. They showed me a picture of the wounds, and I went down there and asked the doctor at the morgue her opinion of what had happened, this was all part of trying to find out what had happened. She thought that they had been shot as snipers. I told her then that it was impossible, I'd been to the motel. The wounds that he had went *down*, which would have been impossible if they'd been shot from the outdoors in, they would have had to shoot up to that level. Later on her testimony was completely different; in court she did state that they were indoors, as to how the wounds had been inflicted. I saw Mr. Gill there, too; we talked a little bit then, and I told him I would be trying to get something started to find out what really happened, and get the policemen who had done this.

"I called him later, and he took me around to some of the boys, Lee Forsythe, Sortor, and Michael Clark, took me to their homes, and they told me what had happened. They were very afraid. If he hadn't been with me, they wouldn't have said anything. They were in a state of shock, which can easily be understood. They showed me their busted heads, they were all bruised. After hearing what they had to say, it was obvious that this whole thing had evolved just the way it was being told: how these people had come in and lined up and beat them up and shot some of them.

"So I called Detective Schlachter again. He still insisted that they were snipers, and that the police shot and killed them through the windows, and that was when I told him definitely that he didn't know what he was talking about, and that he should investigate the thing, that this was his job. I did at that time give him the names and phone numbers and the addresses, but he said he hadn't been able to talk to anyone on it because he didn't even know who was there. After I gave him their names and numbers, he did go out and talk to them."

3 | Riot Victim

"*I*, Clara Raven, M.D., *certify that I performed the autopsy on* Auburey Pollard, aka [also known as] Unknown Man #104, *deceased, and that the attached description is correct and accurate. In my opinion the cause of death is*: Shotgun wound of chest.

"*Gross Diagnoses*:

"1.   1½" gaping wound of right anterior axillary line, 6" beneath the axilla, with fracture of the 6th rib with maceration and penetration of right and left ventricles, laceration of the aorta, multiple penetrating wounds of both lungs and liver and fractures of 11th thoracic vertebra and pellet punctures of the 7th, 8th, 9th, 10th interspaces left chest posterior axillary line.

"2.   Multiple shotgun pellet wounds of interior right chest wall.

"3.   Bilateral hemothorax.

"4.   Large 2" x 1¾" grazing laceration of medial surface of right arm, 6" beneath the axilla.

"5.   Abrasions of posterior portion of right forearm and right forehead.

"Status: Riot Victim."

Other significant information:

"There is marked tearing of the muscle [of the right upper arm] with abrasion and burning around the wound. . . ."

Carl Cooper, "aka Unknown Man #105," had suffered "multiple shotgun wounds of chest and abdomen with penetrating wounds of lungs, heart, liver, stomach, and aorta" and "multiple compound comminuted fractures of left upper arm." There had been massive bleeding of chest and abdomen. Ten buckshot pellets had been recovered from the chest wall. There was a shotgun wound on his left thigh.

Fred Temple, "aka Unknown Man #106," had received two shotgun wounds, one in his right breast at the nipple, the other in the lower chest wall on the left side, penetrating his right lung, pancreas, liver, stomach, and transverse colon. The buckshot had gone right through his body, and there was a "mutilating wound" of the back of his left elbow. "Shotgun slugs and 2 pieces of wadding recovered in right chest cavity."

Tests for drugs and alcohol in all three cadavers were negative.

4 | He Did Go Out

Detective Schlachter testified in court:

"On July 27, 1967, I talked to Eddie Temple, brother of Fred Temple. . . .

"On July 27, at 3:50 p.m., I talked with Witness Cleveland Reed. On the same date and at the same time I talked with Naomi Reed, the mother of Cleveland Reed. Took his statement in her presence. . . .

"On July 27, at 4:53 p.m., I talked to Roderick Davis in the presence of his mother, Rosa Davis. . . ."

5 | A Building Full of People

"I called Conyers's office," Eddie Temple told me, "and I talked to Leon Atchison, and I told him what had happened, and I told him how frustrated I was about not getting any support, and that I knew that this thing was bound to be whitewashed by the Police Department if possible. He said they had a building full of people who were making complaints. This is what got us in contact."

6 | I Was Making Inquiries

On Friday, July 28, Detective Schlachter had a rather frustrating afternoon, according to his testimony. "At 2:35 p.m. Detective Smith and myself went to 8733 Arcadia, talked to Lilly Calloway regarding the whereabouts of a witness. I believe that was Forsythe, Lee Forsythe. . . . On July 28, I went to the home of James Sortor, and I talked with his sister, Judy Sortor. That was on July 28, 1967, at 3:05 p.m. I was making inquiries as to where James was." He did see Clara Gilmore that afternoon at 5:15 p.m.

7 | The Conference Was Put Off

"I did take Roderick Davis to this press conference that was supposed to be with John Conyers down at the Sheraton-Cadillac, and Sortor, Mr. Gill brought Sortor down there, so we had two people give the story to the *Free Press* and the *News*. One of the reporters said it was too hot for them to handle. John Conyers was not there but people were expecting him, so the conference was put off until that Saturday morning. None of the papers ran the story the next morning. Kurt Luedtke from the *Free Press*, he had called, he was trying to get some additional information, he said he was going to run a story. And he asked for authorization, based on the information we had given him, to have the *Free Press* have a pathologist check the bodies."

The Pollards and Gills also gave permission for the *Free Press* autopsies.

8 | Walking in My Door

"They got word to Chaney," Mrs. Pollard told me. "They put him in a boxcar, on a shipping plane, where they ship anything, carloads—as long as they got him back from Vietnam. Auburey died that Wednesday morning, and Friday evening they had Chaney back here, he was walking in my door."

9 | Just That Afraid

"The next news conference"—on Saturday, July 29—"I did take Roderick Davis," Eddie Temple told me. "This one, Conyers was there, and there were several concerned groups about being brutalized." An ad hoc committee had been formed to handle alleged violations of citizens' civil rights during the disturbance; it included Conyers, Congressman Charles Diggs, State Senator Coleman Young, the NAACP, the Wolverine Bar Association, the ACLU, and the Michigan Civil Rights Commission. "This was primarily to find out the basis for all these complaints. There were volunteers taking statements—not in shorthand, but long-hand—and there were several people there with their heads all busted up and their bodies busted up. It took a tremendous lot of effort to get these boys to go to these news conferences. I had said I was going to get in touch with the police, and it scared them to death. They were afraid to death of policemen. When these policemen let the ones go that they did let go, they told them that they'd better not tell or they was going to kill them. And they believed it. I mean when you see somebody shoot somebody down, you believe that they'll shoot you down, too. They sincerely believed that the police were going to shoot them down. This took a lot of begging and pleading. I had to use the deaths and justice to try to get them there. They were just that afraid."

10 | To Frighten Him

NAME: *Roderick Davis*   INTERVIEWER: *Lois Lewis*
    "Police beat Mr. Davis about the head 7 or eight times.
    "Police ask him questions and when he attempted to answer them he was told to shut up and was beaten.
    "Was robbed by Police of 15 or 20 dollars. Took wallet and haven't returned it. (Was not given a receipt for his articles.) Shoes.
    "Smashed his fingers with a gun.

"Forced to lie down on floor spread eagle and fired shots into floor in an attempt to frighten him.

"When finally permitted to go home was subjected in abusive language to march away with his hands in the air barefooted. Told not to look back."

11 | At Close Range

Dr. Robert J. Sillery examined the bodies on Saturday morning for the *Free Press* at the three funeral homes to which they had been removed. In the case of Fred Temple, whose body was at White House Funeral Directors, the funeral was to be held that day, and "the body," Dr. Sillery's report said, "was completely clothed and laid out in a casket. It was not possible to remove the body from the casket. The clothing covering the chest and abdomen was folded back, and only those portions of the body so exposed were examined." Dr. Sillery's reports served to confirm in every respect the autopsy reports of Dr. Raven, who must surely be the most appropriately named morgue lady in the United States. Together the autopsies proved beyond doubt that the boys were shot indoors, at close range.

12 | Sure, It's the Police

At eleven ten a.m. on Saturday, Detective Schlachter interviewed Michael Clark.

At one p.m. he talked, according to his testimony, "to a *News* reporter, two of them, Kurt Luedtke, Barbara Stanton, and Dr. Sillery at the scene of the Algiers Motel." What Luedtke and Miss Stanton, who were from the *Free Press*, not the *News*, had to say, with the backing of Dr. Sillery, apparently did not please Detective Schlachter. In an article later Miss Stanton reported that he was "yelling that everybody is playing cops-and-robbers and tracking all over his investigation."

"Sure," she quoted him as saying, "it's the police who were the villains. You just watch and see, when this is all over it'll be the fault of the police, all over the country. Police start riots, police start trouble, police do the killing. Yeah, it's all the police-man's fault, always the police."

13 | Find the Truth

In the Fish Room of the White House, in Washington, D.C., at almost this very same time, President Johnson was greeting the members of his Commission on Civil Disorders, who had con-vened for their first meeting. In his remarks to them he said, in part:

"One thing should be absolutely clear: This matter is far, far too important for politics. It goes to the health and safety of all American citizens—Republicans and Democrats. It goes to the proper responsibilities of officials in both of our parties. It goes to the heart of our society in a time of swift change and of great stress. . . .

"So, Mr. Chairman and Mr. Vice Chairman, let your search be free. Let it be untrammeled by what has been called the 'conventional wisdom.' As best you can, find the truth, the whole truth, and express it in your report. . . . "

14 | The Odor of a Case

S. Allen Early, Jr., a very tall, powerfully built Negro attorney with a somehow somber and world-weary expression, whose mind worked at electric speeds, who wore stylish tweeds, and whose big hands flopped as he talked with great clarity on any subject that presented itself, seemed to me, when I met him, to have a strangely ambiguous style. A graduate of the Yale Law School (1944) who had lived for some years in New York, then Europe, then Washington, he could carry off an easy Eastern sophistication; yet he seemed to be burning, at the center of his life, with banked fires. He had served for four years, from 1959 to 1963, as Assistant Prosecutor for Wayne County, and perhaps that had been a harrowing post. I had heard that he had been through a domestic tragedy.

On Friday, July 28, Allen Early told me, a client called him and said he knew somebody who knew something about the Algiers killings. "He turned up with the two girls. I listened to their story, and having been a prosecutor I thought I recognized the odor of a case. We didn't know then what was going to happen. The police were trying to find the boys, and we thought the girls might possibly be in some danger. I had the bright idea of hiding them on a boat—a friend's boat; I used to have one, but this belonged to a lawyer friend of mine, a forty-three-foot '67 Chris-Craft. I had keys to it. It was at the City Marina. I took the girls over and stashed them aboard; they seemed to like the set-up. This was more or less at my back door—I live just a block from the marina—and I went to do some grocery shopping, left the girls under guard of my partner, Elliott Hall. They suggested that they'd like to take a little walk around Belle Isle, and they took off—borrowed a quarter apiece. That was the last Elliott saw of them. I tell you, I felt a bit of consternation, when I got back, to find out that we'd been duped by those little girls. They hitchhiked back uptown, and we eventually found them trying to get back to the boy who'd been harboring them. Bubba Carter persuaded them to go with us. . . ."

15 | We Just Thought We Would Move

In the conspiracy hearing, Julia Ann Hysell was cross-examined as follows by Attorney for the Defense Norman Lippitt:

Q. What is your name, please, witness?
A. Juli Hysell.
Q. How old are you?
A. Eighteen.
Q. Where were you born?
A. Columbus, Ohio.
Q. When did you move to Detroit?
A. The end of June.
Q. Of what year, please?
A. '67. . . .

Q. All right. Were you employed when you were in Columbus, Ohio?

A. Yes.

Q. And what were you employed as?

A. A beautician.

Q. And how long were you so employed?

A. About six months.

Q. Did you graduate from high school?

A. No.

Q. How far did you go in school?

A. About eleven and three-quarter years.

Q. Who did you live with in Columbus, Ohio?

A. My parents, and then I had an apartment of my own.

Q. Who did you come to Detroit with?

A. Karen Malloy and Nancy Stallnaker.

Q. And was Karen Malloy also from Columbus, Ohio?

A. Yes.

Q. What was your reason for coming to Detroit?

A. We just thought we would move to Detroit.

Q. You just thought you would move to Detroit?

A. Uh-huh.

Q. How did you get to Detroit? What did you use for transportation?

A. Some kids came up. They were coming up this way so they brought us up.

Q. And where did you stay when you came to Detroit?

A. Pontchartrain.

Q. And how long did you stay at the Pontchartrain?

A. A week.

Q. Why did you leave the Pontchartrain?

A. Because it was too expensive.

Q. Well, did you pay your bill when you left the Pontchartrain?

A. My parents paid mine.

Q. I said did *you* pay your bill when you left the Pontchartrain?

A. No.

Q. Did you run out on the bill at the Pontchartrain? . . .
A. Yes.
Q. All right. Now where did you move from the Pontchartrain Hotel?
A. At the Pallister, I believe. . . .
Q. And how long did you stay at the Pallister?
A. A week or so.
Q. And what were you doing for a living at the Pallister Hotel?
A. I wasn't doing anything for a living. I was on vacation.
Q. You were on vacation?
A. Uh-huh.
Q. How long did you remain on vacation before you went back to work?
A. I haven't went back to work yet. . . .
Q. All right. Now when did you move to the Algiers Motel?
A. After we left the Pallister.
Q. All right. And when was that? Can you give me a date?
A. I can't remember. [In her statement to the police, earlier, she had given July 22 as the date; Karen had said July 21.] . . .
Q. And what apartment or room in the Algiers did you take when you moved there?
A. 12-A.
Q. And did you take it along with anyone else?
A. Karen and Nancy.
Q. And did Nancy stay there then until the 26th of July? Was she there on the 26th?
A. No, I believe she left the 24th or the 25th.
Q. So that left you and Karen in that apartment at the Algiers Motel?
A. Yes. . . .
Q. You were registered at the Motel, were you?
A. Yes, I was.
Q. In your name?
A. No.
Q. In what name?
A. I didn't register personally. Someone else registered.

Q. Who registered?

A. Someone else.

Q. Yes. Who registered for you, Miss Hysell? You are under oath. Who registered for you at that Motel?

A. I don't know.

Q. How did you get to that Motel originally?

A. I took a cab.

Q. A cab physically took you to the Motel and you got out of the car, of the cab, right?

A. That's correct.

Q. Now, there came a point in time and place when you were registered, is that not true?

A. That's correct.

Q. Did you walk out of the taxicab and into the office of the Motel?

A. No, I didn't.

Q. Where did you go?

A. I walked over and was talking to some people.

Q. And then did you go and register at the office?

A. No, one of the fellows registered.

Q. Who registered?

A. I don't know. It was somebody Nancy knew. . . .

Q. Did she go to the Algiers Motel with you?

A. Yes. . . .

Q. And how is it that you knew to go to room A-12?

A. Well, we stood there until they came back with the key.

Q. And I asked you who this was.

A. I am not sure. I don't want to say.

Q. In your best recollection and judgment, who was it?

A. I don't know. There was four or five fellows standing around.

Q. Did you know any of them?

A. Not then.

Q. Not then?

A. No. I had seen them.

Q. Did you know them subsequently?

A. I know them vaguely.

Q. What are their names?
A. I don't know their last name. . . .
Q. All right. Did you thereafter learn their names?
A. Their first names. I never bother with last names. . . .
Q. How much money did you originally come to Detroit with?
A. A couple of dollars.
Q. And how much did it cost you to stay at the Algiers Motel every evening you were there?
A. Ten dollars.
Q. Ten dollars a night?
A. Uh-huh. . . .
Q. How did you pay for this?
A. My parents sent me money.
Q. Your parents sent you money?
A. Uh-huh.
Q. How did they send you this money?
A. Western Union.
Q. And how often did they send you money?
.A Any time I called them and asked for it.
Q. How much money in total have your parents sent you since this thing took place?
A. Oh, probably about a thousand dollars. . . .

16 | Sanctuary

The riot had by late Saturday afternoon pretty well subsided. One crucial problem the city had was where to put all its prisoners. More than seven thousand had been arrested, and almost all were being held on high bail. Wayne County Jail was crammed, and so were police hoosegows and garages, both at Headquarters and at the precincts; busloads of arrestees had been sent to Jackson State Prison and the federal prison at Milan.

Late Saturday afternoon, Wayne County Prosecutor William Cahalan, a man with a smooth, waxy complexion that makes him seem exceptionally scrubbed and decent, as a public prosecutor should be, and with a tendency to trip over little words in his speech, which makes him seem eager even under pressure, as

he should be, too, went (as he told me later) to city-owned
Belle Isle, in the Detroit River, to inspect the bathhouse there,
to see whether it could serve as a place of incarceration. It
was, eventually, made into one, and it was dubbed Belcatraz—
"with every cell a showerbath." Police Commissioner Ray
Girardin told me that access to Belle Isle, over a single bridge,
had been shut off early in he riot. There were memories of
Detroit's vicious race riot of 1943, which started there; and
there was, besides, a sudden concern about two private clubs
that leased quarters there on public ground, the Yacht Club and
the Boat Club, which excluded Negroes from their membership
—even "white" Negroes who owned yachts (according to J.
Anthony Lukas in *The New York Times Magazine* of August
27, 1967: among the yachts that had lined up along the course
of the annual speedboat race in the Detroit River on the Fourth
of July, 1967, nineteen days before the riot, at least thirty were
owned by Negroes). This made Belle Isle a peaceful sanctuary,
and after his inspection of Belcatraz, Prosecutor Cahalan joined
Joseph Schirmer, a photographer, on Schirmer's yacht for a
session of sociability and escape from the worries of office. The
interlude was destined to be short.

17 | A Great Probability

"Attorney S. Allen Early called and said that he had the two
girls who were involved in the incident," Leon Atchison told
me, "and that he wanted to bring them down and give a statement along with everybody else. Because our temporary office
was in the Retail Store Employees Union Hall, and they had to
close at five o'clock, we had to advise everyone who wanted to
make complaints after that time to come down to Nathan Conyers's office, and of course the Justice Department was in town
at that time also. Early brought the two girls down, and Mr.
Davis and Mr. Temple and Cleveland Reed and Charles Moore
came down to Nathan Conyers's office and gave statements. And
the Justice Department, Mr. Bob Murphy, was also there. Mr.
Murphy wound up with all of the material.

"It was clear to me that their statements were enough alike, and they didn't really know each other, that there was some substance to it. We felt that if you added the other ingredient, that the police had failed to report the shootings to their superiors, it was really the motel employees that reported the bodies, then there was a great probability that the police did in fact commit murder there.

"We had faith that the Justice Department would move in on this matter and see to it that if the Prosecutor's Office and the Police Department failed to do the kind of job that should be done, they would do it. Everyone there felt, all of the witnesses and ourselves, we felt that would be the case. We didn't have any faith in the Police Department investigating itself on this. Mr. Cahalan, the new prosecutor, came in with a pretty good reputation, but we had to take a sort of wait-and-see attitude on what he was really going to do. So therefore we went the federal route, to make sure that something was done.

"We're not sure how the *Free Press* found out that we were having this meeting at Nathan Conyers's office. During the meeting Mr. Luedtke called from the *Free Press* and asked us not to release any information that we had gathered at this meeting, because he felt that it would jeopardize his investigation; he really felt that he was on top of the situation.

"But S. Allen Early, for some unknown reason, on a pretext of taking one of the girls [Karen] out to get a cup of coffee, took her over to the Prosecutor's Office," which summoned Mr. Cahalan posthaste from Joe Schirmer's yacht. "And the next thing we knew the police, the Prosecutor's Office, was calling us, asking for the other girl. Senator Coleman Young took the other girl over. That was their first contact with the two girls."

18 | Oh, God! Oh, God!

Eddie Temple had gone straight from the press conference earlier in the day to his brother's funeral at White House Funeral Directors. Larry Reed and Rod Davis were late. "I went over there," Larry told me, "but I couldn't make it in. I tried to get there late, so I wouldn't have to look at the body. It was already closed when I got there." One of the Temple twins, Herbert, also missed the funeral. "He was a blue baby when he was born," Mrs. Temple told me, "and the doctor warned me the child might have trouble. He took a car, about a year ago, and they sentenced him to one to one and a half years up at [the Michigan State Reformatory at] Ionia. They held him downtown for four whole months, and he's had nearly a year up there." "He could have come," Ella Temple Clark told me, "they would have let him come, but he would have had to have two policemen escorting him, and Mother couldn't stand the idea of having *policemen* at the funeral."

"Carl," Mrs. Gill told me, "didn't have no front, he didn't have no chest, no stomach, no privates, no organs, or nothing." (The charge of deliberate castration of Carl Cooper was to come up later. Both autopsies noted shotgun wounds of the left thigh, but neither made any mention of damage to Cooper's genitals. Dr. Raven's diagram of the anterior view of his body shows this wound as on the outer part of the thigh, and she wrote, "There is a large area of abrasion of the left anterior thigh region, measuring approximately 4″ x 2½″, with a number of punctate wounds in this abraded area." Dr. Sillery wrote, "The wound here is superficial and involves only skin and subcutaneous tissue." As to the radical and damaging nature of the other wounds there was no doubt in either doctor's report.) "They had Carl padded, you know," Mrs. Gill went on. "He couldn't hold the fluid. He was pretty well messed up. The undertaker told me that they worked with him all day to get him ready for showing. Took all day. He said, 'Don't touch him,' because I mean they had to change his hands the next day where he was turning dark, they had to pack him, he couldn't hold the fluid, you know."

Carl's funeral at the Swanson Funeral Home was described in a supplement on riots in the September-October 1968 issue of *Trans-Action*, a magazine published at Washington University, St. Louis:

"Cooper's funeral was a Jessica Mitford affair held in a funeral home so 'tasteful' that it looked like an architect's drawing rather than a building in use. Clark was one of the pallbearers. 'I knew Carl since we was little kids.' Cooper's family and friends seemed the sort known as 'the good people of the Negro community.' They were decorous people, well-dressed and driving good cars. They were not necessarily middle class, but they were urban people, not poverty-stricken Southern migrants dressed uncomfortably in their mail-order suits and Sunday dresses. The body was lying in an open coffin. The minister offered his comforting best to a background of weeping. After everyone had passed the body, curtains were drawn across the front of the room, hiding the pulpit and the body. Suddenly, the room erupted in a surge of emotion. Women screamed and several charged the curtain only to be led away by attendants. The family seating section lost all semblance of regularity as women began to rock back and forth, and soon everyone was moving around the room. The funeral director eyed his watch; another cortege was waiting to move into the chapel. The women who had been led away went back into the room. The minister offered more words and then the curtains were reopened and Clark and the other pallbearers moved the coffin out to the hearse."

"Those calls and letters," Mrs. Pollard told me, "commenced to come in before the funeral and after the funeral. The letters were dirty letters. One of them said, 'I'm a National Guard's wife and damn proud of it,' said, 'Negro hoods running the streets, they will not stop until they all be stuck like a zombie,' they wasn't supposed to be living, and all that. 'Your pimp-ass son, we're glad he's dead.' Your pimp-ass son. How in hell she know he was a pimp? He was drawing compensation, a pimp ain't going to work in no factory. The phone calls, once it was a man and once it was a woman, they saying if the police got any time, they would see that I'd be dead. They said I'd die a little harder than Auburey died, said he died hard enough, but if the police got any time, if we pressed any charges, must remember we'd die just like him. If anything happened to a police-man, well, I'd get a worse death than my son got. Way I feel, I ain't got too much to live for anyway.

"See, when I taken Chaney to the undertakers to see Auburey, you know, we got ready, I was going to touch his head, you know, I wanted to feel of him, you know. Undertaker told me, he say, 'No, no, don't touch him.' Said he just got him pieced together, because they naturally tore him up. Said, 'Don't touch him, Mrs. Pollard.' The undertaker was the R. T. Wilson Funeral Home. I don't think he'd been in business too long, but he said that if I would subpoena him, he'd come into court and tell just what kind of shape he got him out of the morgue, be-cause they cut him up so bad his mortician had a hard time trying to put him back together. They did a awful bum job on him. That's the reason I sent the *Free Press* man out there, after he told me they done cut him up so bad I just figured we could take an autopsy too, you know. So when they took this autopsy they didn't see no whiskey or beer or alcohol or dope or *any-thing* on him.

"So then when they told me, 'Don't touch him,' Chaney, he started to hollering and screaming and going on, hollering, 'Oh, God! Oh, God!' You know what he said? 'Momma, they don't kill them in Vietnam like that! They don't torture them then shoot them or blow them up when they got through with them. Momma, they don't stand them up and beat their face off before they kill them,' he said. 'Momma, they did worse than if they caught one of them Vietnams out there.' We had to carry Chaney out of there. He just went to pieces. He said, 'Just wait till I get my men over here. Just wait till my crew comes. When my crew comes we're going to show them something. We'll set them booby traps. We'll bomb them. We know we can get them. Just wait.' Till all the police looked at him like they was going to kill him. See, I knew he was out of his head. He'd say, 'There's a man out there following me.' He didn't trust nobody. wanted to lock everything up. He thought everybody was go-ing to kill me."

19 | Executed

On Sunday, July 30, Joseph Strickland, a star reporter of the Detroit *News*, having traced Robert Greene, the paratrooper veteran of Vietnam who had been at the Algiers on the night of the killings, to his home in Hopkinsville, Kentucky, flew down to Hopkinsville with Detective Schlachter and Assistant Wayne County Prosecutor Jesse B. Eggleton. On that same day, as it happened, Kurt Luedtke of the *Free Press* decided to break the long silence about the Algiers incident.

Luedtke's front-page story, which hit the stands Sunday evening, was unsensational; on inside pages, another article gave details of the *Free Press* investigation. Luedtke wrote that the paper's information "indicates that the men were killed inside the building and not by police or soldiers firing into the house. . . . Officials now fear that the three Negroes were deliberately executed."

One of these officials, according to Luedtke, said, "The big question is who did it, and there are a dozen theories about that."

20 | I'll Never Forget That Face

Strickland's story from Hopkinsville, which appeared on the front page of the *News* the next morning, was sensational indeed. "An eyewitness located here by *The Detroit News*," it began, "told Detroit and Wayne County investigators today that he saw a white National Guard warrant officer shoot to death two Detroit Negro youths at a Woodward Avenue motel during the riot."

Strickland quoted Greene as having said, presumably to him, "I saw the National Guard officer kill two of the boys." Greene, Strickland reported, "said he would be able to identify the National Guard officer. . . . 'I'll never forget that face.'" (Greene, however, who was taken from Hopkinsville to Detroit by Detective Schlachter after the questioning, was unable to pick that face out of the line at a show-up in the Detroit Police Headquarters that very next night; this peculiar episode will unwind itself later in this narrative.)

On page 17, that Monday morning, the *News* printed a transcript of Prosecutor Eggleton's questioning of Greene, and it turned out, if one read far enough, that Greene had not in fact claimed to have seen a National Guardsman kill two of the boys; he had seen a warrant officer take a boy in a room and had heard a shot. "Then," he said, "the guy next to me, they took him to A-4. The officer told him not to take him to A-4. He said, 'Take him to another room.' And he took him to A-5, I think it was A-5, that's the back room there. We heard another shot fired, and he came out and said, 'That nigger didn't even kick.'"

Q.   "Was that the warrant officer also?"
A.   "Right."

21 | Joy

If Detective Schlachter, flying back to Detroit with Witness Greene, was delighted, as one can guess that he was, to have had the heat of the Algiers Motel case removed at last from the Police Department, his joy was to be short-lived.

I I

Three Cops and Three Days

4

The First Day

Sunday, July 23

1 | If We Had Started Firing Then

David Senak—twenty-four years old; five feet nine inches tall; three-year veteran of the Detroit police force; enthusiast of the clean-up, or vice, squad; winner of two citations; unmarried; Baptist; with a boyish pink complexion that flushed and paled markedly in response to the flow and ebb of emotion; with an attractive smile which pushed deep dimples into his cheeks; called by some Dave but also the bearer of two other nicknames, of which he told with a humorous sparkle in his eyes, the first an anagram of his name, Snake, and the other given him by an aunt, "Inda," which, he said, means snake poison in Slovak—sat at his desk in his den at home, under the snarling fangs of the stuffed head of a wolf shot by an uncle of his, beside a carefully kept file of his exploits on the force ("I like to look back and see what I've done"), and he told me this:

"I was working plain-clothes on that Sunday morning—I was on clean-up, we were arresting prostitutes, well that particular month we were on numbers mainly, because we were working days—and I was scheduled to work at ten a.m. They called me about five thirty or so from the station and told me that there was a disturbance of some sort and we were to come in uniform that morning as soon as possible. So I called a partner of mine that lives around here, and him and I went in to the station together; we got there about six, a quarter after six, and the men were milling around, and I was put on a scout car at first, within the precinct. Just shortly after we got on the street they called us back, and they formed us into units to go over to Twelfth, Tenth Precinct, Twelfth Street.

"We went over there, and they put us out into a task force. I think the first time I saw Twelfth and Clairmount was around eleven o'clock, we drove by it, and the riots themselves, it seemed like they were contained within one block, and there were very few people in the street and a lot of police officers. Mainly people were looking out their windows at the time. Then around maybe an hour after that things started getting a little worse, where they'd be calling for us, 'Police officers in trouble,' and we'd be going from one police-officer-in-trouble to another. We'd just break up a crowd in one place and they'd be congregating in another. This brought us to about one o'clock—six or seven officers in trouble; we made one raid on a drug store that the window was smashed, and we got two or three prisoners from there and took them in to Number Ten and went back on the street.

"And then we got a run to Philadelphia and Twelfth. We proceeded east on Philadelphia toward Twelfth, and we were just getting to Twelfth Street—it was an officer-in-trouble run —and these two colored came running from between the houses, and they each had a brick in their hand. We had three scout cars, four men per scout car, and I was in the lead scout car with my sergeant, and they came running up point-blank range and one of them threw a brick through the front windshield of our car. It cut my sergeant, hurt the driver a little bit, but we jumped out and this other fellow threw a brick through the second scout car. Well, they got the one guy right away, and I chased the other man, and I thought my partners were behind me, and he ran two houses to the west on Philadelphia and then cut into the back yard. I was chasing him. All I had was my night stick. He had gone through the corridor between two houses and was starting into the alley and I was fairly close to him. As soon as I hit the back yard, two colored males attacked me from either side. I did a head dive. Luckily I was wearing gloves at the time, and I landed on cinders and tore the gloves up and my pants, ripped my shirt. One of the men had my night stick, or was picking it up, so I started to draw my gun, so he saw this, so they split. In the meantime the other guy had come back and he was just ready to kick me in the face. I grabbed him by the leg and had a little westling match with him, and then the women—people that had no business at all as far as rioting or anything just came out of their houses and they were starting to yell at me, so I saw the crowd was building back there, so I let him go and tried to get my men. I yelled for a couple officers, and by the time we got back, he was down the block. And the same thing generally happened all day.

"My sergeant was just inches away from being killed by a five-gallon jug that prior to being thrown at him contained gasoline.

"We made a stand on the corner of Philadelphia and Twelfth. We had one occasion during the day where a man actually— you see, the mob was coming up the street at us, and we had twelve men there. We cordoned off an area around a fire apparatus of some sort, and we had orders to just hold this area, so they were coming up the street, and there were a good thousand of them—I think that's a small estimate, really—and they were throwing rocks, rocks and bottles, anything they had, and it looked like rain they were coming down so heavy. And as they were coming they were breaking the windows on the stores on either side of them, and just looting, just open looting. And so this one fellow ran in front of them, and he had a chair and ran about three stores ahead of the mob, threw this chair through a window, went inside. It was a beer and wine store, and liquor, I guess. He emerged a short time later with a wooden box of fifths—whiskey; and this guy took one of the fifths out, we were standing there, and this one officer was to one side, and he took one of the fifths and threw it at him. And the officer didn't see it until it was just about at him. And so this was an outright Breaking and Entering, Felonious Assault, and Inciting to Riot. And so the officer told him to halt. And the man picked up this whiskey and was going back into the midst of the crowd, so the officer had some sort of rifle on him, raised it, and the rifle was jerked out of his hands! The sergeant said we didn't want to agitate these people. And this was the general trend of the situation.

"The riot laws are very lenient toward mobs. Twelve people armed or thirty people unarmed constitute a riotous mob, and you can tell them to disperse, take the force necessary to protect yourself, and to protect the community from them. No one took the initiative to do this. We had cars with PA systems. I believe that if we had acted before they started looting, and before these people saw the instigators go and actually in front of us burn places down, arson, which they all know is an offense punishable by imprisonment, you know, a felony, they saw this, they saw the people carrying gasoline cans into stores and actually burning them in our presence and nothing done. And after that it was ridiculous. If we had started firing then, we would have just agitated them more. We couldn't have controlled them. But I think that had that officer shot that man—he was so blatant that he walked up to the store, threw the chair through the store window, went inside there, stayed there for a matter of a few minutes, came out with a wooden box, fifths of whiskey, and threw one of them at us. If he had shot him there, the crowd was such that they were more scared and apprehensive, they didn't know what to expect. They were feeling us out, see. Now this was an outward act of violence, and he committed three different felonies within a matter of minutes, and had the police officer acted and told the man to stop and if he hadn't have stopped, shot him, I think the first instinct of the crowd wouldn't have been to rush us, as it might have been later, but to have dispersed, because they would have been fearful. Now this in itself wouldn't have solved things, you know, this one shooting. But I think maybe had they shot at the beginning, we may have saved those forty-some lives that were killed, and a lot of innocent people that were killed, by shooting the people that were at fault."

2 | I Don't Remember Exactly

Under cross-examination in the conspiracy hearing by Attorney Konrad D. Kohl for the defense, Michael Clark was asked about his activities on the first day of the riot. The following exchange took place:

Q. All right. Where were you then?

A. I don't remember.

Q. Well, so far you told us you were at your mother's house sometime during that night.

A. That's right, but I don't remember what time I arrived.

Q. Well, did you stay there after you got there until dawn?

A. I fell asleep, yeah.

Q. Were you there Sunday morning, Mr. Clark, if you know?

A. Yes, I was there Sunday morning.

Q. All right. Now that takes us to Sunday. What did you do during the day Sunday?

A. You mean while the riot was going on?

Q. Yes, sir.

A. I went over to my cousin's house.

Q. Will you tell us, please, where your cousin lives and what your cousin's name is?

A. What is my cousin's name?

Q. Yes.

A. Rodney Norman.

Q. Rodney Norman?

A. Uh-huh.

Q. And where does Mr. Norman live?

A. The address where he lives now, I don't know where he lives now because he moved.

Q. Did there come a time, Mr. Clark, when you eventually returned to the Algiers Motel?

A. Yes.

Q. When was that?

A. It was the same day, that Sunday.

Q. It was on Sunday?

A. Uh-huh.

Q. All right. What time did you arrive at the Motel?

A. I don't remember exactly. It was light outside.

Q. What is your best recollection?

A. I don't remember.

Q. Was it during the day?

A. I said it was light outside. . . .

Q. Was it before noon?

A. I don't know.

Q. You have no recollection?

A. No.

Q. Sunday night were you at the Algiers Motel?

A. I am going to tell you now I don't remember where I was back then. I don't write it down in a diary where I go.

3 | What a Hell It Was

Ronald August—twenty-eight years old; five feet ten inches tall; five-year police veteran; clarinetist in the police band; one commendation; slender, dark, and straight; with a gentle voice; with the slightly enlarged jaw muscles of a man who clenches his teeth; devoted husband of Genevieve, father of Doreene Linda, two and one half, and Denise Jean, one; parishioner of St. Raymond's Roman Catholic Church; member of the Home Owner's Club—sat in the spotless dining alcove in his house, over his shoulder a commemorative China plate, bursting with China flowers, given to him and his wife on their wedding day, and told me this:

"They called me up seven o'clock Sunday morning, got me out of bed in fact. I planned on getting up about eight and going to church and going to see my folks. It was my day off, naturally. And they told me to report as soon as I could possibly get down there, that they were having trouble. I says, 'What do you mean, trouble?' He says, 'I don't know, they're just having trouble in the Tenth Precinct, and they're calling everybody in.' So, naturally, I says, 'I'll be in.' No choice in the matter, see. So I called my folks and told them I wasn't coming out that day, and I got dressed and went down there and stood around for about an hour, and then they put us on a DSR bus and shipped us over to the Tenth Precinct, where I stood around about four more hours. And then they brought a crew in that's been on the street quite a few hours, all—I won't say bruised up, I won't say bloodied up—they just looked beat. And I hear them complaining about what a hell it was out there on Twelfth Street, but I didn't have the opportunity to ask any of them personally just what was going on. But as I visualized of what I saw then, I would think it was the heat from the fires that made them look so rugged.

"They put us in a paddy wagon and took us out there. Gee, it looked like everything was burning. They took us down Twelfth Street as far as they could go, and there was people swarming everywhere. All they taught us about riot control with horses and different riot formations they teach us, V formations, and so on and so forth—I didn't see any of that used. Maybe they used it and it didn't work, I don't know.

"Anyway, they put me over on Fourteenth Street, and I believe it was Lawrence, maybe it was Collingwood, maybe it was Seward, I don't know, it was in that locality, and they put me there with another fellow that I went through high school with —by the way, he played clarinet also, we knew each other quite a while—and they told us to seal off the area. And there was police officers all up and down the block. We were to let nobody in, but let them out. And I don't care what they're carrying out, bushel baskets full of whiskey, tape recorders, cameras, televisions, they were to be let out. But don't let nobody in. Little six-year-olds with wagons full of brand-new underwear, socks, and shoes. Carrying everything out."

4 | Trying to Get Something Free

At first Lee and Sortor denied that they or their friends had done any looting. I was a more or less official-looking white person, and they had too long a habit of awareness that anything they said might be used to punish them to talk openly about the first phase of the riot. Like Michael toying with the lawyer in court, they put me on.

There apparently was, on that first day, a feeling of unwonted elation among those who ran in the streets. An articulate young black nationalist whom I met, a student at Wayne State University with a bright, fluid mind, told me, poking at the nosepiece of his horn-rimmed glasses to push them into place, fingering the tuft of beard under his lip: "There was a new thing, a new feeling, out there on Twelfth Street. I was out there Sunday. It was between noon and two o'clock that the feeling changed. After all those years of having the man in control—Detroit's an affluent town, Detroit's black people are well off—not middle-class, not even lower-middle, but upper-proletariat, I mean a cat can finish high school and get a job at a factory and buy a Pontiac and ride around and all, but the man has his finger on you every minute of every day. I mean, 'Show up at *this* time,' and, 'Do *this* on the assembly line,' and every minute of the day it's been what *he*'s said. And you get home, and the man is your landlord, and so on and so on. But out there, there was suddenly a realization. Man, the whole thing was *reversed*."

Another young militant at Wayne State, a girl with a carefully groomed natural hairdo, who talked with what seemed to be great honesty about black revolutionary ideology, hopes, and difficulties ("One trouble is—let's face it—we're all middle-class, and the hardest thing for us is to make contact with the folk—

the real poor"), and about that first day: "On Twelfth Street everybody was out, the whole family, Mama, Papa, the kids, it was like an outing. . . . The rebellion—it was all caused by the commercials. I mean you saw all those things you'd never been able to get—go out and get 'em. Men's clothing, furniture, appliances, color TV. All that crummy TV glamour just hanging out there." She was not the only one I talked with in Detroit who regarded television as the opiate of the white masses and the *agent provocateur* of the black masses. Some years before, watching TV along with most of the eleven children of the black farmer I was visiting in Holmes County, Mississippi, I had seen how, to the poorer blacks, the lily-white commercials act as an ironic affront and, even more, an ironic encouragement to violence. On the shows gunfire is commonplace, and what is more, it is necessary; it sells products. Virtue triumphs but the outlaw is mighty attractive—every day, every hour, he is sanctioned by the pretty white girl in the commercial lighting up and taking a deep puff as a preliminary to romance, or caring about her soft hands even when washing the dishes, or naked in the shower behind the ripple glass, arms raised to the white, white lather in her blond, blond hair.

"I thought it was real ridiculous," Thelma Pollard, Auburey's sixteen-year-old sister, said to me. "I wouldn't call it a riot. When it first started off I'd just call it everybody trying to get something for nothing, you know, because everybody was just breaking in and stealing things, trying to get something free. That's the way I thought it was."

Trans-Action quoted an unnamed youth, who was in the main part of the Algiers on the night of the shootings, on Sunday's looting: "I heard a friend of mine say, 'Hey, they rioting up on Twelfth!' I said what are they doing and he said looting. That's all it took me to get out of the house. He said the police was letting them take it; they wasn't stopping it; so I said it was time for me to get some of these diamonds and watches and rings. . . . People . . . were trying to get all they could get. They got diamonds here, they got money here, they got clothes here and TV's and whatnot. What could they do with it when they bring it out except sell it to each other? That's all. They're just getting something they haven't got. I mean, I bought me some clothes from somebody. I have exchanged whiskey and different things for different things. You know, something I wanted that I didn't have. This was a good way to get it. I really enjoyed myself."

Mr. Gill, when he told me about that Sunday afternoon, played down the joy. "I was laying down," he said. "It was about five thirty, I'd been down about twenty-five minutes, and I was just dozing. Someone unlatched the door; it was these kids with a whole lot of shit. I said, 'Where'd you get that?' Carl said, 'Oh, they're rioting, they're rioting.' So Carl and them got ready to go out, and I said, 'Man, don't go out,' I said, 'because somebody's going to have to pay for this. They're not going to let you just get away with it.' I kept telling them, man. I don't think they enjoyed it, because everybody was scared. Most of the people I met, they were just doing it, but they still had this fear." There was undoubtedly a generational gap in the experiencing of pleasure in the uprising and, indeed, in the looting itself. Of the 7,231 persons arrested altogether in the riot, 4,683, or just about two out of three, were between the ages of sixteen and twenty-eight, and only 981, or 13.5 per cent, were over forty.

Several months after the riot the boys began to relax and open up. Sortor murmured to me one day, "Sure. We was doing a bit of looting." Some days later he said that the friends had looted some clothing from a store on Grand River and they had also looted some food, "but Punkin and Melvin put it in their car and took it home." Another day he said, "Me and Auburey got a couple radios, me and him went down, then he went on home. We sold them. Different people down the street, they'd buy them. You just be walking down the street, or you'd either be sitting up there, and somebody say, 'You selling that radio, man?' You say, 'Yeah, yeah, I'm selling it.' 'I'll pay you so-and-so for it.' 'Okay.' We got fifteen dollars for them."

"Auburey came back home, you know," Thelma said to me, "he came back and he said he seen this box sitting in the street and he picked it up. My mother told him to don't be picking up that stuff and be carrying it home. He was scared and he thought somebody might have seen him picking it up and he took it back down and he came on back home. And he sat home the rest of Sunday looking at television because he was scared to go out. You know, he'd get scared if he'd find out he was going to die or something like that, you know. My momma said they'd kill everybody, so he stayed home."

5 | The Suspense of the Whole Thing

Robert Paille—thirty-one years old; six feet two inches tall; two hundred pounds; two-year veteran of the police force; one commendation, numerous meritorious awards; veteran of the U.S. Air Force (clerical work, supply, Stateside); former Explorer Adviser, Boy Scouts of America; unmarried; Catholic; pronounced cleft in his big chin; apparently unable to encompass all he meant to say in his speech and so given to appending rag-tags of inchoate continuation at the ends of clauses, "there," "all that there," "everything else there"—sat in his parents' small home that burst with house plants and whatnottery (under a table a fire extinguisher he had purchased after an alarm that his house would be fire-bombed), and he told me this:

"I guess the main thing was the suspense of the whole thing, you know, you never knew how far it was going to go. It was confined to that area at the time there, and they were just burning it up, and we thought that it had to be stopped somewhere, but everybody felt that we could have done more. It seems that we had orders not to do anything, just block off the area. And these people, in the meantime, I could see them right from my post over there, I was blocking off the street, and it just seems that they were just running all over the place, wild and that, right down the street. There were some people carrying TV sets, and you could see them going right in the house. I saw more crime transpire that one day than I saw all two years I been on the force. And there was nothing I could do about it, because I didn't have the orders. And right where we were stationed there, there was a—the Motor Traffic Bureau, these were the fellows, you've probably seen them in previous riots there, you know, motorcycle pants and all that there. These fellows here were standing by with their bayonets and everything else. These are the fellows that ride the motorcycles and drive alone in cars. These fellows, you know, were ready and everything else there. Standing by for orders. All this is transpiring and they're just standing there. Nothing they could do.

"Well, there was a lot of rumors as to what was happening, but the main thing seems to be that the Mayor gave the order not to do anything. He's the commander-in-chief, more or less, in the city here, and it seemed that the Reverend Hood"—Nicholas Hood, only Negro member of the seven-man Detroit Common Council—"who was his adviser at the time, and—who was that other figure here? Well, there were two figures mainly there, they told him that if we showed any force of arms, that these people would become real violent, and they would likewise respond. And so he says, 'If you let us go out there and talk to these people, we'll calm this thing down and it will be okay.' In the meantime all these places were being robbed and everything else, and they went out and nothing happened. And this gave them enough time there, this was the time when they started burning.

"Well, I feel that we should have some kind of a status quo. Because in the past we haven't had too many of these problems and that there. It just seems that the more you give these people the more they want, and they feel now that with these riots and everything else there, they can get everything they want free. And by just using a little bit of violence, they can get anything they want. And this is a wrong way of basing any type of thing.

"I think we should have more power. The policemen should have more power. And when these things do break out in the beginning, they should be handled in the beginning. They should give the police power to take care of these things.

"I feel that, you see, like B. and E., that's Breaking and Entering, the law states—and we have been repeated this again and again in our squadrooms—that if you find a man breaking and entering, if you do not know his identity, and if you have reasonable doubt to believe that he's coming out of the premises there, you know, having breaking-and-entered and so forth, that you can shoot him. I feel that these people should be treated likewise. If they're breaking into these places here, they should be made examples of, if you shoot a few of them there, you know, the serious violators there."

6 | Loot Being Sold

From Detroit Police Department Disorder Log:

"3:50 p.m. Radio Run. Loot being sold at Algiers to 'man named James.' Cars pulling in."

7 | A Production Line

"On the next corner," David Senak told me, "south of where we were, there was a dry cleaner's. We saw these people coming up with five-gallon cans of gasoline, they busted this big window and had a production line set up, where they were passing out this clothing—and it was funny, probably they were stealing their own clothing, because this was all secondhand stuff, you know, these were items that they'd brought in to be cleaned. Well, they were passing this stuff out by the handfuls, and then they took these five-gallon cans of gasoline, took them in there, and put the place afire. And this was all in the presence of uniformed police officers. And this was the general trend of the whole situation."

8 | Pure Chance

When they were in tenth grade at Pershing High School, Roderick Davis and Larry Reed, who had been singing in choir together, and four other boys, school friends, formed a rock-

and-roll group, to play in school talent shows; they called the group the Dramatics. As they improved they began to want to go into business, and they played wherever anyone would have them, free, for publicity. One Friday night in 1964 they were singing at a place called Mr. Kelly's Barroom, and, as Roderick said to me, "people were hollering for more. A lady came up after and asked did we want to become a recording group. Did we! So we came down to the Golden World Recording Company the next Sunday and auditioned—sang ten or twelve things plus some we'd wrote ourselves. A month later we cut our first record.

"One time in 1965 we were watching a group called the Contours do a show, and we saw the M.C. call out the names of the guys in the group, and each one came out sliding and jumped up on the opposite side wall and came back doing splits. This gave us the idea for our routine, we used it ever since. Each one, see, takes a lead, we'll take a fast number, break the band except for the drums, and then go into a dance, one at a time, every man for himself; after that the band's back in. Other groups have begun copying our routine now, makes us sort of mad."

Now with five members—Roderick, Larry, Ronald Banks, Larry Demps, and Michael Calhoun—the group began to get bookings and would make, for most engagements, $350 a night.

Each year at the Fox Theater—an extraordinarily gaudy cavern on Woodward near the downtown area, one of those gilt-encrusted extravaganzas from the roaring twenties, tumultuous with sexy multicolored plastic sculpture, a heavy old dream palace, a haven in recent years for skin flicks and horror movies—a week-long show of music and entertainment is staged, called Swinging Time Revue. The Dramatics got a spot, along with the Parliaments, J. J. Barnes, and other more or less known artists, in the '67 revue, and they had been doing two shows a day, complete with their wild solo dances, on weekdays, and three on the weekend days. They sang "Groovin'," which they had adapted from a number by a white group, the Young Rascals; "I Want a Love I Can See," from the Temptations; a number called "Inky Dinky Whang Dang Do"; and some numbers of their own, "Bingo," "Somewhere," and "All Because of You," which Supersonic had recorded four months before.

Early that Sunday morning Larry called Fred Temple to see if he wanted to come and help out as valet at the Fox that day—"help keep our clothes up," Roderick said to me, "and hand us towels to wipe away—we'd get pretty hot—fasten cuff links, stuff like that." The boys wore red pants, white shirts, black vests, and greenish-bluish iridescent jackets. Fred told Larry he didn't think he should go, because he was laying bricks for his uncle seven days a week, and he was supposed to work; but he decided at the last minute to go to the Fox.

"I used to mess around with Herbert, Fred's brother," Larry told me, "then we sort of drifted apart, and I got to be friends with Fred in Noland Junior High. We took graduation pictures together. Then we went on to Pershing. At first he didn't like to talk to girls that much, didn't like to be bothered with them. I used to introduce him to girls, we met quite a few girls together. When we dropped out of school Fred got a job with Lee's Nursery, and then he worked with Ron, Ronnie Banks from the group, at Chrysler last year."

"Fred was a nice quiet guy," Roderick said to me, "friendly and popular with girls or anybody else. He liked to give rather than receive. Every time someone would come and ask for a dollar, he'd give it. Or if not, if he didn't have one just then, he'd promise to do something another time."

On that Sunday afternoon, just after the Dramatics had finished their second show, "A man came out on stage," Roderick told me, "saying a riot had started, everyone should go home or to the nearest hotel or someplace safe like that. So we left out."

It was midafternoon. It was muggy outside, the temperature was about eighty-five degrees, the sky was overcast, and there had been a trace of rain a little earlier. A hot fresh wind was blowing out of the southwest, and on the wind, above the city, the boys saw dark smoke rising from many quarters.

"We got on the Woodward Avenue bus," Roderick said,

"going north to get home quick as we could. A few blocks after we passed Grand Boulevard, the bus stopped, and there was this whole line of people wanting to get on, when this policeman got on and shouted, 'Everybody get out and get someplace out of the way because there's liable to be shooting right around here."

The six boys walked a block north, and there, right across the street, on its twin pedestals, was the inviting neon palm tree, the inviting name: Algiers Motel.

"It was pure chance," Rod said. "I'd never been there before in my life. We thought we'd try it, had the money from the show, you see, they'd paid us two hundred and fifty, we each had fifty dollars, so we thought we'd see what it would be like to stay there. Mainly we wanted to get off the streets. I was the oldest one, so I purchased the room. It cost eleven dollars a night."

The Dramatics, all six of them, were checked into room A-5 in the big building in the back. As soon as they were installed there, Fred Temple called home to tell his mother where he was.

9 | Everybody's Taking Everything

Charles Moore, a forty-one-year-old shear operator at Rockwell Standard who told me that he earned $15,000 last year and that his wife earned $10,000, lived in a predominantly white middle-class neighborhood in northwest Detroit, near Oak Park. He had been suffering from a coronary insufficiency and had arranged to enter Ford Hospital the following Saturday for some tests. (The day I first met him, some time after the riots, Moore was an indignant father, shaking his head over "today's kids." He said he had entered his two daughters, Jane, who was in ninth grade, and Barbara, in fourth, in a private school, mostly for white children, called Lutheran West, and was paying $600 a year tuition "to help them get something better than I've had." Moore, a quick-tongued man, had experienced among other difficulties in two decades no less than thirty-three arrests, sixteen of them for traffic violations and most of the rest for quarrels of one kind or another. Just the day before, he had been telephoned by a store called Allington's in the neighborhood and had been told that Jane was being held by the store; she had pilfered some hair curlers. He went and got her—charges were not pressed—and asked her why, *why*. She had said, "I just want to be like the other kids, Daddy. They said I was trying to be elite"—she pronounced it *ee-light*—"because I wouldn't steal, and because I go to school with white kids." During the riot, he said, one of the girls had said to him, "Everybody's taking everything. What did you get, Daddy?" "They seem to think," he said, "that there's some kind of prestige in it, or something— take because everybody else is taking!")

That Sunday Charlie Moore drove in his '66 Cadillac across the river to Canada with two friends, James and Norah Adams, who were staying in room 14 in the main part of the Algiers Motel. During the day they had heard about the riot on the radio, and coming back they were searched at the bridge. Driving up Woodward Avenue, Moore stopped at a red light and was waiting for the light to change. Two police scout cars were directly in front of him. The driver of the one nearest him, a policeman, jumped out, apparently to chase a looter. The car started backing up, and it ran right into Moore's car. Moore had vainly blown his horn. Immediately after hitting the Cadillac the scout car shot forward and plowed into the other scout car; then it backed up again and came back at a higher speed and hit Moore's car again.

"See, what had happened," Moore explained to me, "when the driver jumped out he reached up to the gearshift lever to put his car in neutral but he put it in reverse instead and ran off and didn't notice. Then a state trooper sitting in the back, see—they were working mixed teams, city police and state police—he reached forward to put it in neutral, but just then they hit me and it jogged him so he put it in forward, see. And then the very same thing happened at the other end of the line, only the other way around, so wham! I got it again. We had quite some discussion. They had to tow away the rammer there—a City of Detroit car. James and Norah took a cab on to the Algiers. The disturbance was going on all around us, and while we were arguing there, the man heard a brick go through some glass and just jumped in his car and took off with my license! Man! I had to report for a lost license at the First Precinct, see. I didn't want to get caught without a license in the middle of a riot. By the time I finally got to the Algiers, James and Norah weren't there, they had went to her sister's."

10 | The Least of My Problems

"So there I stood," Ronald August told me, "without a comfort relief, without a cup of coffee or a drink of water, and it started getting dark, and you could see the sky lit up from the fires. There'd be a fire here, then a half hour later there'd be one over here. When it got dark enough, we urinated in the alley, which was against a city ordinance, but that's the least of my problems, urinating in the alley.

"Finally this colored lady came out, and she had a bottle of orange pop, and I was so damn happy to see that bottle of pop! It was around ten o'clock at night. I got off at about four o'clock the next morning. It was about twelve hours right there, plus the time I was in the station before I was posted there. That's all it actually was that first day."

11 | How Auburey Was

"Auburey stayed home Sunday night," Mrs. Pollard told me. "I'll tell you how Auburey was, as long as my husband was at home nights, with me, he'd just go on and stay out. But Pollard was working that night, you know, and Auburey stayed, because he didn't want me and my daughter to be at home by ourselves."

12 | Kind of Hard Sleeping

"Sunday night," David Senak told me, "I got through work about two thirty, three o'clock. I came home, and I was black with soot, my uniform was torn, my pants were shredded on one side, shirt was torn, and I was just covered with soot because we were in the middle of fire for six or eight hours straight. So I came home and took a bath and went to sleep and got up about ten o'clock in the morning. It was kind of hard sleeping that night, because I was still a little shaken. People on the outside just had no idea what happened down there and still have no idea. It's like somebody coming back from Korea and trying to tell me what happened there, I just can't comprehend. I imagine anybody out there had trouble sleeping that night."

5

Snake

1 | Something I've Always Wanted to Do

David Senak's grandparents on both sides were immigrants from
Czechoslovakia; his paternal grandfather settled on a farm near
Memphis, Michigan, and his maternal grandfather moved to
Detroit, to a small Slovak community centered on Carrie and
Strong Streets, with its own church, Harper Baptist; he worked
for Henry Ford. Senak's father became an accountant (at the
time of these events he helped keep books for Holley Car-
buretor), and his mother worked, too (at Chrysler, as a key
punch operator).

David was born in Detroit on June 18, 1944. He attended
A. L. Holmes School, Osborn High School for one year, and
Cass Technical High School until his graduation in January
1963. He took architectural drafting and building at Cass, and
he designed, among other things, he told me, "a house of my
own. It pretty much suited my idea of what a perfect house
was. Had a master bedroom that was eighteen by twenty-four
feet, quite large, and it had a built-in range downstairs, and it

had my private den, which gave adequate space for mounting trophies and the like." However, in a class in cost estimating he found that the house would have cost, not counting the price of the acre of land on which it was to stand, $175,000. "So I gave up the idea."

David was active in the church, he told me, "from infancy." He attended Sunday school and church "and the different functions" at Gratiot Baptist, and through his church organization he became affiliated, when he was sixteen, with the YMCA, and soon he was employed there—part-time as long as he was in school, full-time afterward. "Within about four years I probably covered just about every minor position in the Y"—attendant for the Youth Department, teacher of gym classes, swimming instructor after he got his life-saving badge at eighteen, and locker-room attendant and "various positions." "This gave me," he told me, "a general liking for the public, and I still have it."

While he was working full-time at the YMCA, David began part-time studies at Macomb Community College, in the liberal-arts curriculum; but shortly afterward, a friend of his who was a junior executive with Hamilton Carhartt Overall Company told him that the firm was in the process of moving its inventory from Detroit to Ervine, Kentucky, and that the company needed a man in its shipping department. "I cut my classes at school down to a minimum," he told me; he served the firm for about six months as shipping clerk and then, for six or eight months longer, as shipping superintendent. He returned to Macomb for one semester full-time.

In May 1965, he told me, "I put my application in for the Police Department. This was something I've always wanted to do, and it became more evident after I'd worked with children at the YMCA, and it's just been a more or less natural thing for me to want. Instead of being a doctor or lawyer, I chose the Police Department as a profession." He was told that he would have to wait for his twenty-first birthday. "So I kept in touch with them, and it was the day after I turned twenty-one that I took the entrance exam." Screening took about three months, and on August 2, 1965, he enrolled at the Police Academy. On October 28 he was stationed, in uniform at last, at the Thirteenth Precinct.

A week later, however, he changed uniforms: He enlisted in the Air National Guard for a four-month stint. "I had an obligation to fulfill," he explained to me, "and I didn't want to take two years from the police force to go into the service, and so I took the Air National Guard because it was a means whereby I could serve my obligation and at the same time continue my Police Department work." Most of his tour was at Detroit's Metropolitan Airport, and four months later, at the beginning of March 1966, he was back on the force.

2 | It Really Impressed Me

"The first week in March," he told me, "I was reassigned to the Thirteenth Precinct and probably the second or third day there I was assigned to the cruiser. This was a four-man scout car, three plain-clothesmen and a uniformed man, and they were assigned to the general precinct to do only the most important runs, like hold-up runs in progress, and the like, and they had occasion to help raid a blind pig"—it was a raid on a blind pig that touched off the Detroit riot of 1967—"and it was Sergeant Vic De Lavalla and his crew that busted the pig, and we were assigned to just back them up. Well, it really impressed me, and the crew chief, Patrolman O'Kelley, took a liking to me, so he introduced me to Sergeant De Lavalla, and shortly after that he recommended me to go on clean-up. And so that started a sort of a career within a career, and I've had many experiences on clean-up."

3 | I Really Looked Bad

"Clean-up basically deals with blind pigs and prostitutes and numbers men in daytime. In my very first week, we were working on night crew, and we were called in by the inspector, who was Inspector Loftus at the time, and he was notified by a colonel of the Salvation Army, I believe it was, on Rivard, that they had a blind pig that was operating only on Sundays. These men would be paid on Saturday night, and the colonel would see them by eleven o'clock Sunday morning, and they'd all be drunk, and he said the only thing that could be happening would be that they'd be visiting this blind pig in the morning. So these are very secretive, basically. There was no way of him finding out through his sources where this blind pig was, so he wanted one of our men to more or less infiltrate his ranks and find out where it was, get a drink and bust the pig. Well, the inspector really wanted the place, so they asked me if I would 'join the Salvation Army' and try to find out where it was.

"For a week prior to the time I went to the place I wore a white sweatshirt and white Levis and didn't change at all, didn't comb my hair or shave, and I really looked grubby about Saturday. I was to go there Saturday night and get acquainted with the men and the following morning try to get one of them to take me to the pig, and then get my drink and somehow contact my crew. This was all sort of makeshift because we didn't know exactly what we were running into. The arrangements were made for me to have a cot in there, and the only thing was to convince these other fellows that I was just one of them.

"So I went over to a buddy's house and told him what had happened. Him and I bought a case and a half of beer, and another couple of friends came over, and I just started drinking. About nine thirty or so I was quite inebriated, so it turned out that my friends had to drive me to the place and just drop me off, and I stumbled in to the Salvation Army, and this fellow wouldn't even talk to me—they have a policy of not admitting drunks. I tried to explain to him that the colonel had told me to come here, but the words just seemed to be a little incoherent, and it took me about fifteen minutes to explain to him that I was a friend of the colonel. So finally he did admit me and take me to a cot.

"It was really an experience. I was in such a state that everything was a little exaggerated. I walked into this big auditorium-like deal, and they had cots in rows, and on Saturday nights these men, you know, drink a little bit; they bring bottles in with them, you know, and sneak them. And so they were laying all over the place. Some of the men were vomiting, and stuff like this, and everything just seemed to be overemphasized. So he took me to a cot, and I laid down there, and I think the situation, more than anything else, made me a little sicker than I would normally be, so it was a very disgusting night, as a whole.

"I got up the next morning, and my eyes were bloodshot, and I really looked bad. I don't even think my mother would let me into the house. So I stumbled downstairs and I couldn't eat breakfast with the guys, so I just started talking with a couple of the fellows, and during my conversation with them I had established the fact that I was just a fellow in transit, I was from Ohio, I hitchhike around the United States, and because of my clothes and my general appearance, they believed it, and this one fellow, he was about fifty years old or so, it just so happened that this was how he got started on the road, and so he took to me, and in about an hour and a half or so we killed a bottle of wine that they had, which didn't help my hangover any, and they invited me to go with them to this blind pig.

"Well, I went inside the place. They gave me a drink. I'd had wine, and the guy gave me a bottle of beer. I couldn't stomach it, and I vomited on his floor. After vomiting on his floor, the fellow didn't want to serve me any more, and according to court procedure you have to have evidence in your possession, to establish the fact that you did make a purchase inside of a blind pig. Everything was great except for the fact that I had no way of notifying my crew; he wouldn't trust me to use his phone. So finally he told me if I'd leave his premises, he'd sell me a bottle of wine. This was beautiful, because I could leave the premises and call my crew and go back there. So I did. I paid for the wine, left the premises and walked three or four blocks to a pay phone, called my crew and met them. Then I went back inside the pig, and as soon as I was in the premises and drinking there, they busted the place. At the time I was told by my sergeant to go and lay down in the back seat of the car, because I couldn't even participate in the raid. . . ."

4 | We Subdued Him

"My first citation was just after I got on the job, March 20, 1966. Two elderly people came out, and they were really terrified, because there was a man that had attempted to break into their house, and they lived on the ground floor; he'd smashed their window and was halfway in when they started screaming so loudly that he left. When we got the run we got a description of the man. So we started patrolling the area. Usually when you get a run like that and you can't get the fellow right away you go back to the station. Well, what we did was just a little out of the ordinary, we figured he may be in the area yet, waiting for us to go, so we circled the blocks, maybe five or six times. This one time we circled I saw this fellow between the houses in the shadows, just caught a glimpse of him. So I yelled at my partner, 'Slam on the brakes.' My partner pulled in to the curb, left side to the curb, rolled down his window, and yelled to the guy to come out of the shadows; he didn't get out of the car. I was still a rookie, so I was told in training in the Department to always get out of your car when you're investigating anyone. So I got out of the passenger's side, which was toward the middle of the street, and walked around the car. And this guy was coming toward my partner, who had his head stuck out the window, Roy St. Onge was my partner's name. I saw that the guy had something in his hand, so I yelled to Roy to get his head back in there. And I grabbed the guy, and he had a rock in his hand, and he was real close to smashing Roy and taking off, see. So we subdued him, arrested him, and got him back to the station. They had a line-up. Turned out to be the same guy. So they wrote us up for a citation."

5 | Something I Wonder About

One day I asked David Senak, "What makes a good policeman?"

"A police officer," he said, "is probably a unique person. Most police officers with a little experience could probably tell you within a few months of a new officer's tour of duty whether he would probably make a good police officer or not, and whether he's going to stick it out. In the late forties it was sort of difficult to get a job, and a lot of people resorted to being a police officer, simply because it was an easy way of earning a living. I think these are the police officers right now, as a whole, that give the general public a bad opinion of all of us."

Then I asked, "What do you think are the qualities that a man needs to be a good police officer?"

He paused, and finally answered in a low voice, "Perseverance." Then he added, "You've got to be dedicated." Then, as if still answering my question, he said, "I think one bad aspect of my life as far as the Police Department goes is that I never really fell in love with any girls up to the point where I joined the Police Department. And then afterward, the type of work I did on the force reflected a sort of bad attitude toward women in general." Here he gave a slight laugh. "And I have a tough time, you know, bringing them up to the level of a police officer's aspects of a woman."

"How does that work out? How do you mean that?"

"Well, see, I've arrested maybe close to a hundred and seventy-five, maybe a hundred and eighty girls, and taken them to court and gotten convictions for Accosting and Soliciting. These girls come from all different backgrounds. You couldn't name a background that a girl hasn't come from. I've had many different situations where girls would, after the accosting is made and the arrest is made, they would try to give you a background so you'd be a little softer on them. I think not so much being a police officer as doing vice duties has on the whole given me a bad outlook on women in general. I know a lot of vice men that are married, you know, and have married after vice squad, that seemingly are happy, so I just probably never have found, you know, maybe the right girl. It's something I wonder about, whether I will, and, you know, whether it is because of my vice duties or not, or my police background."

This subject came up again another day. "I know the problem myself," he said, "and I say half the battle is knowing the problem, but in my case I know the problem, and I know all women aren't prostitutes, and I know all women don't have a checkup with everybody they come often in contact with, but I think subconsciously it affects me. I go out with a lot of real nice girls, and I just can't seem to, you know, get really attached to them. I like to be friends with people a lot more than I do—girls tend to want to become attached right away, and I'd rather have them as a friend. You know, it sort of makes for conflicts. It's hard to say what I feel inwardly. I know the problem. I just can't—I'm not even sure that's why, maybe I just haven't found a girl that I want to settle down with. Maybe she just hasn't come along yet. But I figure, you know, that there's got to be someone. I've gone out with quite a few girls, you know, you—maybe everyone feels that way when they—for different reasons. It may not be the police experience that has governed that."

"Do you think," I asked him, "that this has made you think of women as essentially evil, or more apt to be criminal than men?"

His answer was: "Who gave who the apple?"

6 | Select Areas

"Eighty per cent of the work on the clean-up squad," he said once, "is colored. At least. The only time we get white girls probably would be Third Street, Second Street, select areas where a lot of white people go, you know. Where they're not conspicuous."

7 | A Typical Accosting

He opened a drawer of his file, rummaged awhile, and drew out a write-up. "This is a typical accosting," he said. "This is what I'd say in court in front of a judge." And he read: " 'On March 22, 1966, at approximately 4:10 a.m., while driving my private car north on Brush at Canfield, defendant waved me to the curb. I pulled to the curb and got out of my car. The defendant then approached me, unzipped my pants, and attempted to put her hand on my privates. As she was doing this, she stated she would give me a straight lay for ten dollars, plus the cost of the hotel room. I then identified myself as a police officer and placed her under arrest for Accosting and Soliciting. Date of trial was adjourned to April 12th, 1966, by Judge Maher. A plea of Not Guilty was entered. Sentenced by Judge Maher to ninety days in Detroit House of Correction.' It's interesting the reason that she adjourned was that Judge Maher was on the bench, but she knew why she was trying to adjourn it, because the judges change by the month, she was trying to get another judge. See, he was taking the place of another judge, he's a traffic-court judge, normally, and he's real tough over there, he believes a criminal should be prosecuted to the full extent of the law. These prostitutes were really getting zapped!"

8 | Some Judges Like It

"In an Accosting and Soliciting, which is the charge you take a prostitute under," he told me, "the court requires the initial accosting to be done by the prostitute. There can be no overt act on your part to solicit anything from her, so all you can do is drive down the street and hope that they signal you in some way to pull to the curb. If they don't do that, you know, there's nothing you can do about it. The way most of these prostitutes work is they'll stand at a curb and wait for the people to stop for a light, or something like that, or just after a light where they're just speeding up, and then they'll call them to the curb, they'll call them or they'll wave them.

"The second half, the soliciting, it's a two-part deal, where they have to give an act and a price. On the act, I usually, in my cases I stick to the exact wording of the prostitutes, and a lot of my partners go to court and the whore'll say, 'A suck and a fuck for fifteen dollars,' see, or, 'A half-and-half for ten dollars,' and the officers when they go to court will say, 'An act of oral perversion and an act of sexual intercourse with the defendant for the sum of such-and-such.' I don't know whether it's better or worse, but I usually just stick to the exact wording of the prostitutes. 'Around the world.' 'A suck and a fuck.' 'Sixty-nine.' 'A half-and-half.' 'A French.' Some judges like it and some judges don't.

"Often they'll say, 'How much can you spend?' The courts will allow you to say whatever price you give. And then they can say, 'Okay, that's good enough.' I hear the prices are a little higher now because the trade is a little less after the riots, but when I was working you could get just about any price you want, depending on the area you choose—the lower-class colored girls, higher-class colored girls, lower-class white girls, higher-class white girls, the colored call girls that'll come to your room, the white call girls. Generally on the street it would be five or ten dollars."

9 | Real Clean-Cut-Looking

"There are special places to work queers," he said to me, "and special police officers, too. Like I used to be a whore man. The whores would take me because I sort of more or less have an innocent-looking face, and I can dress real clean-cut-looking, and a lot of their conception of a police officer is a slovenly-looking guy. They look at them in a bad light to start with, see. I worked with prostitutes, but my partner Bill used to work with queers mainly. As easy as it was for me to get a prostitute, I had a heck of a time getting a queer, talking a queer into believing that I was trying to solicit him—or, you know, make him solicit me."

10 | On Being a Fanatic

"A lot of times we'd pick up a prostitute coming in, back into the station. That's what I mean about my crew. We're fairly unusual. We work almost all the time. My sergeant was a fanatic. He's such a good officer that you can overlook some of the faults, like going for months and days without eating—you just don't take lunch. We used to eat in our car; we had a place over on Canfield that we'd get self sandwiches, you know, real large sandwiches. Well, when it came time to eat, if we were in the area, we'd swing over there and buy some sandwiches and go back into the productive numbers area and just circle around there looking for numbers as we were eating. We were doing two things at once.

"We worked nights on blind pigs—days we usually worked eight-, eight-and-a-half-hour days—but nights on blind pigs we used to work from eight at night on Thursday, Friday, and Saturday night all the way to eleven o'clock in the morning. Because we'd get these blind pigs right at the end of the day, right at the end of our evenings, and then we'd have to process all these people, and make reports for court, and then one guy'd be elected to take the person to court, or the people to court, and it would be hectic.

"Bill and I, one time we were due to get off duty at two o'clock in the morning, and we were drinking in this one bar on Woodward—we also investigate liquor complaints in these bars—so we were drinking in this place, looking for something or other. It was about a quarter of two, we were coming back into the station, and these two prostitutes accosted us, and normally, I know a lot of guys would just pass it up, because it was too close to quitting. But we didn't. We had no idea of passing it up, and we got two of the best cases we ever got, they just laid everything on the line because we were a little high, and they just let caution to the winds, so to speak, and we took them in, and it turned out we had to work two hours overtime making out the paper on them. We missed our bowling that night; we were supposed to bowl with some people out at an all-night bowling alley. But we did it! When you have dedicated police officers, they *work*."

11 | The Teacher

"I was quite pleased," he said, "that I had an opportunity to learn from my sergeant. He's a dedicated man, he's the most dedicated man in the precinct, or in the city as far as I'm concerned. He's taken more abuse than any one police officer I can think of, and he's still a working sergeant.

"Sergeant De Lavalla's been on the force for twenty-three years. This man is a fantastic police officer. He's gotten three departmental citations. (I got two regular citations, and I was supposed to be given four more, when the riots came; naturally they can't give a person a citation if he's suspended.) Very few people get departmental citations; very few get one in a lifetime. He's gotten three of them, and he's gotten so many just regular citations that I couldn't even give you a rough estimate.

"I wish I could tell you some of the stuff Vic was in. He got his stomach slashed from end to end by a queer in his younger days as a police officer. He stands a good chance of dying from hemorrhaging if he gets hit in the stomach. That hasn't stopped him one bit from being out there. If any one of us gets in trouble, he's the first guy helping us. Last year he spent a month straight in the hospital because he helped one of my more ignorant partners with a drunk. The guy was in plain clothes and he jumped a drunk before identifying himself. What you're supposed to do is put your badge in front of the guy's face, let him see it, identify yourself verbally, and then place him under arrest, and if he fights you, then, that's it. And this guy jumped his drunk and then said he was a police officer. The first instinct of the drunk was to start fighting. So Vic grabbed him, got him in a bear hug. And he was laid up for a month because of that. He cracked a narcotics ring when he was in the Narcotics Bureau that extended over to Europe. And it was all due to his work. That was one time they gave him a citation; they gave him a citation for the queer; they gave him a citation for going into a burning building."

12 | How a Girl Gets Started

"They say society can't get along without some prostitutes in order to satisfy some people," he said. "They use the excuse that if there weren't prostitutes to satisfy these people they'd become sexual degenerates and start attacking children and stuff like this because they couldn't get their sexual desires appeased. But I don't think a sexual deviate goes after prostitutes anyway. Because I talked to prostitutes—just talking—and they say there are some people that have really odd sex drives in different ways, and they want them to do unusual things; and most prostitutes will go along with it as long as it doesn't hurt them, but they say the number of people who do this are very insignificant. Most of the Johns are businessmen from all walks of life that for some reason or other—I mean, their wife is pregnant, or something like that—they feel that working off their anxieties off on a prostitute is a lot better than hurting their wife in some way. There are a lot of reasons they can give you that make you stop and think and say, 'Well, some aspects you could look at and say, "That's all right. You know, it has its place." ' But then you look at the prostitutes from my angle, and as far as I'm concerned they're just as bad criminals as rapists and anything else, because they contribute to any crime that you can name.

"There isn't a crime that I can think of offhand that you couldn't involve prostitutes or pimps in some way. Rape. Rape! Just thinking about rape you would say, 'Well, how could a prostitute or a pimp be connected with that?'

"But how do most prostitutes start out?

"You know, you don't just say, 'Well I'm going to be a prostitute.' Because you get women from Grosse Pointe, which is a very wealthy section of town, and they become prostitutes —and why do they become prostitutes? Not because they need money, but they want to please some guy, some pimp. They go to a bar downtown, and they meet this guy. He's smooth, you know. So she falls in love with him, and pretty soon he doesn't have enough money for something or other, and she wants to buy him something, and he says, 'On my bed.' This is common to him, you know, this is like drinking a cup of coffee in the morning—to know whores and everything. So she says, 'Well, it may not be that bad.' So he fixes her up with a real high-class guy—at first—and then he breaks her in, and he's shacking up with her all the time, so sex isn't that immoral to her any more as it used to be, and after a while it becomes just a chore. And after they get enrooted in the thing there's no way of backing out, because the pimp won't let them back out. They've been had, see? They've already given their money to him, they've already started, and most of the time they love these pimps. It's hard to believe, because the pimps beat them with clothes hangers. They'll take a clothes hanger and double it up and beat their backs, see, because the backs don't matter, the back isn't going to bring in any money. Johns don't look at the backs anyway, so they can beat them black and blue. I've seen a lot of prostitutes'll wear a real lowcut dress in the front and high-cut in the back because their backs are all bruised up. And they show us this stuff, they show us where the pimps beat their backs.

"So it initially starts with a rape. A pimp will rape a woman, and a woman will—well, it's a rape. A virgin is molested and she doesn't want to be. She comes from a halfway decent background, a lot of times; but it's done, see. And then he says, 'What if we have a kid? You going to turn me in? You going to send me away to jail?' These people have lives that you wouldn't believe.

"This one pimp, he owns a bar, down on Woodward, now, or not Woodward, on Gratiot—this guy started out in our precinct. Little punk, eighteen years old when he started out. Right now he's twenty, two years from there now, he's got at least ten girls working on Third Street, black and white, and he's got girls working in his bar down on Gratiot, in an all-white neighborhood, prostitutes, and he owns this place. And he owns a Cadillac and a '67 Malibu convertible. And he paid cash for both of them. He's got his own private attorney that just works for him. Twenty years old. And he's not even a citizen, as far as I know. He wasn't then. He was a citizen of Canada.

"Some of the girls that you meet when they first start out are clean, respectable girls, they're in transit, a lot of them are in transit and they go to Wayne State University. They start going with some shady character who takes them to a couple of bars downtown like the Roxy, they meet these hoods down there, fall in love with one of them, and then it's only a couple of steps down. It's like narcotics, when they start out with marijuana and go to smoking opium—it's so *stupid*."

13 | Fostering the Flames

"How much do you think that prostitution and pimps have to do with race difficulties in general?"

"I think that if it weren't for them to foster the flames you wouldn't have anything."

"Why is that?"

"Because any trouble I've ever seen that they've attributed to racial trouble in the city, like officers in trouble where they're trying to arrest a person, and he starts screaming, 'Brutality!' and the people come outside—they've always been due to either prostitution or pandering of some sort. Illicit practice. We have most of our trouble with white Johns coming into the colored neighborhood. Most of the time they'll look for prostitutes on John R or Brush, and there are certain sections that are predominantly colored, and prostitutes in other sections are white. Just by the corner you can almost pick your kind of person. And I can remember many a time where guys will come into the station, and they're just beaten to a pulp and cut up. You wouldn't believe the extent that they're molested. And it's due to them cruising these areas for prostitutes, see, not knowing what they're doing, and either going into a house of prostitution and waiting for their tricks and being molested either by several prostitutes ganging up on a John, or the prostitutes' pimp, who sizes the man up as being worth taking. And they'll have prostitutes that'll have their pimps inside the closet of the room that they take the Johns to. And it's a rather precarious position once your pants are down and you can't do a whole lot of struggling. You're at their mercy. I wouldn't even venture a guess as to how many Johns get themselves beat up and in trouble and just don't want to report it."

14 | The Murphy Game

"The Murphy game," he told me, "is a big crime in Detroit." (Police Commissioner Ray Girardin had described the Murphy game to me: "I think it came from Boston originally"—and he began to talk with an Irish accent—"where the fellow would say, 'I know a lovely woman, name of Mrs. Murphy, who's dyin' to give it to you. Just pay me. She's waitin' for you up on the second floor.' The Murphy man collects. There's no woman there." All rolling of Johns by pimps, using their prostitutes as lures, is now loosely called Murphying; so even is stealing by gangs of prostitutes.) "Every weekend without fail," Senak said to me, "there's at least one man that come in to the Thirteenth full of blood and saying that he was looking for a girl and they jumped him. You'd be surprised how six or seven girls can work over a really tough guy. They could be on the street and do it. In fact they had one instance at Palmer and Brush, where the whores would wait till four or five o'clock in the morning, you know, when there was just barely a few cars on the street, and they'd line up right across the street, ten or fifteen of them, and the guy would be so petrified that he'd slam on his brakes and stay there, and the girls would stay in front of him, because they knew that the guy wouldn't run them down, the other ones would swarm around his car, open his doors, they went so far as to break the vent windows to open the doors—they'd have hammers with them—beat up the guys, steal their clothes and their wallets, and let them go."

15 | Trolling Alone

"I had a prostitute one time," he told me, "I got a case on her on a Sunday morning as I was coming in to work. I used to go down Chrysler Expressway, and then come down Brush, just to see if there were any prostitutes on the street. Well, this one happened to be a new one to me, and so I made the move then. She was colored, this was a colored neighborhood. I drove by her, and she waved at me, so that I pulled in to the curb. She gave me half a case, she gave me a price as I recall but she wouldn't tell me what she'd do, she said, 'We'll talk about that inside.' According to procedure I wasn't supposed to go inside with her because I didn't have a back-up crew.

"This turned out to be one of the most notorious houses of prostitution in the precinct. She took me to her room, and she told me what she'd do, and at that time her pimp jumped out at me and knocked me down to the ground. He had no idea I was a policeman; they have more or less of a policy, the pimps do, that is—the prostitutes will fight you, a lot of them are known for fighting—but if the pimps have any idea there's a police officer around they won't come anywhere near the area. He thought I was just a John, and it was going to be a Murphy.

"So he knocked me to the ground, and he started, he kicked me a couple of times, and as he kicked me, my gun fell out. I usually carry it in the back of my trousers without a holster, because a lot of the prostitutes will frisk you before they give a complete act. So the gun fell out, and I grabbed for it, and as soon as he saw the gun he just took off.

"I got the prostitute on that deal. He ran out the door, and I got the prostitute and ran after him. And a cruiser was coming by, and he ran down the alley, and they caught him later. As I recall, the warrant was denied on that, because they took him for Attempt Robbery Unarmed, and he made no overt act other than an assault, so they kicked the case. This is something that police officers contend with every day. Most judges go on the premise that police officers are paid to risk their lives, and a robbery against you as a citizen isn't the same in any respect as a robbery against a police officer, because a police officer is supposed to have the means to protect himself, so the judges feel the person shouldn't have to pay so highly for it.

"I was reprimanded later by my sergeant for going into the place. We have a policy, only to protect our own men, to have back-up all the time; normally we work in twos or we work in two cars, where one car will back up the other car while we're trolling, that's what we call it, 'trolling for whores.' The sergeant, he was just concerned with my safety more than anything."

16 | Nice Couple

"We used to stop for coffee in this one place on the night shift," he told me, "and it was about two thirty or so, we were drinking coffee upstairs. I had to go to the bathroom, so I went downstairs, went to the john, I was coming out, and this fellow bumps into me. He says, 'Hey, I haven't seen you around here before.' I said, 'Well, we just stopped in, I'm with a couple of boy friends of mine upstairs.' He says, 'Is there anybody in the men's lavatory?' I said, 'Yeah, there are a couple of people in there,' He said, 'Well, let's go into the women's lavatory,' and we were right next to it. I said, 'Okay.' So we go inside, and as soon as we were through the door, he backs up against the door and starts pulling down his pants—and gives me a case. And it was kind of funny, because there were a lot of queers upstairs, see, in this one place—it's known for police officers going there for coffee, it's centrally located, plus it's near some queer bars, see, and this was after the bars let out. So I didn't want the other queers in the place to know I was a copper, because I used to play the bars. So I told this guy that we were going to walk through this area and to keep his mouth shut, and—you know, you've got to be forceful with these people, you can't count on them. So I went through there, and I had him by the arm, you know, like a lot of these queers walk hand in hand, well I was walking into there, so it was perfect; walked right by those queers, and not a one of them—you know, they looked up and they'd say, you know, 'Nice couple,' and all that stuff. They had no idea, you know. We did it so well, my sergeant didn't even know I went by with him! So I ended up waiting the car for about twenty-five minutes, till he got suspicious from me not coming back for my cup of coffee."

17 | It's No Profession

"Queers," he said "fight a lot more than prostitutes. You can see why, if you look at it. A prostitute earns her living at this trade. If she's busted, she just takes it in her stride, more or less, most of them, this is generally what happens. But a queer, it's no profession to him. He could be anything from a ditchdigger to the vice-president of General Motors Corporation—not saying that the vice-president of General Motors is a queer. But there have been very high and well-thought-of people that were convicted, or at least went to court as queers, and on morals charges. So you got a different batch of people, and these people are going to—boy, they'll do just about anything. You can't trust them, see. A lot of them are family men, they have a lot of them that are married, and this one guy I got happened to be a fireman. This is another thing, that maybe my crew and my sergeant are different from a lot of police officers in Detroit, maybe, but a lot of police officers felt that because he was a fireman he shouldn't be convicted or taken to court for accosting. Well, we didn't think that, you know. I got a case on the guy, and that was it, and that's the way we feel with prostitutes, you know. Some prostitutes curry favor with a lot of police officers—or not a *lot* of police officers, but police officers—and you know they figure they should have favors done to them, and we just didn't feel that way. And this fireman, we took him to court."

18 | The Right Testimony?

"I had a case with a queer," Senak said, "with a judge from Dearborn. He was sitting in because we had a few of our judges died close together, and we couldn't have an election, so they brought these judges in to take their places. And this queer I brought in, I read the testimony—to get a case on a queer, you need everything but the cost factor; it's the same charge, Accosting and Soliciting—and in the testimony the man offered to fuck me, and I had 'fuck me' in quotes, and the judge looked up and said, 'You sure you're reading the right testimony?' Because a lot of times these officers, a lot of their cases will be almost about the same, because it doesn't vary that much, with prostitutes, and you get a general trend the way you work and you can usually write them up similarly, so the judge figured that I had got a prostitute the night before also and got the cases mixed up, see. I said, 'No, your honor, this is what they call it. They usually refer to it either as a fuck or a brown.' And when I said 'brown' he knew what I meant. The queer's attorney was all hopped up about that, too, because he figured that there was going to be a mistrial, that I'd used the wrong wording—but the guy himself knew that it was true, because he used it!"

19 | Privilege in Court

"You know," he said, "you can't send a policewoman out on the street and let her have a John accost her, because the John might be influential. And if you take him to court you may find out that the John is high in society, so they don't want to step on anyone's toes."

20 | Prejudice and Fear

"This," David Senak said, "is a kind of a bad subject. I don't know how you can take this. A lot of police officers aren't really college-educated, and, you know, they haven't the greatest vocabulary in the world. You couldn't ask them to give you a definition of prejudice and expect a real dictionary definition. Over the years, see, after so many people say, 'Well, you're prejudiced because you believe in something,' they don't know that prejudice means 'a prejudged conclusion.' So right off, their definitions are wrong—policemen's conclusions are anything but prejudged in the first place. But they use the word, because people say, 'You're prejudiced.' Or 'bigoted.' If you could find a word in the middle that would express 'drawing a conclusion based on fact and personal experience'—well, that is what police officers generally feel. But they would tell you that police are prejudiced.

"Of course, these are dangerous grounds, and I'm giving you what I think. You take me. People say, without knowing me, they'll say, 'You're prejudiced, you know, because you're a police officer, so you're prejudiced.' Well, we're not prejudiced, I'm sure of that. But we do have certain conclusions, but they're based on fact, and they're not conclusions singling out any race, or anything like that, even though police officers will say, as a general statement, 'I don't like coloreds,' or, 'I don't trust coloreds'—because they happen to work in a colored area.

"I talked with some New York police officers, and depending on the area you're in, you're going to get a different opinion of who he dislikes. Some police officers in New York that work in all-Puerto Rican areas are going to be all anti-Puerto Rican. Most police officers can't realize that they're not anti-Puerto Rican or anti-colored, or anti-any-group-in-specific. They're anti-crime.

"This is hard for a lot of people to believe, and I did a lot of thinking about it, and this is my conclusion. They are actually anti-crime. Because you deal with a certain people—and I've had a little psychology, and conditioned responses to me are the center of the whole problem. And if people can believe that police officers have no way of knowing that they're being propagandized by their surroundings, they'd probably look at them in a little different light, a little better light. Policemen have no way of deciphering from just incidental things whether it's right or wrong, or whether it's going to lead to their being prejudiced or not.

"A good instance is: A few weeks ago I read in the paper where the people in Brewster projects were saying that the police officers in the area—now this is a different precinct, the First Precinct—they were saying that police officers were shirking their duty and being prejudiced. And they use this 'prejudice' so loosely it's pitiful. But they said they were being prejudiced because they weren't coming to runs in Brewster projects as fast as they were in white areas.

"Well, police officers, one, are colored as well as white, they work integrated crews, so what one police officer does another police officer does, regardless of color. [At the time of the riot, there were approximately 250 Negro police officers in Detroit out of a total of approximately 4,400.]

"I happen to know, from personal experience, of one example of why police officers may not bust lights to get to a run in the Brewster projects. More examples of this could be evidenced if you wanted to talk to other police officers. This one instance was where we had a run over there, it was a Friday or Saturday night, it was real crowded out, a lot of people, and too many runs for just one precinct to cover, so we had to go in there from Thirteenth on a run. It was an Attempt Robbery in progress—I can't remember whether it was Armed or Unarmed. So we got over there real fast, we just went down Mack, and we were there in a matter of seconds. Got over there and the guys were fighting in the middle of the grass of one of the houses. Jumped out of there. Got the guy—he had attacked an old man. They were two colored people. This old man backed off so we could deal with this guy. Well, we were wrestling all over that ground with him. After a little while we got him cuffed. We had five thousand people out there, screaming 'Police brutality!' and rocking our scout car. Wouldn't let us leave with the guy. And this man, this colored man who was standing there, he couldn't do a thing, the colored man who was being attacked. They didn't care about him. It was police brutality against the robber! For subduing him. In a colored neighborhood.

"Well, a lot of police officers, they'd just—it might not be evident, they might not say, 'Well, next time, I'm going to slow down and I'm not going to go over there very fast. Maybe the guy'll run away and I won't have to take this abuse.' But in the back of his mind he realizes this, whether conscious or otherwise, and the next time, if he's a little ways away and there's a red light, well, he'll stop for it! And he'll know that he's stopping for it because he doesn't want to go there. He may not realize the reason, and then when he tells someone else, 'Ainh, I don't have any trouble there any more, because I don't get there so fast. I wait till the trouble sudsides.' And then the people say, 'Well, you're shirking your duty.' He's not shirking his duty because he doesn't know it.

"We have colored neighborhoods in our precinct where men will respond just as fast as any other neighborhood in the city, and this is the truth. I wouldn't lie at all, and I don't have to, you can ask other police officers. The people never give you trouble, very seldom have a run there, but when you have an emergency there, you get there. There are other areas, on Third Street, that are full of white people that do nothing but give you trouble—not to the extent of the Brewster project, because they're not as united in white areas as they are in the colored against the police officers, but they still do give you trouble, and police officers in that area will do the same thing they do in the Brewster projects. They're afraid. They're inwardly afraid."

21 | I Came Close to Shooting Him

"My other citation," he told me, "was for an incident I had on Garfield and Brush. I was trolling for prostitutes at the time, and I turned the corner, and this prostitute waved to me, and so I was going to pull in to the curb, but it was all parked up, see, so I went slowly and motioned her to follow me around the block. So I turned the corner.

"Apparently she had some other John that tried to pick her up, and she got detained. Then in the meantime I was waiting for her, and these two guys came walking down the street, toward Brush, going west, and they saw me, and it's obvious, in a colored area like that, if a white man stops he's looking for a prostitute, so they opened the door and got in, and said, 'You want a girl?' I said, 'Yeah, that's what I'm here for.' They said, 'How about that girl walking on the other side of the street?' And I knew her, see? I said, 'Okay sure.' I could still get Accosting on them if I can't get the girl. So I said, 'All right, good.' So they said, 'Well, how much money do you have?' 'Five dollars.' They said, 'Well, give me the five dollars and I'll go get you the girl.' I said, 'Oh, no. Oh, no. I've had this before. You'll just run off with my money.' He said, 'How do I know you have the money?' So I kept my money in my left-hand pocket, wound up, so I pulled it out, and I had me ten or fifteen dollars there. I said, 'Here, I got the money. You get me the girl and I'll give you the money. I'll give *you* five dollars, too, when you come back.'

"I guess the guy got greedy, then. What I figured, their normal intent was just to get me a broad, or, if they could, get the money, and disappear. But he got shaky, and he pulled a knife and said, 'I want all your money.' And as he said that he hit me with his one hand in the face, and he went to grab for the money. The money was wadded up, see, and I could get a better grip than him. I had my hand on it. My left hand was occupied with him. And I was reaching back for my gun, so the first guy got out of the car, and this other one followed right behind him. The first guy, I imagine he had thought he was blameless in the Attempt Robbery Armed, see, because he tried to block me getting the guy that actually pulled the knife on me.

"So I pushed him aside, and he started running into an apartment building. I took after this man, the first man, so he started running down Brush toward Canfield, and I pulled my gun, and I stopped, and I told him to halt, I was a police officer. It was real lucky for him that he halted when he did. I came close to shooting him. I was kind of shaken up there. I think I would have shot him if he wouldn't have stopped."

22 | A Girl from the Algiers

"We were in the Seven Seas Bar, across from the Algiers," he told me, "and my partners and I were drinking there separately. I must have been in a business suit, for a reason I'll tell you in a minute. Sometimes I'd be in a suit, as a businessman, as a college student—I wore a beard at one time. I used to play the beatnik. A lot of the areas these girls work, a certain type of person comes through. And on Brush and John R they're mostly colored girls, and you could be anything. You know, they'll take on almost anything. If you go into some of the colored hotels, they have a clientele of businessmen; maybe there's a big office building near the place, where these guys know about this hotel, and the only people that frequent this place are from this one business. So they pretty much know if I come in in a sweatshirt and a beard that I'm not from this business. So I got to dress accordingly, in some places. Some nights my partner will dress well and I'll dress like a slob, and other times we'll switch off, or we'll be working together often, and we'll dress alike.

"So I bought this colored girl a drink, and she gave me the case in the bar, and I said, 'Well, where are we going to go, then?' And she said, 'Well, we're going to go into the Algiers Hotel. I got a room there.' She wanted twenty dollars—because it was unusually high. I said, 'Well, am I going to have to pay for the room, too?' And she said, 'Oh, no, I have my own room in the hotel, that's included in the price.' So I said, 'Okay,' so we walked over there, and as we were walking my partners came up, and we arrested her.

"She mistook me for the sergeant, when we finally made the arrest on the girl, so I must have been dressed pretty good. My partners were both kind of perturbed. So that's why, as I look back on it, I was probably wearing a suit and they were just

wearing shabby clothes, so she just took me for the sergeant—
and these other two fellows were older than I was, see."

23 | It Takes a Special Guy

At different times I asked Ronald August and Robert Paille what
they thought of David Senak as a policeman.

"Dave," August said, "is a hell of a good police officer. They
don't come any better than Dave. It takes a special type of a
man to be a policeman, I think. They don't just come out of the
thin air. If it was an easy job, which I think most people think
it is an easy job, all you do is drink coffee, they tell me. But
he has ambition to fight crime, so to speak. He was a good vice
man, or a good clean-up man, so to speak. You put him in plain
clothes and put him out there on the street, and he knew the
tricks of the trade. Now when I talk about tricks of the trade,
he knew how to mix in with the queers, with the homosexuals.
Now me, to give me a job like that, I'd shrink down to this
big"—a thumb and forefinger an inch apart. "I just don't want
nothing to do with it. But Dave was a—I worked a little clean-up
myself, trying to make a sale on a Sunday, you can't buy whiskey anytime on Sunday, but buying beer before noon is taboo,
so I worked clean-up for a week. I don't know, you go down
there and you talk chummy-chummy to the bartender, and then
you turn around and slap him on the back with a summons. I
didn't care for that kind of work. It takes a special guy—I'm
trying to explain to you what it takes to be a good police officer,
and then it takes something else to be a good vice man. It's just
a different experience altogether. But Dave Senak is—well, let
me stack him up against myself. I think he's a better police
officer than I am, because he's just got the knack, let's say."

Paille said, "I can't speak too much for David Senak there
but I feel that he's young and he could stand some more experience. He had been on the clean-up squad quite a bit. He was
probably pretty good in that. But I don't think he's been out in
the street too awfully much. In fact, I think he hasn't almost as

much time as I do. I don't know, to me it seems that he could stand some more experience. I think every officer has to make a decision, you know, which could be deliberated for hours in court and everything else there, you know. But you've got to make the right decision. Something like that, when you get the riot and everything else there, you know, you know it's imperative that you make the right decisions. But everything happened so fast, you know, it was hard to really keep track of things."

6

The Second Day

Monday, July 24

1 | Taking Them In

"I went back in the next day," Ronald August said. "Actually the schedule was set up for twelve noon to twelve midnight, but you had to be there at quarter to twelve for roll call, and you were lucky to get out of there by three o'clock in the morning, or maybe two o'clock. We put in a good fourteen, fifteen hours a day, easy.

"In the daytime it was relatively quiet, except for looters. There was some fires that second day, I recall. They sent us over to what they called the Kiefer Command, which was set up over at the Herman Kiefer Hospital there. They picked a crew of us, twelve men, eleven men and one sergeant, twelve of us, and they picked out three scout cars, put us in the cars, and we were going along in a three-car unit consisting of twelve men. And we made runs, making arrests, and the arrests were actually all looters, in the daytime.

"We didn't know where to take them, there were so many of them. They had it set up you took them where you were working in the locality; we were there at Number Ten, at Livernois, but we were taking them where we thought we could get in and out the fastest."

2 | We Thought We Were Safe

"We didn't eat Sunday or all day Monday," Roderick Davis said, speaking of the Dramatics and Fred Temple in their room at the Algiers.

"The two youngest ones, Ronnie and Michael, they went swimming in the pool, and the rest of us just stood around watching. So that is how we ran into these girls that were living in the main motel part, these go-go girls from Chicago. We had met them there in Chicago when we did a show at the Regal Theater." In court Rod was able to name three of them: Laroyce, Carol, and Bertha; he could not recall the fourth name. "We didn't even want to know the other people there.

"Most of the time we were just in the room. We all called home to keep our families from worrying. The police never bothered us, not that day. We thought we were safe in there. We smoked cigarettes all day."

3 | A Small Scratch of Paper

At the first murder hearing a police officer named Edward Lalonde was questioned by Assistant Prosecutor Avery Weiswasser, for the People, as follows:

Q. What is your assignment of duty?

A. I am at the Thirteenth Precinct in charge of firearms at this time. . . .

Q. What was the procedure of issuing guns to personnel during the riot, and various vehicles, when they were assigned to caravans, especially?

A. I handed an officer a gun and wrote the name down on a

small scratch of paper that I had. When the officer turned the gun in, I crossed the name off, and when the small paper got full I threw it away. . . .

Q. What type of guns were they, riot guns?

A. Both shotguns and rifles; and they were for the most part owned by civilians in our precinct. . . .

Q. Now these shotguns, what gauges were they? Do you know?

A. Mostly twelve-gauge.

Q. What type of gun?

A. All different types, sir.

Q. Were they single-shot bores or magazine types?

A. They were mainly pump shotguns and semi-automatic shotguns with four or five magazines.

Q. And what type of ammunition was issued to any police officer?

A. Twelve-gauge, double-O.

4 | Real Nice

"Next morning," David Senak told me, speaking of that Monday, "they told us to come in at twelve. So we were there, and we had a roll call, and they split the station into two groups, one had to stay in the precinct and the other one went to Tenth to reinforce their units over there. And so they assigned me to a car, and most of our duties was in and around Oakland, because the day preceding, of the start of the riots, they also burned Oakland out, pretty much to the ground. And so we were contained in that area, chasing people away from the buildings and stuff.

"That day I was carrying a shotgun from the Department that they issued to us. The third day I carried my own gun. An officer always prefers to have his own gun. You're taking your life in your hands when you use someone else's gun. Every gun is a little different. Personal guns are registered with the Department—I mean sidearms would be, not rifles and shotguns. Anyway, the shotgun I carried that second day was from the station; I think it was a Browning automatic or something. Real nice gun."

5 | Haul and Run

"Auburey would fight," Mrs. Pollard said to me one evening, "but he ain't going to fight against no gun. Because, he tell me, that quick a person will draw a gun, he'll haul and run in a minute."

"Monday," Thelma told me another time, "he went down to the corner store and bought a lot of potato chips and junk like that, and after that he stayed home on Monday, too."

6 | Nothing You Could Do

"We were driving," Robert Paille told me, "we were patrolling back and forth, we were all inside these vehicles and that, with guns and that, and all you could see was through a little small glass there." Monday was a hot, windy day; the temperature hit ninety degrees in the afternoon, and the wind blew twelve to seventeen knots from the west; the humidity was not excessive. "And when they told you to jump out, you got out there, and you stood in formation across the street, you know, and they were throwing bottles out and everything at us there, and we'd look out for each other. We'd say, 'Watch out, there's a bottle coming.' There was nothing you could do. There was one fellow there, he had a watermelon there, and he was throwing watermelon at the photographers and everything else. Nobody was safe. But you had nothing you could do. You just stood there. You got into your vehicle, you drove to another location, and while you were driving there they were burning up that location you had been at." By the end of the second day 731 fires had been set. "Nothing you could do. Then you'd get out there and you'd stand out there, and I noticed these people on the side, they all had smiles on their faces and everything else, just like they had just accomplished something. I couldn't understand that, and I asked one fellow, 'What's wrong with you people?' And he said, 'If you think you've got it now, just wait until later on; we're going to really get you fellows,' and that. So this was the general impression I got from these people: They didn't want any help or nothing, all they wanted to do was take over themselves."

7 | Anarchy, More or Less

"This wasn't actually strictly a race riot," Ronald August said to me. "That's not my idea of a race riot. It was racially involved, but a race riot is where the white and the colored clash. I didn't see this at all. To me it looked like anarchy, more or less. The percentage of agitators in the colored people, and the rubbydubs in the white people there were also agitators—all started looting and raising hell, so to speak. If people want to call it a race riot, that's their prerogative, but a race riot is not geared in that way, I don't believe. Maybe I'm wrong."

8 | Not Within the Confines

Michael Clark, under cross-examination in the conspiracy hearing by Attorney Kohl:
Q. Where did you spend Monday?
A. I don't remember.
Q. And when you say you don't remember, you are telling this Court under oath that you just have no recollection, right? It is just not within the confines of your mind . . . ?
A. I don't know if I was at the Algiers or over to Momma's or over to my cousin's or where I was.

9 | A Lot Were Screaming

"I don't want to seem to be exaggerating any," Ronald August said to me, "but they must have had five, six hundred stacked in the garage there at the Tenth, and we'd take them in there, and it was a mess. They took your picture when you brought an arrest in, because they were all giving phony names. A lot of these people we brought in were screaming we were violating their constitutional rights, and civil rights, by taking their picture. And a lot of them were intoxicated, because they had quite a bit of access to the liquor stores."

"The area where they kept all the cars and that there," Robert Paille said to me, "it was like a big garage that they had them all sealed in there, and they had these tanks and everything else lined up along the outside there. You could see the people just bulging out of these places. We had different shifts, you know; some of us would go there and some of us would stay in the precinct. I've been on a detail over there, where I had to guard prisoners when they were coming out. Put them in buses and took them away. And they were, you know, all mad and everything else there, ready to fight."

10 | Senak's First Killing

Detroit Police Department, Report on Case Investigated for Warrant Recommendation, Complaint Number DD 386913: "Patrolmen Donald Van Loo, David Senak, and William Croft were assigned to Scout 13-6. At approximately 1:25 p.m. on July 24, 1967, they were on routine patrol driving north on Second Avenue, Patrolman Croft was driving the automobile, all the officers were armed with 12-gauge shotguns. At Euclid Avenue they noticed the front window of the Food Time Market partially broken out and a colored male, later identified as the deceased, stepping out of the window carrying a bag and some bottles. Patrolmen Van Loo and Senak exited the scout car. . . . "

Joseph Chandler's widow said later that he had gone out at about one o'clock to get her a pack of cigarettes.

"I saw this fellow," David Senak told me, "climbing out of a fresh hole in the side of a supermarket window. I was in the back seat; my two partners were in the front seat. The driver slammed the brakes on, we jumped out of the car, the man saw us and started running across us. We were coming north on Second, he started running south right across us into the alley, and just before the alley he dropped the packages he had in his hands, he had some whiskey, wine or whiskey, groceries of some sort. It was a fresh B. and E. I hollered for him several times to stop as he was running across us; he paid no attention and then he turned into the alley. My partner [Van Loo] and I followed. We were both carrying shotguns. I called two times while he was in the alley for him to stop, and then we fired on him. I fired two times, I guess, and my partner fired three times at him. The man didn't slow up at all. Gad, I couldn't—I still can't believe it. Went up the alley for about a house or two and then cut over, back north. He hit a fence and vaulted the fence. One or both of us fired as he was going over the fence— this was a range of eight to ten yards, close. And he vaulted this fence and just kept running. And my partner, who was in the car [Croft], cut around the other side, but he couldn't get there fast enough to get this guy, and in the meantime there were people coming out of the store, so he blocked the entrance of the store, and so we just went back there and assisted him, thinking that this man got away."

Report, Complaint DD 386913:
Chandler "climbed over the second fence (height of fence four feet six inches, covered with a vine which extends above the fence to a height of five feet six inches) and continued for approximately twenty feet, where he stumbled and fell. The deceased got up and continued diagonally across Euclid and between the houses on the north side of the street (130 & 150 W. Euclid). The deceased then ran east in the alley north of Euclid, east of Second, to the rear of 119 W. Philadelphia . . . "

"We hit the man," Senak said, "with I think four shots, and we hit him three times in the legs. I can't believe it. This man must have been in top physical shape. We were shooting double-O buck, hit this man three times in the legs, he didn't flinch, and there were witnesses all around who saw this. Man didn't flinch. He vaulted this fence, and apparently he was hit while he was going over the fence, didn't hurt him a bit, or seemingly. . . ."

Report:
" . . . where he attempted to crawl under a car parked in the rear of that address. Mrs. Alline Sims of 119 W. Philadelphia saw the deceased attempting to crawl under the car and immediately summoned her husband, Joseph Sims. The deceased asked Mrs. Sims for a drink of water and told Mr. Sims not to call the police but to get his wife at 81 W. Philadelphia. . . . "
Mr. Sims did, however, call the police. "Scout 13-7, manned by Patrolmen Edward Riley and William Peplinski received a Radio Run to 119 W. Philadelphia: 'In the rear a shooting.' "

"We had no way of knowing this," Senak told me, "because we were in the station making arrest cards out on the three people we had caught in the building. This was an unrelated incident as far as they were concerned. We called in the shots to the Homicide Bureau, that we had taken shots at someone but they were uneffective. Later they told us the shots did take effect. . . ."

Report:
"Scout 13-7 conveyed the deceased to Ford Hospital where he was pronounced DOA at 1:45 p.m. by Doctor Tauber of the Hospital staff. The deceased was suffering gun shot wounds to the right foot and right buttock. On July 25, 1967, an autopsy was performed on the body of the deceased at the Wayne County Morgue by AME Clara Raven, who gave the cause of death as shotgun wound of the right buttock, penetrating liver and right lung with massive hemorrhage, Chart #5604-67."
I asked David Senak, "Was it routine at that point to call in shots?"

He replied, "Well, we weren't that busy then. See, at night, at night you—I imagine there are so many shots fired at night that you just couldn't.'"

11 | A Sandwich

"They had to start some more men to Ten, as I remember," Senak told me, "so they shoved my two partners to Tenth, and then they kept me in the station for a while. They were having prisoners booked and photographed in the station. It was real hectic. The station was just a big jumbled mess then. They had Guardsmen there that were just coming on, and Guardsmen that hadn't been given anything to eat for ten or twelve hours. Food started coming in about Monday afternoon from the officers' wives; the inspector's wife made some sandwiches, the first sandwiches they got was from the police officers' wives themselves. I had a sandwich."

12 | Just Staying Around

"Monday Auburey was home," Sortor told me, "then we went over and was staying around Melvin's house. He came around there. We just stayed around."

13 | No More Jeering

"I was scared," Ronald August told me. "I can recall, the second night, laying underneath the scout car being shot at. And my radio, the walkie-talkie, was telling us to evacuate the area, although, hell, we were afraid to get from underneath the cars. We were in the Thirteenth Precinct, LaSalle, I know the street was LaSalle. We had windows smashed out; there was one particular Ford wagon we had, that the radiator leaked. What happened I don't know, but they were using everything they could find that would roll on wheels. Cars that were waiting for the scrapyard they put back on the road. But we'd run from one end of the precinct, and we'd get there, and either there'd be nothing there or you'd make an arrest, and you'd take him in to the station, and I don't know, it was quite a mess.

"One fellow in the station was shot, they had a machine gun, and I don't know what all the guns they had; this was the police officers posted around the Tenth Precinct, and so on and so forth. One fellow was shot trying to escape. And after that, these people were tame. I mean, no more jeering us or calling us any names. After that shot rang out, there was no more noise. I believe it was the second night, Monday night."

14 | Partially at the Algiers

Mr. Kohl, continuing his cross-examination of Michael Clark:

Q. Now Monday night, Mr. Clark, where did you spend your time? Where were you?

A. Which Monday night are you talking about?

Q. Well, we are talking about the 24th of July. The riot started Sunday as you indicated, or Saturday night, and now we are over to Monday. You have already testified you don't know where you spent the day. . . .

A. Wait a minute; the night before it happened?

Q. That's right.

A. Where did I spend it?

Q. Yes, sir?

A. Partially I was at the Motel.

Q. I beg your pardon?

A. Partially I was over at the Algiers.

Q. When did you go to the Algiers on Monday?

A. I don't remember.

Q. When did you leave the Algiers on Monday?

A. I don't remember.

15 | You Couldn't Defend Yourself

"I was just like everybody else," Paille told me. "You never knew when somebody would take you off or something of the sort there. I understood that there was a few of these snipers had these night scopes where they could actually see in the night through the scope there and pick you right off, no matter if you had the lights off or not. We used to patrol the streets with the lights off and all. If they had something like that, you couldn't defend yourself. We all thought that there was some organization behind it, that there were some experienced men there behind those guns, and there were quite a few people shot up in there by it and all. We never knew what to expect next. Like one time there I had gone out there and a building was on fire; it was at night. And the firemen were being shot at, we couldn't see where the shots were coming from. So the firemen they just got out as soon as they could, you know. Slid down these poles and everything else and took off. There was nothing you could do. They were shooting from dark windows and everything else. You can't see them anywhere."

16 | Night Ride

"I went to the Algiers that night," Charles Moore told me, "but Adams wasn't there. In the lobby I saw this white girl, about eighteen or nineteen, talking on the telephone; she was pregnant, and she was crying, and I heard her telling her mother that she was scared by all the rioting and she wanted to get home and she couldn't get a cab to take her to the airport. So I offered to drive her out there. I'd never seen her in my life before. She wanted to get to Columbus, Ohio. Her name was Nancy [Nancy Stallnaker, traveling companion of Julie Hysell and Karen Malloy]. So I drove her out to Metro; it was about two o'clock in the morning. She bought a ticket, but she couldn't get on a plane until the next morning, so she asked me to take her back. So pretty soon they stopped us, here was a state trooper stopping us at a roadblock, me with a little white girl in a miniskirt, giving Algiers Motel as her home address. Minute I tried to say anything, he said, 'Sit there and shut up.' I had my temporary license—from where this other guy had run off with my real one; and now the guy tells me, 'It ain't stamped right.' We had to sit there fifteen, twenty minutes. Searching the car. She's crying. She kept saying, 'They're going to shoot us.' So I finally just took off without my license, wasn't stamped right anyway, guy says. I just drove off. Nobody bothered us. I let her off at the annex at the Algiers. Adams was not in his room, so I just went on home."

17 | Rooftop Chase

"Then," Ronald August told me, "I can recall going across a rooftop trying to get this sniper. I was going across the rooftop, and this wire came off a telephone pole, out of the alley, and you know how they'll come across these flat roofs about ankle high. I kind of scratched my face up."

18 | Don't Get Near the Doors

"Fred had called me on the Sunday," Mrs. Temple told me, "and I'd told him to get home, get a bus Monday. He said, 'If the buses are running I will get one.' I forgot to ask the address. He'd just said, I'm on Woodward.' So the next evening, Monday, he called and told me not to come for him, they were shooting near there. I said, 'Don't get near the doors, son.' And he said, 'Tomorrow for sure I'm going to try to get home.'"

19 | Back Out

"They had so many people being booked," David Senak told me, "that they didn't have enough men to fill out the arrest cards and process them, so that I had to stay in the station and help them until I went back out on the street later that night, but just for a little while, and then we came back in. Nothing happened. I started at twelve that day, and I think I got home about two thirty that second night."

I asked him, "Did you sleep any better that night?"

"No."

7

An Out-of-Doors Man

1 | I Lost Interest

Robert Paille told me the story of his life:

"Born in Detroit, I'm thirty-one.

"My father and my mother were both raised in Canada, on a farm, they were Canadian-French. And my father's always been hard-working and that there, and he was a lumberjack since he was fourteen years of age. He's always had a hard life because his mother and father died before he was fourteen. He's always had to dish things off for himself, but he's never missed work, as far as I know. He's always gone from one job to another. He's dead right now. He was a lumberjack in Canada, and over here he was a carpenter. We both built this house over here, my brother and I and him.

"Well, I attended St. Ambrose, first grade, and afterwards went to Carstens, and I attended that up to the fourth grade, and then went to Servite High School, and I graduated from there. My main interest in school was science. That's the reason why, you know, I was interested in high school and all. I went to the University of Detroit for a while, studied chemistry, I decided to change over to chemical engineering, but I soon lost interest in that, so, later on, I attended part-time in Wayne State University, and then I went to the service—my father died '57.

"I was in the service there for four years, '57 to '61, I was doing supply, I was in clerical work, over at San Francisco, Hamilton Air Force Base, it's about twenty-five miles west of San Francisco. I was Airman Second Class when I was discharged.

"When I got out of there I went to Michigan Tech, and I took up geological engineering. I attended that for about two years, and kind of lost interest in that, too, you know.

"So eventually I came back here to the city. I've had lots of jobs. Prior to going into the police force, I was with the city here as an operating engineer, heavy equipment operator. I enjoyed it over there, I enjoyed the work, but I felt that I would be more interested in law work and that there, you know, and I joined the police force. I felt it was a better job and all. So I looked into it there, and I went through the Academy and all, became a policeman. I graduated out of the Class of May 10th, 1965."

2 | Different Sports and That There

"My main interests and so forth are the out-of-doors. Like hunting, different sports and that there.

"I've belonged to the Scouts, and I've always had a good record with the Scouts and that there, and when I quit I was an Explorer Adviser. I was in charge of the boys fourteen years of age and older, and that was over here at a school over here.

"When I was in high school I played some football, I played tackle and end, and I attended all the intramural games there when I was at Michigan Tech there, you know; we had these sports to keep us going up there. I played everything they had up there.

"I like duck hunting, and I usually go up around Orchard Lake, or over there in Mt. Clemens. And I like hunting deer; I usually go up around Grayling, in that area, that's where I usually hunt. That's where I went last year. That's about mid-state. It's pretty nice up there. You have to go in the mountains, you know, at that time of year, because, you know, the acorns are up there and everything else, and the deer will be on that. That's where I've gone the last two years, anyway."

3 | Shooting Down a Muslim

"I have a lot of meritorious awards," he told me, "about six of those, and I just received a commendation. It covered a multitude of things there, the meritorious and all covered a fifteen-hundred-dollar Armed Robbery holdup, where we apprehended one of the people there, and a man who was terrorizing a jewelry store, and another one was about a week before the riot.

"There was this kid, we arrested him for suspicion on Armed Robbery, and he didn't want to come with us. He said, 'You can kill me if you want to,' he said, 'but you're not going to take me in.' So we went out, you know, and we told him he was under arrest, and what the charge was, and we started to put handcuffs on him. So this kid spins around, and he hits the other officer and everything else, and gets behind the officer and takes his revolver out and uses him as a shield. And in the meantime here, I was there, you know. I couldn't do anything at the moment; my gun was still in the holster and all. So the officer dove between the cars and left him in the open. In the meanwhile this boy was backing up, with his gun in his hand there, and he's pulling the hammer back on it, so I immediately went down to the side there, pulled my revolver, and I shot him. I shot one bullet. It hit his arm, grazed off. It dropped him down, and he was unconscious. So we took him to the hospital. There was another man that was hurt as a result of the bullet there; hit him in the head, bounced off of it. So we took them to the hospital there, you know. The one I shot, he was okay. He was out of the hospital the next day, in fact, and the other man was released the same day.

"That was a young Muslim that I shot down. He turned out

to be a Muslim there, he was using an assumed name, and he was positive in the show-up there for Armed Robbery. He had a warrant on his person there, for his arrest, in regards to a Felonious Assault."

4 | The Blue Flu

Two months before the riot, Detroit's police officers, outraged that the city had not budgeted a pay increase, rebelled against the pressure they felt was being applied to them to write more and more traffic tickets, which bring the city revenue. They began a slowdown; from mid-May to mid-June only 21,109 tickets were written, compared with 74,001 in the same period the previous year. The city retaliated with disciplinary action. Suddenly, in the middle of June, a large number of men began calling in sick; they were said to be suffering from "blue flu." At one point almost a third of the city's patrolmen were either claiming to be sick or had been suspended.

"Yeah, I was involved in it," Paille told me. "We don't have too much arbitration measures in the city here, and we got to use what means we have available. I got the blue flu, and I was almost suspended one time because of that. I'd been called off sick and everything else there, and they told me, you know, I should be getting back to work and all. And at this time they were going around, the sergeants were collecting the traps from various officers and that—your traps consist of your badge, your gun, and everything, all your essentials, your ID card—so they were just ready to come out to me, in fact I beat them by half an hour, went out to sick bay, and I went out to the doctors there, and they told me to go back to work."

5 | The Center of Crime

"I thought the morale was fairly high, you know, just before the riots there," Paille said to me. "But there was always the same thing, you know—that they weren't getting enough pay and all. It's true, because it's a rough job. I've seen more in that precinct in two years than I have been told would be in any other for about ten, because that's the center of crime, it seems, in the city, in that area.

"It's primarily a colored precinct. The only real experience I've ever had with coloreds prior to going into the police force was when I was in the service. We slept in open bays in the Air Force and that. There was sections of the room, you know, that they conglomerated in. I got along fairly well with them, except when they started playing their radios at night there, you know. They turned this offbeat stuff on, spiritualistic stuff and everything else, start telling jokes and all. Be tired, you know, from work and that. I'd tell them to shut up or something there, you know, and these fellows here, you know, would talk back and call you every name under the sun.

"But other than that I had a lot of good colored friends in the service."

6 | That Immorality They Have

"I've saw a lot of nice Negro homes there," Paille told me, "poor people and all, but they're real clean homes and that, and they're decent people and all. But there's not enough of those places, there's other places where a fellow is making two hundred and fifty dollars a week, I've seen that, a construction worker, he didn't have one single good stick of furniture in his house. We had to vacate a man like this already. A construction worker, two fifty a week, he couldn't afford to buy one piece of furniture. What does he use this money for? That's what I'd like to know. And the answer I got was pleasures. So these people here, a good part of them are immoral. Any policeman knows that, in those areas. You've got to get at this basic problem. Lot of people told me you should separate the children, you know, from these people here, because they're influencing these kids here. This is what's going to make tomorrow! These people. But something's going to have to be done with that immorality they have. If you pour funds into them there, that's not going to help them. They've got to have that pride. Basically I believe they're more immoral than corresponding white people and all. Because you get a lot of these families over there, you know, and you'll find there's prostitutes and everything else there."

7 | A Whore as a Hero

"I think," he said to me, "that prostitution has a bearing on these riots, because in the past here we have the Cynthia Scott case here." At three in the morning, on Friday, July 5, 1963, Patrolman Theodore Spicher (twenty-eight, six feet three, 200 pounds) stopped his patrol car to question Cynthia Scott (twenty-four, six feet, 193 pounds), who was walking south on John R, near Edmund, with her left hand full of money—forty-three dollars, the man who was walking with her, Charles Marshall, said. Spicher and his partner tried to pull Cynthia Scott, who had had eight convictions for prostitution, to his scout car for questioning, and the policemen said she pulled a knife. Spicher shot her in the back twice as she tore herself away, and shot her again in the chest as she wheeled, half facing him; and she died. A week later civil-rights leaders assembled a protest meeting of seven hundred at police headquarters, 1300 Beaubien. She came to be known as St. Cynthia. "She actually led parades afterwards," Paille said to me—though that could not have been, because she was dead. "She was a hero in their eyes. And they claim that was because of her color and all that there. Actually, when you make a whore or prostitute a hero, that's something else, you know!"

8 | A One-Time Deal

"I've gone out with a lot of girls and that there," Robert Paille told me, "and I've come pretty close, at times, you know, to marriage and that, but I've never felt that I've met a girl that I really wanted to marry. Because marriage as far as I'm concerned is a one-time deal there, you know. You don't get married a thousand times like some people do. I mean, you get married and you're married for good."

9 | A Sentimental Atmosphere

David Senak had nothing to say about Robert Paille; although they had ridden together on that Tuesday night, he said he hardly knew Paille.

"Bob Paille is a very likable fellow," Ronald August said, "kind of a sentimental atmosphere when you get to know him. Maybe when you talk to him you'll think he's on the muscle. I don't know, I think I am, myself. Maybe sort of on the defensive. I feel like I've been kicked around a little, to be honest with you. You can get a broader picture by just that kicked-around statement, because I think I'm getting a raw deal. But Bob's a nice guy."

8

The Third Day

Tuesday, July 25

1 | In the Stomach

When the police officers of the Thirteenth Precinct reported for work on the third morning of the riot, they were greeted by a shocking piece of news. One of their colleagues, Patrolman Jerome Olshove, had been killed.

"It happened Monday night," David Senak told me with great emotion. "Heard about it Tuesday morning. At morning roll call. They told us. We knew when we came in. Shotgun in the stomach."

2 | Olshove's Death

At three o'clock that morning, according to witnesses, a car full of uniformed men cruising down John R passed, at the corner of Holbrook, an A&P store where looters were at work; a single shotgun blast was discharged from the car.

A few minutes later, according to the police warrant report, a Thirteenth Precinct scout car manned by Olshove (pronounced *All'-shuh-vee*), Roy St. Onge, and William Bolgar responded to a radio run to the A&P to check for looting. On arrival they found a man named Albert Phillips standing in front of the store, his face bleeding from shotgun wounds; Phillips collapsed on the parking lot. He was taken to Detroit General Hospital later (and was discharged after three weeks).

The officers, seeing two men looting inside the A&P, shouted to them through the broken window a command to come out, and they did—Danny Royster, a twenty-year-old, and Charles Latimer, nineteen. According to the police report, the patrolmen ordered the looters against a wall; Latimer obeyed and Olshove handcuffed him; Royster hesitated, and Bolgar and St. Onge, who had a twelve-gauge shotgun in his hands, shoved him.

A twenty-seven-year-old woman named Claudette Wilson, who, aroused by he earlier shotgun blast, was peeking through a second-story window directly across Holbrook from the A&P, testified in court that one of the men had come out as if to surrender, "but it seemed as though an officer went to hit the other man. When he tried to retaliate they began scuffling, and both men appeared to grab for the shotgun." St. Onge said Royster tried to grab the gun and it went off. The shot killed Olshove.

(Royster and Latimer were later both charged with first-degree murder, even though the latter was handcuffed at the time of Olshove's death. As of this writing, the men were still being held untried in Wayne County Jail.)

3 | Crying Like Babies

"I take it," I said to David Senak, "that this was the source of a great deal of anger."

"It sure was."

Then after a long pause, during which his face reddened and he seemed to be having difficulty breathing, he said with feeling, "We had guys there at roll call that were like brothers to him, couldn't go on the street for a half hour, forty-five minutes. They were crying like babies.

"He worked a cruiser. If it had been a regular patrolman it would have gotten a good response, but Olshove was just a real well-liked man. It hurt even more, when a good man went. Everyone knew he was supposed to quit that Thursday to take a job with IBM. If the riots had held off for another week, he'd never have been there." A career police officer, Olshove, at thirty-two years of age, had been studying police administration at Wayne State University, and had also been taking community leadership courses in spare time. He had won twenty comendation and citations. "I'd been in the cruiser with him, and cleanup work also at times. Only the best police officers make the cruisers. He was a very young police officer. The cruiser, that's the heavy car. Three plain-clothesmen and one uniformed driver, and they're picked because they know their business, they know the precinct, and they only handle the most important runs, the holdup runs in progress, and when they're not doing anything, if it's a slow night, they help clean-up.

"Athletic, very congenial. A lot of police officers are gruff and hard to talk to. Jerry wasn't like that. Police officers are very clannish, and when they have new rookies come in there, they're not readily accepted until they prove themselves, and Jerry always had a nice word for everyone. He was on the golf team, the Police Department golf team.

"The men got real excited at first. One of the sergeants came up and said, 'Nah, he's not dead,' he said, 'he's in the hospital. He's going to be all right.' This was two stories. This was to cool the men off. But it took a worse effect when people saw that our own supervisors were lying to us.

"He left a little four-month-old kid."

4 | Out of the Algiers Area

"And there's another thing," Senak went on. "My partner, the fellow Bill that I've told you about, arrested one of the guys that shot Jerry, who are held now for his shooting, about a month before, for beating up an elderly man, a seventy-five-year-old man, just about half a block away from the Algiers Motel. They jumped him on the street and beat him up. They were out there, one guy had the old man down, the other guy was pushing his head into the concrete. If they would have given them five more minutes they would have killed the guy. Bill and his partner caught these guys, took them downtown, and had they been retained in jail for this offense, they wouldn't have been out there. And who knows how many other crimes would be curbed by just a little more diligence?

"Holbrook and John R"—where Olshove was killed—"are very close to Woodward and Euclid"—where the Algiers stood —"and this man was attacked almost a month before right in front of the Algiers. In fact, he made a citizen's complaint to Cavanagh, and Bill got a copy of the letter; so Bill got a citation. And they said that the Algiers Motel is a detriment to the neighborhood, and they would like to have some way of curbing the crime in there, because they'd been having all kinds of trouble like this. And he said that the man that jumped him came from the Algiers Motel. He said they jumped out of the Algiers Motel area. And later the one man that was connected with Olshove's killing was one of the guys Bill caught out there."

5 | A Gun at My Head

At about eleven o'clock Tuesday morning, Rod and Larry told me, at the Algiers Manor, in room A-3, which had two double beds, four of the Dramatics—Fred, Rod, and the two Larrys— were lying in bed, two by two watching a movie on television. The other two, Ronnie and Michael, had spent the night over in the main part of the motel with the Chicago go-go girls. Suddenly, at the door of A-3, there was a loud knock, the door flew open, and the room seemed to swarm with uniformed men.

"They looked in the closets," Rod told me, "in the drawers, under the covers. One of them put a gun to my head and shouted, 'Get up!' They took us outside. . . ."

6 | Everybody Started to Laugh

"They came there that morning," Sortor told me. "They came in asking for dope or something. We"—Sortor, Auburey, Lee, and Michael—"was all in Lee's apartment. Soldier walked in and he asked where the stuff we smoked was at, or something. I said, 'I don't know what you're talking about.' He started searching the room, they didn't say nothing about no loot, they just came in, asked for that grass. We laughed at this one guy, because he told us to go outside, he said, 'Move!' Didn't nobody move. He started hollering, and everybody started to laugh."

"I was in bed when they came in that morning," Lee said to me. "They got me out of bed and made us go outside and go on the wall of the main motel. They lined us up sort of the same way they did that night." The boys were taken out through the French doors at the back, which opened on Lee's apartment, A-5.

In his testimony in the conspiracy hearing, Michael tried to say that Ronald August was there that morning; but Michael's testimony on that occasion, as we shall see, was pretty wild. None of the others supported that testimony. "Some of them say," Lee told me, "that was the same men as came that night, but I wasn't sure. I seen that private guard that morning." Melvin Dismukes told me later that he had been present at one search, whether at this one or a later one I could not be sure; he said that one of the boys—he thought it was one of those who were killed that night—"was calling me names. Tom. Black mother-fucker." Sortor said there were two girls there that morning, "girl named Virginia and this girl named Ann; they were staying there."

"When they lined us up against the wall," Sortor went on, "they searched us down, going through our pockets and stuff. Everybody had money on them; I had about a hundred dollars. They wanted to take it, they said we didn't need this money. The police said we didn't need it. They just went in our pockets, you know, took it out, said, you know, 'We should keep this.'

Then they gave it back to us. They said they were going to take us to jail. Inside they found two knives, that's all, and they found this tape recorder in there in this other room, in room A-1; they took that. It had been there all the time, before the riot even started, and they took that on out. I knew the fellow had it when I seen him, but I didn't know him by name."

In the conspiracy hearing, Lee Forsythe was cross-examined by Attorney Kohl as follows:

Q. You were there then. Do you know that some weapons were seized?
A. I do. . . . I saw the officers and the National Guardsmen come in and take them out.
Q. And what did they take out, if you know?
A. They didn't take any weapons out of our annex, but I seen them take something out of the Motel part.
Q. What weapons did you see them take?
A. Rifles and shotguns.
Q. Rifles, shotguns? How about pistols?
A. I didn't—I didn't see anything.
Q. Would you tell us, please, how many rifles and how many shotguns you saw them remove?
A. I didn't count them.
Q. Granted perhaps you didn't count them, but do you have any idea?
A. No, I don't.

"They jumped Auburey that morning," Sortor told me. "They asked him Auburey's name. And Auburey say he was working at Ford's. And they just jumped on him. Just told him to get on up over there, you know. He got against the wall, guy asked him something, and I guess Auburey hemmed, then he hit him in the back and alongside his head." ("You see," Mr. Gill said another time, "Auburey was a real slow talker. They'd ask him something, he wouldn't look like he's thinking. I guess that's what got him killed.")

"Then they told us to go on back in."

There was more imprudent laughter by the boys. I am not clear about the chronology. At some point, according to Sortor, this happened:

"We was trying to open the front door. You know, the guy said, the door was locked. This here guy telling us through the glass, 'Don't move,' So he said, 'Stand there.' So this other guy, he hollering, 'Open the door! Open the door!' This first guy here still was telling us, 'Don't move,' and was getting ready to shoot in at us, you know. So the policeman, he says, 'Don't shoot any of them. Don't do that.' So he didn't. So he took his gun—he was a little guy, this was a National Guard man—and broke the glass out and cut his hand, you know. We had to laugh."

7 | What Was That About?

"When the small Guardsman cut his hand," Roderick Davis said to me, "the boys laughed at him. I wonder if that could have been why they came back.

"After it was all over, Larry said, 'What was that all *about*? Man, one of them was pointing a gun right at your head!' "

8 | He Checked Out

"The guy from A-1," Sortor said to me, "he came back that Tuesday after they had came in that morning, he wasn't there when they came in. He came back mad, say, 'Them fucks took my tape recorder.' He got his clothes and he left. He checked out."

9 | They Checked Out

"Them girls"—Virginia and Ann—"they'd had enough of that. They checked out."

10 | Someone Been Whipping You

After the search, Auburey got dressed and went home, and he took a bath. "He told my other son," Mrs. Pollard said to me, "and told him not to tell me because I'd get upset, that the police had been in there and raided the hotel and beat him in the back. Cause I wouldn't have let him stay there if I'd known that. He called me in the bathroom and asked me to wash his back, and that's unusual. And his back was all whipped up. I do know he was beat in the back because I washed his back, and I said, 'Ow! Oooh!' I said, 'Auburey, you been beat in the back!' And he said, 'Aw, no, Momma, ain't nothing happened to my back.' And I said, 'Yeah, son, someone been whipping your back, because you got great whips all in your back.' And he said, 'Yeah, Momma, the police whipped me because they couldn't find nothing, so they whipped me.'

"He went back over there. I never would have went back to that hotel if it had been me. I never saw him after that."

11 | A Routine Day

"Tuesday I worked in the Thirteenth Precinct again," David Senak told me, "and that was just a—could I say a routine day, as there were riots? Patrolling and, you know, arresting a few people here and there for looting.

"That third day I used a rifle during the day and a shotgun at night. I used my cousin's gun, he had a gun with a scope on it, I guess it was a seven- or eight-millimeter German gun, and I used that during the day, because we were having a lot of sniper fire during the day, and a shotgun was ineffective. So I used his gun during the day with a sniper scope. I call it a sniper scope because I'm in the Air National Guard, but it's just a regular scope that's mounted on a pretty heavy gun. Seven- or eight-millimeter Mauser. Turned out not to be too accurate."

12 | To Be on Your Own

"It was quiet all day the rest of Tuesday," Roderick Davis said to me. "The stores opened up, and we went across to the Lucky Strike Market, corner of Woodward and Euclid, and we bought some rolls, apple turnovers, milk, pop. Three or four TV dinners. The other three went home Tuesday. The youngest one, Ronald Banks, his parents came and got him, and he came back to get Larry Demps and Michael Calhoun—only lives five or six blocks from there, and he just walked back up and the three left together. Fred and Larry and me, we just stayed on and watched TV."

I asked why they had decided to stay.

"It was a kind of a two-way thing," Roderick said. "We had the money to pay up to Wednesday morning, and we decided to see what it would be like to be on your own."

13 | The Whole Day

Michael Clark, under cross-examination by Attorney Lippitt in the murder hearing:

Q. What had you done that day?

A. What did I do the whole day?

Q. Uh-huh.

A. Do I have to answer that? I went over to my sister's, came back, slept, ate, watched television, listened to the radio. Walked, went swimming, and that's about all.

14 | I'll Be Back

During the day Carl and Lee and Sortor stopped awhile at Carl's house. "When we came out to Carl's," Sortor told me, "Miss Margaret told us to go on and check out, you know, come on home. So we were going to get our stuff together and come on home."

Mrs. Gill—or Miss Margaret, as the boys called her—told me, "Carl was going with a girl named Patty. In fact, she was in jail during the time. She was in there for, you know, looting. There, too, he was trying to stick around the Algiers for her to call, because she didn't know my number. He knew that she'd probably try to catch him at Michael's. Before he left here to go back he called over and asked Michael had she called.

"They left here for the hotel—whenever he left home I knowed where I could reach him. They took tapes and they was going to play around. And I was cooking a turkey dinner, and I said, 'You going to come back and eat?' And he said, 'I'll be back and have a piece of meat,' you know."

As he set out for the Algiers Motel on a riotous afternoon, Carl Cooper made a natty sight; he was wearing brown loafers and brown socks, orange trousers, a brown sports coat over a white dress shirt, and a white straw hat.

15 | What's Happened to These People?

"Frank came over there," Sortor told me, "a guy named Frank Parker, so we went back over to his house. I went around to Auburey's house on the way. I said, 'Well, Frank told me, "Come on over to my pad, man." I'm going to pick up my coat.' Which this coat was mine already, before the looting started, see, this coat was mine, so I said, 'I'm going over there and get it.' So we went on over there, went to Frank's house, stayed over there for a little while. So it was some friends, six of us, you know, in the car, so we were riding, going back over to the hotel. We wouldn't have got stopped, see, but this here guy, I guess he started shooting at the police over there, and they told everybody to turn around and go back down Fourteenth, so we turned around, and we had to go all the way down to the Boulevard, and the police, they pulled us over down there, I guess it was because there was six of us. A police car told us to pull over. Then a jeep ran alongside and bumped into us, forced us up on the curb. They got us out and pushed us around down there and lined us up around this big tree. They took my coat. They said whose coat was it. I said it was mine, it was in my hand. It was a cashmere coat, cost about seventy-nine dollars. 'Where did you loot this out of?' I said, 'I didn't loot it.' So the guy hit me up the side of my face. So I said, 'I ain't loot that coat. I had this coat last winter and I just left it over at Frank's house over there, because I had another one, another that was a lighter coat, like a pinstripe coat, I had that, so I wore that.' They was searching us down. Auburey got hit then, back of the head. Auburey was just telling them he was working at Ford's. Guy told him to shut up and hit him. So they told us to get back in the car and go ahead on. So I said to Auburey, 'Man, what's *happened* to these people? They gone crazy.' "

16 | You Could Have Won a Lot

By about seven o'clock, Lee, Carl, Auburey, Sortor, and Michael had all gathered in Lee's room, A-5; they had brought two friends with them, Melvin Pratt and Heywood Lester; and Michael's sister and brother-in-law, Brenda and Rodney Norman, also joined them there—and perhaps one or two others.

"We just got tired of watching television," Lee told me. "Started to gambling. This guy Melvin Pratt was winning; he picked up maybe two hundred dollars."

"We was shooting craps," Sortor told me. "We was shooting twenty dollars, something like, twenty-five. You could have won a lot."

"They said when they were shooting crap," Mrs. Gill told me, "Auburey was saying, 'When I die, cremate me.' Sometimes you can sense things."

17 | I'm Not Going out There

The curfew hour came and went; they were still rolling dice. Finally, at nearly eleven, all but Carl, Michael, Auburey, Lee, and Sortor decided to leave—or, at least, all but one of those others surely did. I believe that one, who was wearing a yellow shirt, may have lingered after the rest.

"When the other boys left the motel," Mrs. Gill told me, "the other boy, he told Carl to come on with him. Carl wanted to come, but Carl was really scared to come out. He said, 'Man, I ain't going out there, be shot up in cars and things,' said, 'I'm not going out there, I'm going to stay right on in here. You ought to stay, too.' He tried to get them to stay, but it was eleven o'clock. Carl kept saying he should have went home. Auburey sitting there and saying, 'When I die, cremate me.' So I don't know if the boys had a feeling, or what."

18 | A Whole Bunch of Shooting

Michael had called his mother before his sister left. "I called my mother," he testified in the conspiracy hearing, "and told her my sister was over there. And then my mother told me that she heard it was, they was doing a whole bunch of shooting over on the Expressway, and to tell my sister and them to go back the opposite way, go towards, go towards, go north—yeah, go north and then go down to Davison and come."

19 | Something Was Fixing to Happen

Earlier in the evening, Mrs. Gill had visited a friend. "I was out there," she told me, "and I don't know, I never had that feeling before, just felt like you was out there by yourself, and something was fixing to happen any minute. I was over at a girl friend's house, and I just said, 'Take me home.' It was before the curfew, and the streets was empty. Actually that was the first time I'd been out riding since the riots, and I think that maybe I didn't realize how bad it really was. Just by hearing it over the news and all. But to be out there!"

Carl called her after the friends left, Mrs. Gill told me. "And he said, 'Well, it's after curfew, and the cabs won't come now,' he says, 'the cabs has stopped, you know,' he said, 'so I'll come home the first thing in the morning.' I said, 'Okay,' I said, 'but in the meantime you call me back, you call me back when you get ready to go to bed, let me know what room you're going to be in.' So he said, 'Okay.' And that was the first time he ever came out and said he was scared. He said, 'I'm really scared.' "

20 | We Decided We Were Hungry

Under cross-examination in the conspiracy hearing by Attorney Kohl, Juli Hysell testified as follows:

Q. Then do we understand that on Tuesday evening, the 25th of July, you were in room 2?

A. That's correct.

Q. And who was in room 2 with you?

A. Karen Malloy.

Q. Just the two of you?

A. Yes.

Q. Did you leave that room?

A. Yes, we did.

Q. When did you leave?

A. I imagine it was around midnight. I am not sure about the time.

Q. There was shooting in that area, wasn't there?

A. I never heard any shooting.

Q. And so what caused you to leave room 2 at approximately midnight?

A. Bubbles came to the room and asked us if we wanted to go to his room and play cards and listen to the radio.

Q. And what is Bubbles' name?

A. Bubbles.

Q. No, I say what is his name, not his nickname.

A. Eli Carter.

Q. Was Eli Carter staying at the Motel?

A. Yes, he was. . . .

Q. Did you at any time date Bubbles?

A. No, I didn't.

Q. But Bubbles was paying your way at the Motel, wasn't he?

A. No; he was giving me money if I needed it.

Q. But you didn't need it because you could always get it from your parents, we are led to believe.

A. I didn't send home every day for money. . . .

Q. So, midnight on the 25th you are invited to leave room 2 by Bubbles?

A. No, Bubbles—yeah, oh, that's right, yeah. He asked us did we want to go play cards, and we said no. . . .

Q. Well, what else happened?

A. We got up, and we had been watching television, and we got up, and we decided we were hungry, but we knew we couldn't go out on the street because, you know, of the curfew and that, so we started walking around the pool, because there was some people there that, you know, they had food at the Motel.

Q. They had what?

A. Food at the Motel. And some of the people that were living there had some food. And Carl Cooper was standing by the pool, so we started talking to Carl. . . .

Q. And what happened?

A. We just started talking to him.

Q. Did you know him?

A. Yes, we knew him. We had met him a couple of days before.

Q. Yes.

A. And, you know, we told him we were looking for some, you know, food and that. . . .

Q. Some food?

A. Because we were hungry. And he said that Lee had some food over in his apartment, and we were welcome to go over there if there was anything we liked.

Q. And where was Bubbles at this time?

A. He was in his room, playing cards. . . .

Q. Then what did you do, Miss Hysell?

A. We went over to Lee's and fixed hot dogs. . . .
Q. Did you know Lee?
A. No, I just met him then.

21 | A Puzzle

"I called back over there about twelve," Mrs. Gill told me, "and talked to the girl on the switchboard, and she said she couldn't accept any calls, and I said, 'well, why?'—you know. And she said, 'I just can't accept any calls right now. Soon as I get a line clear.' And I said, 'Well, what's going on?' And she said, 'Nothing. It's quiet over here.' So that was a puzzle to me, you know. Like I say, I was nervous for some reason, you know. You hear all those bullet shots around, you know, shooting around, you don't know what to think. What made me really nervous was when he told me he was really scared."

9

"Quiet and Respectable"

1 | B or C Average

"I was born in Royal Oak," Ronald August began. "Well, my birth certificate states it's Royal Oak Township, which I believe now is called Madison Heights. March 27, 1939.

"My father's a tool grinder; he's done this for the last thirty-some years, he's been in this trade. My father was brought up in Grand Rapids. He ran away from an orphanage, as I recall him telling; at the age of sixteen he came to Detroit. His parents weren't deceased, they were separated, and he, along with his two other brothers—he has three brothers, but as far as I know, the two of them out of the three were in the orphanage with him in Grand Rapids.

"My parents moved here in this same vicinity of town, Northeast Detroit, when I was approximately four and a half years old, and I started kindergarten in the fall of '45, and I went there two years, at Burbank Elementary. Then I switched over to St. Jude Catholic School, that's on East Seven Mile Road, and I went there to the eighth grade. My grades were, I'd say, maybe a B or C average."

143

2 | A Dislike of Getting Knocked Around

"I liked building model airplanes," he told me. "They were never, I would say, a really advanced, complicated kit, but I did a lot of that. And I was always messing around with electricity or electronics, and I remember building my crystal set, and gee, I haven't seen a crystal set for quite a while now. Then my dad bought me a Heath radio kit, and I built the radio, and I remember the electric train I had. It was older than I was when I got it, a Lionel, and I had two engines; my dad bought it used. And oh, it ran for a good many years. I still have it, but it doesn't want to go any more. The tracks are rusty, and I guess the cold attic doesn't do it any good.

"My interest in sports—I like sports, but I was never that enthused to get out there and get knocked around that much.

"When I was a boy, it seems to me my dad bought me a new bike when I was about ten years old, and I practically lived on a bicycle. We'd go on bike hikes, and I can recall one time calling my dad up at four o'clock in the afternoon—he got home about then—telling him to come and get me, because I broke the chain on the bike. My mother always knew where we were at; she'd pack us a lunch, and we'd take off maybe ten o'clock in the morning, and there was at least three of us, two or three of us. I can recall most of my boyhood just riding that bike. I rode up to school, I even rode it a little bit to high school, till it was stolen, and then I never had a bike after that. I walked."

3 | Always the Toughie

"I had one brother, he's five years younger than I am. He is somewhat different than what I am, I always believe. He's more or less of the sports enthusiast, where I never was. He was strictly the varsity type all the way through school.

"We've always had a good brotherly-love relationship, as far as brotherly love will go. He was always the toughie, where I was more or less just satisfied to do something not as strenuous as he was doing. He was all the time wanting to play football, he'd be going to basketball practice and things of this nature, where I was just happy to, well, go play cards, go play Monopoly, and things of this sort, or go on a bike hike, or go down to the City Airport and see the airplanes. Well, he didn't do these things. In fact, when he got his bicycle, he wouldn't even change a flat tire; either my dad did it, or I did it, or it sat in the garage. His interests were strictly nothing mechanical; he just wanted sports."

4 | Tinkering

"My first car came along when I was sixteen. I always regretted my first car, because it never ran. It was a 1946 Ford. I swear, I'll never have another Ford. I was working in a gas station, and I was too young to pump gasoline, so I was washing windows and sweeping and my primary task was washing automobiles, which got to be a very good-paying proposition in the wintertime, because you just couldn't keep up with the cars that came in wanting a car wash.

"This fellow pulled in the station one day with this '46 Ford, with a for-sale sign on it. It was noisy, but I figured, 'Well, that can be fixed.' Where actually it could have been fixed, but not on the wages I was making, because it needed a new manifold, and if you recall the '46 Fords—this was another pastime of mine, I just loved to tinker with automobiles—you had to put a fuel pump in them bloody things every six months if it wasn't every six days. I just got it home, and I was real excited about having a car, and after we ate dinner that night, I said to my mom, 'Come on, we'll go for a ride.' I got in her and it wouldn't start!

"I only had that car three months, and between putting in new fuel pumps and changing the transmission or something, it was just sitting there all the time in the garage. I sold it at a loss, for forty-five dollars; I'd paid sixty for it. That was sort of a poor investment."

5 | C to A

"I recall starting Denby High School," he said, "and went there two years. Ninth and tenth grade I went there. I had a C average. And then in '56 it was that my dad—the company moved. He worked for Palmer Bee for thirty years, the Palmer Bee Company, and they moved to Marysville, Michigan, so that's why I just put two years in at Denby. Consequently after we moved up there to St. Clair, Palmer Bee went out of business or went bankrupt, I don't know what happened, but they disappeared. He kind of followed them up there to keep his seniority without any rewards as far as financial status goes. But then he worked for Mueller Brass, Port Huron.

"And then I started at St. Clair High School, which would be my junior year, and I graduated from there in June of '58. My last two years that I finished up, I can boast of an A average with a few B's."

6 | The Old Danceable Items

"This is one part I forgot to mention," he said, "where I had a very good interest in music. I played saxophone and clarinet, and at the time I did a lot of playing in a small combo, quartet actually, it was four pieces. We enjoyed playing mostly, at the time, high-school dances, parties, and we'd advertise in the newspaper as catering to weddings and banquets and parties. The Blue Lancers. We were going to call ourselves the Blue Notes, but that didn't sound too good, so we decided on the Blue Lancers. We played together about three and a half years, and we could play the polkas and the waltzes and the sambas and rhumbas; my favorites are the old standards like *Star Dust* and *Dream* and *Tondoleyo*, all the old danceable items. I was a tenor, tenor sax and clarinet. I began taking lessons at about ten years old, and I plugged along with the lessons for about three years, and I met this fellow that was a year younger than I was that played the alto, and he was just fabulous. In talking to him, he had a little experience in playing different parties and weddings, and in speaking with him I found where this wasn't getting anywhere, so with his help I learned how to transpose, which was necessary if you want to play in a small combo. About two years after that, I was doing fairly well, I thought."

7 | Softhearted

"Before I was in the Navy," August told me, "I met my wife. At the time she was seventeen years old, I was nineteen. And she comes from a large family, by the way, she has two brothers and two sisters, and they live on a farm.

"I met her in Canada, as I recall. Oh, how could I explain it? I met her in Canada where she thought I was Canadian and I thought she was Canadian, come to find that we lived in two towns on the St. Clair River just eight miles apart. It was at her high-school junior prom, I believe that's how you'd classify this. We were playing for it. And when I met her, she thought, like I said, she thought I was Canadian, but she gave me her phone number, and then when I called her I found out that it was a Marine City number instead of inside there. It was at the Guildwood Inn in Sarnia, just across the bluewater bridge, and I believe it's more or less traditional, they went over there every year. It sounds like having it in Canada, that you're actually going across the continent to get there, but it was only a matter of twenty miles from Marine City. But then we met at this dance, and we dated for about ten months, and we corresponded regularly while I was in the service.

"She was born in Detroit, December 19, 1940, and she moved, I don't know when she moved to the farm—her father has a hundred acres in Marine City, but I don't know, I guess now that it would be fifteen, sixteen years ago. And she grew up on a farm, and she tells me she fed the chickens, drove the tractor, and helped her dad and mother out. When her brother got old enough, well, that relieved her of the outside chores, and she stayed in the house. She has a marvelous personality. She talks all the time, which I guess most women do, but the most striking thing about her is her personality, I mean you just can't help feeling acquainted with her after you've only known her a small amount of time. She's very sensitive, she loves children, and sort of, I'd describe her as softhearted. When I met her, she always wanted to be a nurse, and she was a nurse's aide at the time, working in a hospital in Mt. Clemens."

8 | And See the World

"Then I enlisted in the Navy," August said, "in March, '59, and I had my basic training, I recall, at Great Lakes. From there I was stationed aboard an aircraft carrier, and there is where I stayed until I was discharged. The *Intrepid*, which was classified then as a CVA, or attack carrier.

"It was home-ported out of Norfolk, Virginia. When we were to go to the Mediterranean, it would usually be a seven-month cruise, and we'd go to Naples, Italy; Livorno, Italy; Barcelona, Spain; Cannes, France; Istanbul, Turkey. I went to Rome to the Olympics, either in '60 or '61. Rome is inland; I always thought of Rome as being a seaport. They told us we were going to Rome, so I figured we were going to drop anchor, and there's Rome. But it didn't happen that way. We had to take a bus. And we saw the Rock of Gibraltar; Beirut, Lebanon; Athens, Greece. I saw the Leaning Tower of Pisa—oh, I guess Pisa's around thirteen miles inland of Livorno. I enjoyed it. I enjoy traveling. We made three cruises while I was on the ship, and the third cruise was really six months of saving up to be discharged, because I'd already seen this stuff two years previously, and I was happy just to save a few pennies to come home on. Oh, I'd saved I think around eleven hundred dollars when I was discharged. They paid us in cash on the ship, and you had to fill out what they call a money receipt, you handed it to the disbursing clerk, and told him how much you wanted to draw out of your account, see, and naturally if you didn't withdraw it, it would keep adding up."

9 | Splashdown

"We picked up Scott Carpenter, the astronaut," August told me, "in 1962, I think it was. As I recall, there was our ship, the *Intrepid*, and a couple of destroyers, and we were in the Caribbean. It's just beautiful down there; the water's always sky-blue and not a ripple in it, the only ripple you see is what the ship makes. And we were tensely waiting for the word to—for the splashdown. Nothing was happening. We were just waiting around, and of course we were all in our white uniforms down there, so we'd look presentable when we got on the flight deck, and it was an hour overtime, as it was. We thought something actually disastrous had happened. But finally they told us that— this was right after we had changed to support carrier, we carried nothing but helicopters—so the helicopters were launched, and they flew away, and it was explained to us that the capsule had landed, landing relatively fifty miles away from the ship, and they were flying there to pick up the astronaut. And which they did do so, they got there and picked up Scott Carpenter. I seen him. I have pictures of it. But the idea was that the capsule was still there after they got the astronaut, and in order to retrieve the capsule, one of the ships had to get there first. I don't know if you're a sailor or not, but if you ever hear any talk about a destroyer outrunning a carrier, it won't happen. We did get there first. We picked up the capsule."

10 | Bad News for Ron

"I really didn't have any job prospect when I was discharged," he said, "something around the 28th of February of '63, I believe that's what the separation date was.

"We got married in May, which was roughly six, seven weeks. In '63 I wanted to start in an apprenticeship in electrical work, or plumbing, or carpentry. Any apprenticeship. But the doors were closed then, it seemed to be, because every place I went, they just weren't hiring any apprentices, or if you weren't a skilled tradesman at the time, well, they didn't want you. And the Police Department has always had a recruitment drive, so to speak, where they're always hiring—and I think this is going to last for quite a few years to come, because they need more men and more men all the time. But I went down there and put in the application and within a few weeks I had heard that I was accepted. I learned about a month before we were married.

"There's a little story to that, too. The Police Department has what they call a oral interview, where after your application is accepted and they clear you as far as your past record if you have one or not, then they call you in. They asked me if I was married, and I actually was not married, and I told him I was single. So he asked me when I was getting married, and I told him May the 4th. I don't know who it was, but he stated, 'Well, I have bad news for you, Ron. We're not starting the class, the way it was supposed to be, on May the 13th, starting in the Academy. We're going to start it on the 4th of May. Which would you rather do, be a police officer or get married?' He threw me off balance there momentarily, but I told him I'd rather get married. I told him the party was all set, the caterer was hired, the band was hired, and there was no way of backing out of it. Oh, we had had the hall for over a year. Then he admitted that they don't start classes on Saturdays anyway. He was having fun with me."

11 | Bank Holdup

"We had a bank-holdup-in-progress run," August told me. "They gave it to us and two other back-up cars. And at the time I was on the John C. Lodge Service Drive, which is nothing but a straightaway, and you have no stop signs whatsoever, and I had no turns to make, because the John C. Lodge runs right into Hamilton—this was Hamilton and Collingwood, Detroit Bank and Trust. So I picked up speed. Traffic was light. And I was approaching a light, which I think there wasn't too many lights on the way there. I believe this light was at Pallister. When I got there, I was going about fifty-five, sixty miles an hour, quite excited to be the first one there, and out of the glimpse of my eye I could see a car coming. I was going north, and this car was coming east, from my left, and he was going to run that red light. Well, it was a Tactical Mobile Unit car, blue-and-white, with the city's finest in special radio equipment, highly specialized trained men, and they were making this run also. How we didn't hit each other I'll never understand, but I slammed the brakes on, and he was going too fast even to make the left-hand turn, he kept on going straight.

"But when we got there, we were far from being the first car there; I think we were about the last one there. And here some advertising company was filming an old-time holdup—you know, the gangland twenties, the gangster-type deal with the old black limousine and machine guns and the works. So we pulls up there, here they are standing around with clothes on looked like in the twenties, with this old limousine they had, and the cameras are coming, and it really looked like the real thing except the props just didn't look like 1967. I recall this because I almost got smacked broadside on the way there."

12 | Chasing

"The officers down there to Woodward Station," August said, "you're just not doing your job if you don't get a stolen car at least once a week, and some fellows pick them up on an average of three a week, because they're really prosperous in that area. We were traveling north on Woodward Avenue, and we seen this car. You know, a car thief never tries to be suspicious. They stand out because your eyes are trained. There are a few police officers that seem to have a photographic mind; they can spot a number and tell you it's a hot car. But most of us don't use this method at all. You can look at the plate number and look at the hot sheet, and within seconds you have your answer, but some of them just tell by looking at the plate. I don't mean by your plate being on crooked or looks like it's wired or anything of this nature, either, but a car thief never tries to drive conspicuously, he'll be real careful. But when we got on his tail, he took off, because he knew we had him. And there was three boys in the car, and we were driving a Buick, and they were pulling away from us in a big cloud of blue smoke. Well, anyway, they made a left turn off Woodward, and it was approaching Second Avenue, and they came to almost a rolling stop and they bailed out. And then the car hit a telephone pole, and they all went in all different directions. Between the two of us we caught all three of them. The third one would never have got caught except for the fact that he tripped and stumbled and fell right on his face, so I was able to catch him. My lungs were burning so hot from running and running. I don't jump fences very well, either. But I had a commendation for that incident."

13 | Money Didn't Mean That Much

"The base pay for a police officer in Detroit right now," he said, "is $8,335 a year, which is tops. I started at $5,500, which was the starting salary in 1963. Top salary I was getting last summer would bring me home, after taxes and pension fund came out, hospitalization and whatever else you can think of, about $122 take-home weekly.

"I had one day out on blue flu. This is a very bitter subject. Now, my personal feeling on this was, the pay wasn't that bad, what with the wife working and whatever little thing I can pick up on the side, carpentering work or something; the money didn't mean that much to me, but I just couldn't see this monthly report. Now every police department's got your monthly log sheets and reports you have to turn in, well and good. But I couldn't see where, if you were working a B. and E. car, or doing something very concrete as far as good police work was concerned, and you still didn't have your twenty tickets for the month, you were a bad policeman. Now, that wasn't right. You take a guy that could catch twenty stolen cars in a month, make fifteen felony arrests, and double that amount in misdemeanor arrests, spend half his time in court, plus the other half on his days off in court, then give him a service rating of eighty-five and he doesn't get promoted because of thát service rating, simply because he didn't write twenty tickets a month. This doesn't affect me, because I don't have enough seniority on the job to even get promoted. But the idea and my feelings are, you take the guy that did nothing but write tickets, well, he was the man that was getting points."

14 | Tensions

I asked August what the morale of the Detroit force had been before the riots.

"Very low," he said. "Very low. I know that's sort of a meager answer, just two little words, 'very low.' But there was tensions. I don't think any of us actually expected any trouble last summer. If somebody would have asked me, the week before or the day before, if I thought there was going to be any trouble in the city of Detroit, and I says, 'Well, no, because I don't feel any trouble as far as racial problems come along.' Seemed to me, I been down there in the precinct for three years, and I never seen it any different then than what I started down there. I didn't actually feel anything different."

15 | You're Going to Get Criticism

"Detroit," August said, "has one of the finest police departments in the nation. The men have the ability, they have the desire to do the work, and I don't think their cry is actually more pay. Sure, the money is going to help, but that's not what they need. They need the public's backing. Not the city government's backing, but just the public's general opinion and backing. You see, being a police officer is strictly not a get-a-patsy-on-the-back job. You can do the best job you can, and you're still going to get criticism. You can stop a man for speeding, even catch him on radar, and onlookers are going to tell you you did it wrong, or you didn't use the right approach. I think it's the best police department in the nation, if they'd just let these men be policemen."

16 | No Trouble

"When we were an attack carrier," he said, "we had ninety-three fellows in our Fuels Division, and when we changed over to support carrier we lost about half the division, they transferred them off. I think we had at one given time—let's say when we had the ninety-three men, we must have had eight, nine, ten colored fellows in our division at the time. They had no trouble getting along.

"I know a lot of colored people, and I always got along with them."

17 | Percentages

"When you work a Negro neighborhood," he said, "naturally you're going to have a high per cent of colored arrests. When you're working a white neighborhood, it goes the other way."

18 | Playing This Up

"By the way," he said, "I don't go along with any sort of brutality. I blame your news media for playing this up so much. You get a police officer out there, not only in the state of Michigan, but what they had in Watts, and what they had in Harlem, and all the racial trouble they have across the nation, they never show you what the people are doing to cause all this thing, they just show you what the policemen are doing trying to stop it."

19 | You Have to Be Persuasive

"When you're walking down the street," Ronald August said to me, "and you see a man with a rifle on a rooftop, and you suspect a sniper in the area, you been sent over there to look for a sniper, and you ask this guy to identify himself, and, 'Halt!' and the guy disappears, maybe he runs along the roof and he climbs down a telephone pole, and you haven't got the building surrounded as well as you thought you did, and you miss him, see. Well, say you do run up against him and you catch him, and you're lucky enough not to have any cross-fire, well, I don't go along with the idea where you got to beat the vinegar out of this fellow, but you can't treat him with kid gloves, either. You have to be persuasive in the line of police work when you're dealing with these people. You just can't put diapers on them, and powder them up, and put them in the car. I mean you put the cuffs on them, you put them in the car, and if they give you any lip, you use force to effect your arrest, so to speak."

20 | Very Good Public Relations

"I mentioned to you before," he said to me, "that I had quite a lot of interest in music. Well, the Police Department has a very fine Police Band, which I believe, along with the mounted bureau and your traffic safety and so on and so forth, is very good public relations for the Department. Well, anyhow, I played with the Police Band. I worked straight days."

21 | A Nice Family-Type Fellow

"I'm a police officer," August's partner of that Tuesday evening, David Senak, said to me, "and they could fire me, and ten years from now you could ask me and I'd still be a police officer, whether I'm fired or not. But August I don't think is. I think he's just a nice family-type fellow. I worked with him one time in uniform, and all he talked about was his family, and the band. Just a general nice guy. I worked with him a little bit in the riots, and there was a lot of rough-housing, you know, because after Olshove died, you know, everything just went loose. The police officers weren't taking anything from anyone. If they gave him trouble, August would go out of his way not to give anyone trouble, or not to have to resort to violence.

"He's not a police officer in the degree that my friends are, and myself. He takes it as his job. It's a job. I work as a rigger, it's a job to me. He works as a policeman, it's a job. You could almost say that when I took the oath as a police officer I married the Police Department. And I'm sure my sergeant did the same thing, even though he's happily married. He gave a certain part of his life to the Police Department."

Robert Paille said to me, "Well, Ronald August there, I think he's sincere, you know, he's got a family and all that there, you know, and he's responsible. He's not a leader of men and all that there, you know, but I feel that he's done a good job in the past there, you know. He hasn't been outstanding or anything like that there, as far as I know, but as little as I do know of him he's quiet and respectable."

10

An Alarm of Snipers

Tuesday Night, July 24–5

1 | A Military Man

Theodore Johnson Thomas was, as to habit, a military man. White; thirty-two years old; five feet nine inches tall; with a squarish, upholstered, pyknic figure; curly black receding hair and fleshy face with blithe blue eyes above puffy bags—this outwardly thick-set and inwardly lean and anxious person was a veteran of fourteen years in the U.S. Air Force, twelve of them spent as a teacher of rudimentary electronics for aircraft systems. The Air Force moved him from place to place; he, his wife, and his five children built up a backlog of roaming, and one of his daughters, he would proudly say, had been in forty-seven states.

In 1966, after a five-year station in Oscoda, Michigan, and at a rank of staff sergeant, he dropped out of the Air Force, seeking better pay and opportunities, and he became a process engineer of electrical-discharge machines for General Motors. But, as he said to Ladd Neuman after he became at least locally famous because of his bizarre role in the Algiers affair, "After

157

fourteen years of military life you just don't drop away from it." He looked into Air Force Reserve possibilities and was not impressed; then he visited a Michigan National Guard unit, which happened to need a radar officer—just his dish—and he joined, and after a year and a half, when this experience began, he was rated as a warrant officer.

Warrant Officer Thomas was easily confused by the questioning. As to his education: "Actually," he testified in court, "they credited me with fifty-six college hours—" Attorney Kohl asked, "Who credited you?" "—with GM, approximately." "Do I understand you to mean, or to say, you went to college?" "Yes. Well, with the education I've gotten in the service and with the background—with my teaching experience plus the courses I've taken are credit courses." "Well, have you been in college?" "No, sir, I've been in the service. . . ."

Nor was Warrant Officer Thomas always clear as to the exact sequence of events. He spoke once in court of riot training that his National Guard unit had had. "And when was that?" "I believe that was—it's pretty hard to remember. It was either in the fall or the spring of the year. I can't remember; either last fall or this spring, early. . . . In fact," he added, "about a week before the riot we had the mobile unit squad out at the Armory, and they also went through their riot-control formations for us also. We practiced." "When you say 'they,' what organization are you referring to?" "The Tactical Mobile Units of Detroit. That's the Detroit Police Department."

In a manner of speaking this military man was, at about ten o'clock on Sunday morning, July 23, when the telephone rang in his home, ready.

2 | In Case

"I was put on a stand-by alert," Thomas testified, as to that call. "This was—this told me that Detroit was under a state of, or about ready to go into a state of emergency, and we were on a yellow alert at this time. . . . I was called again around noon or a little after noon and told I should come down to the Armory because we're probably—I'm also arms officer out there. I have the keys to the weapons, the vaults, and I should come down in case something did break, so I went down immediately." At another hearing, he remembered one detail precisely: "I hadn't eaten."

3 | Not That Alert

By Tuesday afternoon Warrant Officer Thomas was ragged. He was asked during the murder hearing how much sleep he had had on Sunday and Monday nights. "I figure approximately an hour and a half, sir. . . . From the time the alert went out—it was ten o'clock Sunday morning—until the time of this incident. Monday morning I had an opportunity to lay down but they moved us. I just got in a sack; my bedroom. And we had to get up. I hadn't slept probably fifteen minutes at the most. Then Tuesday morning I got about an hour, hour and fifteen minutes sleep." Attorney Lippitt asked, "How would you describe your condition at the time you came upon the Algiers Motel?" "Not very well," Thomas answered. "Truthfully, I can't say that I was that mentally alert."

4 | Things Were Extremely Tense

At three o'clock Tuesday afternoon, Warrant Officer Thomas was assigned four men—Sergeant Paul Gerard, Sp5 Thomas Kelly, Pfc. Wayne Henson, and Pfc. Robert Seaglan—and was directed to go by jeep to the Great Lakes Mutual Life Insurance Building, at the corner of Euclid and Woodward Avenues, with orders, as he put it in court, "to protect the building. . . . Inside and outside, we was to protect the building . . . from any kind of disturbance. I mean, a bombing, or fire, or sniper fire." Thomas pulled the jeep right up on the sidewalk, snug against the building. The president of Great Lakes Insurance, Thaddeus B. Gaillard, showed Thomas about the building, gave him keys and left a telephone number to call in case there should be any trouble.

The weary warrant officer's spirits apparently fell dark with the day, and when he and his men heard some machine-gun fire at some distance across Woodward, he testified, "we were very concerned." Everyone was jittery. This was to be, as things turned out, the night of culmination—a night of hallucination. Like a whisper grown too loud in mad imaginings, the word "sniper" scurried around town and became a kind of roar. On television sets across the country viewers sat amazed, that night, if not horrified, at the sight of American tanks rolling through the streets of an American city on the hunt for American citizens, and of military helicopters hovering over Detroit rooftops; memories stirred in my mind, at these images, of the nightmares of Warsaw in 1943, Budapest in 1956, Santo Domingo in 1965. During this insane night Tonia Blanding, a four-year-old black child, with her family and friends in an apartment from which sniper fire had been reported, was killed by a burst from a tank's .50-caliber machine gun when someone in the room with her lit a cigarette and the flaring match was taken for the flash at the mouth of a sniper's weapon; and Helen Hall, a fifty-year-old white woman from Oakdale, Connecticut, visiting Detroit to help inventory some electrical supplies her employers had purchased, was killed as she stood at a fourth-floor window of the Harlan House Motel, just after she had called to other motel guests to come and watch a tank in the street and had yanked the curtain back to give them a better view. This was the night of Detroit's great so-called sniper battle.

In a passage of highly tendentious cross-examination by Attorney Kohl in the conspiracy hearing, Warrant Officer Thomas testified on his state of nerves:

q. Machine-gun fire, you say?

a. Yes, sir.

q. Small-arms fire?

a. Small-arms fire, rifle fire. There was all kinds of shooting.

q. And this was throughout the evening?

a. Yes, sir.

Q. The later it became, the worse it became, right?

A. I'd say yes.

Q. All right, and there is no question whatsoever but what at that point and in that area things were extremely tense?

A. Yes; yes sir. . . .

Q. Tuesday night was one of the worst, wasn't it?

A. Yes, sir, it was the worst for me.

Q. Right, all right, but in this area, on this night, there was a great fear and apprehension with reference to sniping?

A. Yes, sir, this is when the sniping became its worst.

5 | A Man Who Had Made It

Melvin Dismukes, a phlegmatic, big-bodied, twenty-six-year-old Negro private guard in the employ of an outfit called State Private Patrol, had been set to watch the Lucky Strike Supermarket and J&R Patent Medicines, directly across Woodward from the Great Lakes Building, one block up from the Algiers.

Dismukes was a man who had "made it" in a certain way—to the point, if this could be taken as a sign of it, of having been accused by one of the black youths at the Algiers that morning of being an Uncle Tom and a black motherfucker. His nickname suggested a clean-living man; he was called Preacher. Born in Birmingham, Alabama, on September 8, 1942, he had moved with his family to Detroit when he was nine. He attended six different city schools and reached twelfth grade, "with a major of machine technology," in Chadsey High School. He had trouble, at first, finding employment; then landed a job, which lasted a couple of years, as a truck driver with Miami Colored Slab, a company that constructed patios; worked a few months as a "sanitary inspector" in Boulevard General Hospital; went back to patio-building as yard foreman awhile; then finally dug into a good steady job with W. J. C. Kaufmann Company, a construction firm, where, after some time as a laborer, he was promoted into welding, which he had been doing for about three years when these events took place.

For five years he had also worked evenings as a private guard, and he had been given, in the hierarchy of watchmen, a rank of sergeant, chevrons and all. At first he had worked in a residential area known as Conant Gardens, where he would check the doors of some houses and flash a light around others.

As welder and guard Dismukes took home about two hundred dollars a week; thus he provided for his wife, Carol, and daughter, Kimberly, aged four at the time of those events, and son, Melvin, Jr., who was one.

Dismukes had another life, too. As president of the Volunteer Service Club at the Wigle Recreation Center, he was in charge of teen-age dances and roller skating, and he had trained a paramilitary drill team of both boys and girls; he was a volunteer assistant to the coach of the semiprofessional Alonzo Stokes girls' baseball and basketball teams, which were mixed, white and colored, and had been named, once, "Volunteer of the Year"; and at Cass Baptist Church he was supervisor of gym and roller skating.

On Sunday, the day the riot had begun, he had been called in the evening by State Patrol, and he had driven his '60 De Soto, all the way in low gear—for it had been "totaled," he told me, just before the previous Christmas when "a guy came through a red light, injured my back and one hand"—two or three miles to his guard post on Woodward, which he shared with two other private guards. He had stood duty there until seven thirty Monday morning, had gone then to work at Kaufmann's, where, because looting had started in the neighborhood, he had helped board up windows, and had finally gone home to bed. He had gone back out Monday night and Tuesday during the day. Several cars had stopped in front of the Lucky Strike, he told me, as if their riders were preparing to loot; men jumped out, and he and his colleagues had stepped forward from cover they had taken, and the looters had scrammed. Like Thomas, he was edgy. He had been warned that insurrectionists might be driving by with machine guns blazing or tossing out Molotov cocktails.

Dismukes was carrying a .38-caliber pistol and a .350 Magnum rifle that he had bought about a year before for hunting.

He had never actually shot game with that weapon, but he had practiced at a public range at Dequindre and Twenty-six-Mile Road. "If I was going to have a gun," he said to me, "I might as well be able to hit something with it. That gun could stop a car."

When the National Guard jeep pulled up on the sidewalk across the street, Dismukes went over and introduced himself to the Guardsmen. Later he asked Thomas over for a cup of coffee with him and *his* men, and they chatted about the troubles. After dark, and after Thomas had posted two of his troops, Henson and Kelly, on the roof of the Great Lakes Building as lookouts, the watchman-sergeant and the warrant officer spent more and more time beside the jeep, talking and listening to news reports on a transistor radio. "Pretty comfortable," Thomas said in court, "having somebody else out there with me."

6 | Snipers!

At about midnight, the men by the jeep and the men on the roof heard shots near at hand.

Immediately after the sounds of the shots came—"about three shots . . . I believe they were small caliber . . . sounded like a pistol," Thomas testified—Dismukes saw one of his fellow private guards fall prone in the street, he told me, and he thought the man had been wounded or killed; it turned out he had simply hit the deck to protect himself.

Warrant Officer Thomas was not sure, in court, what happened next—whether he rushed first to a telephone inside the building to call for help, or whether he went first to the corner of Euclid "to see if I could see where the shots were coming from." "That," he testified, "is a little confusing."

From the corner, whenever it was that he took a look, he would have seen, directly across Euclid to the south, a Standard garage, with a car wash at the far side of it from his point of view, and, above them, a large billboard saying, "Nobody Undersells woody pontiac and don't forget it"; beyond them, the Algiers Motel; and to the right, beyond the car wash and a parking lot, a big brick building which Thomas thought to be a private house—the motel annex.

Sooner or later Thomas got on the phone inside the Great Lakes Building and called the high-command emergency number he had been given.

"I called the high commander," Thomas testified in the conspiracy hearing, "and that was all I had to do, was tell them our location and I was having trouble."

"What did you tell them the problem was?" asked Judge Frank Schemanske. "I mean, that's what I want to know."

"I said there was shooting, I was stationed at Woodward and Euclid, and we were being fired upon."

III

Auburey and His Circle

11

The Fork in the Road

1 | The Fork in the Road

This is the hardest part of this book to write. I want to bring out before your eyes and ears some aspects of the life of a young black man in a city, in the circle of his family and his friends. My own being has been at a distance from being black, and I want, if I can, to narrow that distance here, at least, by a careful looking and listening. This will be but a substitute for the reality that a black writer could give you at this point; I am what I am.

I have chosen Auburey Pollard as the one for us to try to get to know. Of the three young men who were killed at the Algiers, Auburey was somehow in the middle. White society confronts every black youth in this country with a fork in the road when he is about ten or eleven or twelve; one path takes him on through some schooling, to some jobs, to living more or less "straight," to a never easy accommodation, or to a running conflict, with the rule and demands of the white world; the other path takes him apart, into fighting the system without perhaps even knowing, at first, that he is doing so, into scraps and scrapes, into trouble with the police, into jail, into a hustling life, and at last into a constantly harassed alienation from which no turning back had been devised in Auburey's time, though Malcolm X seemed just before his death on the verge of such an invention. Carl Cooper had a police record; Fred Temple had none. Auburey, very late indeed, was still teetering. He had been in trouble with the authorities once, for hitting a teacher in school, but he was struggling against both the bitterness of his existence and his own combative nature; struggling, at the same time, to have a little fun, and to be as safe as Fred, and to be as bold, as open, and as attractive as Carl. He might have gone either way.

Blood brothers could go divergent ways. One of Auburey's brothers, Chaney, the Marine, was clearly on the "straight" path; another, Robert, who was in prison when Auburey died, was on the path of estrangement. Auburey, as his father said, had yet to find himself.

2 | He Helped Me

When I first asked Mrs. Pollard to tell me about Auburey, her reflex response had to do with health. "Really what bothered me when he was real little," she said, "he was so sick till I had to take him to Ford Hospital. And when he was thirteen I had to have him operated on at Harper Hospital; he had a hernia. When he was real small, he couldn't keep nothing on his stomach, he didn't have too much of a stomach. But they used some chemical drugs, built him up a lining, and after his operation he was pretty strong, a pretty well boy, he helped me around a lot."

3 | I Been Making It

Concisely Mrs. Pollard told me the story of her life. "I been living in Detroit since '43"—the year of the Belle Isle race riot.

"Before that I lived in Tennessee, Knoxville. I left home after my mother died, I didn't want to stay home, so I run off. So I been making it on my own. I worked from one job to another job, but I was figuring someday I could marry and have my family here, which I did, you see I wanted to have my own home, which I did, and I said I wanted to have a nice car for them, which I did. That's just it. Me and my husband was together, over twenty-two years we been together—till this happened.

"I go out and do daywork. I work from one family to another. I worked for one family for ten years, and their kids feel just like a part of me, you know. I been there since they was real small. They treat me very nice. I'm a laundress for them. I keep all their clothes done up. Recently they gave me two days, usually I had just one day. They knew when this happened; I called them, you know, let them know I couldn't come, you know, my boy getting killed like that. I don't much feel like working now. I just can't run away from it. I feel if I could just go on, leave, and go this place and that place, maybe I could forget about things. If I could feel that I could go, you know, from one town to another town, I think I could feel much better. Just see something different and be around different things, you know; I think I'd feel better. I'm not going in my house over there, it makes me sick. I don't want no part of that house. I lived there ever since '55."

The Pollards had five children: Chaney Clay, who was twenty-one when his brother died; Auburey Dows, who was nineteen; Tanner Lorenzo, eighteen; Robert Jewel, seventeen; and Thelma Florence, sixteen.

4 | An Artist

"Auburey went to McMichael," his mother told me, "and he was good on art. He went to Pattengill first. Then he went to a school where they could learn him how to read and write good, because he was sort of hard to learn. Then after he learned that they put him in McMichael; then from McMichael he went to Northwestern.

"He loved to do art, which he was a very good drawer. He was a very good artist, he had papers to go to Woodward Avenue somewhere to a school there, where he could do professional art work. He won two certificates. He made a book of all American ships, I have a certificate to show for it, which it went to New York City and then they brought it back to Wayne State University and put it on exhibit down there.

"My husband was in the Navy, he used to take Auburey to see the ships and show him the different ships he was on, like out to Belle Isle when they had them parked, you know, he'd take him down and let him see the ships he was on. My husband was all over in the war; he was overseas for three years, three years and four months I think he stayed overseas. And he always wanted his boys to go in the Navy, and Auburey said, 'Dad, I'm going into the Navy, I want to be a Navy man.' And Chaney said, 'I'm not going in the Navy because I want to be in the toughest outfit they got, the U.S. Marines.' "

5 | Do for Yourself

"We were just a common family," Mr. Pollard told me. "We laughed, we talked. Sometimes I was liable to go out and buy some shrimp, barbecue them all in the shells, stew them down with butter and pour a barbecue sauce over them, and we sit in the middle of the floor and put newspapers there, and nobody but the four boys and myself, and we'd sit there and jolly-bo gig, because my daughter, she wouldn't eat them; we'd sit there and jolly-bo gig, floor show, get up and go swimming—I swim as hard as each one of them! Get out in the back yard and shoot marbles—I shoot marbles as hard as any one of them! I shoot for keeps, I don't be playing; but you know, after I'm through with them, I'd give them back to them. And we'd play ball, I taught them how to play football, I begged them to play football, I had only one would play football, and he only played in one game; that was my baby boy. But now far as sports, boxing, or being rough, I'd tell them you cannot grow up in this world depending on the other fellow. Know how to do for yourself. Don't take advantage of nobody, but know how to do for yourself. Regardless if it's to make up your bed, fix a peanut-butter-and-jelly sandwich, or clean up your room, shine your shoes, or wash your underwear, know how to do it for yourself. See what I mean? Because you'll go a long ways like that. There's nothing dishonest about that. The good book says, 'God bless the child that has its own.' They don't have to be nothing big, nothing like Rockefeller, now, or Henry Ford. There's an old saying, see, that's like this:

> *"I cannot do the big things that I should like to do,*
> *To make the world forever fair, or the skies forever blue,*
> *But I can do the smaller ones that help to make it sweet,*
> *Through tempests that rise and clouds that pass.*

Now, I got it portionally wrong, but it's really a true fact: Everybody cannot do the big things, but you can do some of the small things that help to make it sweet."

6 | Lifeguard

"He loved to swim," his mother said. "He was a lifeguard one while—YMCA was one of the places, and at Kronk Recreation Center, he was a lifeguard there. He had a card, he was very good, he was a lifeguard."

7 | Right in a Circle

"Auburey, Tanner, Robert, Chaney, and myself, we all used to go swimming," Mr. Pollard said. "We used to go swimming at Northwestern there, and the guys used to say, 'Is that your daddy?' 'Yeah, that's my daddy!' 'He don't look like your daddy.' 'Well, that's Daddy over there.' We were right in a circle. We'd all go swimming, then we'd go home.

"Fishing, the same way. Sometimes we used to go up to

Canada, we'd leave like on a Friday, we'd stay Friday, Saturday, up till Sunday sometimes. We used to fish up around Tilbury, all the way up. We used to even take their mother with us, sometimes. But she didn't want to go because she had to cook—coffee *all* the time. 'That's all I do, is cook.' And she's scared of bugs. We went fishing I don't know how many times. We used to love fishing. You know how boys like to roam, you know, and get out. And I used to take a neighbor's kid, if I liked the neighbor's kid, if he was an adjustable kid, a mannerable kid, an understandable kid, I'd take him, too, with mine. I'd take him right along, and we'd have a beautiful time!"

8 | Looked Like They Had Some Money

Robert Pollard, whom I visited in prison, told me about one time, while he and Auburey were small, when he had drawn his older brother into trouble. "We were just walking around," he said, "and we saw a house, looked like they had some money in it, because it was real big, and they had a lot of stuff in there, so we just went on in. First we knocked on the door. If somebody come to the door, we was going to ask for somebody, a name or something, 'George,' or something like that. 'Oh,' we'd say, 'we got the wrong number.' Like that. 'Excuse us. Sorry.' Walk on away. Wasn't nobody there. The door wasn't open, we had to go through the back. We had two more guys with us, and they took a lot of junk home to their mother and gave it to her. The mother asked where he got that stuff, where all this junk come from, you know, perfume and checkers and stuff like that. His mother smacked him and made him tell. At first he wouldn't tell her, but she smacked him and made him tell. He told her about me and my brother Auburey and his brother, that we went and broke into a house. She called the police and brought the police over to my house. Said I had been a bad influence—*I* was, not my brother—said I was a bad influence on her son."

9 | It's Who You Know

"When he was small," Mr. Pollard said, speaking of Auburey, "he always wanted to box. Well, I used to box a little bit—never was a professional, but I was what you call every-guy-says-he's-good, and I had a hell of a left, I thought, which I did, pretty good for a hundred and forty-five pounds. I was supposed to be a professional after I came out of the service, but you know how guys are, they meet those big-leg girls, and that's *all;* you're through with boxing. No more boxing. You're boxing, but not like *that* no more. So this kid, he always wanted to box, so I shaped him up, I got him sweat pants, sweat shirt, gloves, all that; I used to run him, sometimes we used to go to Northwestern, polices seen us many a day, running. Lot of times, police would say, 'What you doing?' And I'd say, 'Training my son.' He was supposed to fight Golden Gloves, I went to see about him fighting Golden Gloves, but the guy wanted to tell me I had to go back over here somewhere, I don't know where it is, off Genesee, so I never could find it, I'd find it when I wasn't looking for it. But I knew boxing was a dirty racket. I used to tell him, 'It's the dirtiest racket in the world.' It's not what you know in boxing, it's who you know, which"—and Mr. Pollard added this with great emphasis—"*is in everyday living.* It's not what you know. You can know too much, and then you're through. You can know just enough, and you won't make it. You don't have to know nothing, and if the right guy likes you, well, then they say, 'You've won the game!' So this boy, he was a good kid, so I used to train him. He started out, I guess, about fourteen or fifteen. I used to train him all the time. I used to have speed bags, I used to keep two speed bags, I built him a punching rack down in the basement. Then we all lifted weights; I used to have weights for them, too. We'd run maybe, sometimes at night maybe fifteen, twenty, twenty-five laps at a time. And my baby boy, he used to run along with us and laugh all the time. And the fellow, Auburey, it was kind of hard for him at first, because you got to run on your toes, see what I mean, flat-footed is no good for a boxer, and it builds up his calf of his leg, that's what it's for, so he can move at all times. When he loses his legs, he's lost everything. And when he's past twenty-eight, he's through; a lot of people don't know that. So I always told him, you got to keep your legs in good shape. And which he worked for, which he became where he could stand up and defend himself and take care of himself. I didn't have to worry about him taking care of himself, because I knew he had the moves and the stamina to do it."

10 | He Would Help the Others

In time the self-sufficiency in the springy calves of Auburey's legs and in the good left he learned to deliver came to represent his main validity as a person. His friends admired it, feared it, and prized it. It was his pride, and it became his curse, as he began to wonder whether people kept him around because they liked him or because they liked having a bodyguard. "Do for yourself!" His father's ferocious drive for Auburey's independence of spirit and force of fist may have been—saddest irony of a short life—what brought him to the Algiers and to death.

"He was a nice person," Sortor said, as his total characterization to me of Auburey, "but he had a quick temper, you know. If somebody would push him around, he'd fight them." "He wouldn't start fights," Lee said, "but he wouldn't refuse a fight if it came to it. He would help the others in fights." "When something happened to me," his brother Robert said, "like be fighting or something, I'd go get him and he always helped me out. He just could box real good."

11 | Sortor

"Him and Sortor was old best friends," Mrs. Pollard said to me. There were, in fact, starting when they were all eight or nine, two pairs of friends, Auburey and Sortor, and Lee and Carl. The boys all called everyone by first names except James Sortor. He was plain Sortor, or sometimes Brother Sortor. "He don't sound like calling him James," Lee explained to me once. Of course, I did not meet Sortor until after Auburey was dead and Carl was dead—two of his oldest friends—and what had happened had "made Sortor kind of cold," as Carl's mother had told me. He sat, head covered—I never saw him in the house without a hat or head rag on—with a steady stare, almost a glare, his humor coming out in pushes of vocal energy which did not seem to touch his lips in passing but briefly fanned up the embers in his eyes. I came to admire his courage, as he broke himself of the dangerously serious drinking he had fallen into, in his mourning and numbness after the Algiers incident. He had two tones of articulation as he told a story, one straight-out and monotonic, the other, coming whenever he quoted dialogue, suddenly deep-throated, man-to-manly, and exaggeratedly animated; it was as if his words were expressed through two entirely different media. When I knew him, his father, laid off from Chrysler, was drawing unemployment compensation; his mother worked in a laundry; three of his four sisters lived at home.

12 | Fifteen Days in Dehoco

"This teacher," Mrs. Pollard said to me, "his name was Mr. Sunday—I went to school to see about Auburey. He accused Auburey of things he wasn't doing. . . ."

"They said Mr. Sunday was a football coach, or something like that," Tanner, Auburey's younger brother, said to me, giving me what would have to be called hearsay. "He was big and fat, too. He wasn't a bad teacher, he was a nice teacher, but he always made jokes on people in school. And he'd smack people on the side of the head, you know, people who'd been complaining. And some of the students would get mad at him."

Richard Sunday, who was thirty-seven years old when this incident took place in February 1965, had for eight years been teaching "special education," a program for slow students, at Northwestern High School. He recently told Ladd Neuman that in his time at Northwestern he has had three serious discipline cases, and that Auburey Pollard was the first of these.

Everything this teacher says about Auburey has to be measured against one statement he made to Neuman—namely that Pollard was known to be a black militant. If there was anything Auburey, and all of his friends, for that matter, Lee and Carl and Sortor and Michael, were *not*, it was "black militant." There was not a breath of politics in them; perhaps they would have been better off as men had they been able to attach themselves to a political idea. The indiscriminateness of this judgment by a teacher who had had eight years to develop the keenest of insights is exactly equivalent to the indiscriminateness of the executions of such diverse youths as Carl Cooper, Auburey Pollard, and Fred Temple, as if they were all black militants, which none of them was, or snipers, which none of them was, or pimps, which they were accused of being but which none of them was. If Auburey was a black militant in Mr. Sunday's eyes, then he was truly invisible to the man who had him in class every day.

Sunday was frank to tell Neuman that he had been afraid of some of his students. "Some time when one of them is about thirty," he said to Neuman, "down on his luck, out of a job, I wouldn't doubt he'll come back and try to kill me." Neuman asked Sunday why he stayed at Northwestern if he was so fearful of young black militants. "I don't care about color," he said. "This is an inner-city school. I doubt if there's one white person here. I'm proud of my job; I'm not going to let anyone run me out. Our kids know they're getting more help here than they could anywhere else. We're one of the few schools open twelve months. None of our kids was jailed during the riots. We had better attendance during the riots in summer school than our regular attendance."

Speaking of Auburey, Mr. Sunday said, "He probably had an I.Q. of 70, but I can't say that for sure. He was pretty high-strung. He was one of those whose veins and nerves are bulging."

"Auburey told me before it happened," Thelma Pollard said to me, "that he was going to get into a fight with him. He said the teacher accused him of things he didn't do. He called him a hoodlum and the leader of a gang. He said he wasn't the leader of that gang, period. The teacher just blamed that on him.

"See, Central came up to Northwestern—Central's a high school—and they started a fight, and somebody yelled to run and get Auburey, and in fact he could fight real good, and he was beating them all up, so the teacher called him a ringleader, and the teacher called him a punk."

Sunday said to Ladd Neuman that 150 kids from Central High School had come to Northwestern "with guns, knives, and everything," looking for Auburey Pollard. "This is something like New York," the teacher said to Neuman. "There's a gang for every street"; and it was known around school, he said, that one of the gangs was after Pollard.

"That day," Tanner told me, "Auburey was sick and he didn't want to go to school." "He had a headache," Mrs. Pollard told me, "because he had sinus, see, because I took him to a doctor."

"He said he had a headache in school," Thelma told me, "so he asked the teacher could he go home, and so the teacher said he wasn't sick, but he was, and so the teacher called him a punk, so he got mad at him and hit him."

"He accused Auburey of things he wasn't doing," Mrs. Pollard said to me. "Him and Auburey had a few words, so he hit Auburey, before all the classroom, so Auburey beat him up."

"When you're ill," Sunday said to Neuman, "you have to go to the health clinic. At the health clinic, if there's no one home, they won't send them because you know they could go home

and die. Auburey said he was sick. I sent him to the clinic. He
called home and no one was home, so they sent him back. He
got very angry and said, 'I'm going home and no one's going to
stop me.' I told him to sit down at his desk and lay his head on
his hands and stay there. Then I got careless. I usually don't turn
my back—like the old gunman days in the old West. But this
time I got lazy. This time I did, and I got hit across the back of
my head. He hit me with his hands. He had four gold insignia
rings on each hand. They worked just like brass knuckles."
Sunday said he went down on his knees and could hear Auburey
cursing him; and that Auburey went on hitting him on the
arms, back, and head until he was nearly unconscious and another teacher came in and pulled Auburey away.

After this incident, Mr. Sunday felt that incarceration in Northwestern High School would no longer be sufficient for Auburey
Pollard. "He went downtown," Thelma told me, "and took out
a warrant on him. Auburey had to go to court for it." Sunday
told Neuman that his fellow teachers were surprised when he
pressed charges. "They done took Auburey," Mrs. Pollard said
to me, "and had a trial without even telling me. And when we
were back in court, because he was up for sentence, and we'd
gone back, and when the judge read out the ticket"—the judge,
Mrs. Pollard told me, and this will be a matter of interest later in
this account, was the Honorable Robert E. DeMascio—"he say
he going to let the students know they couldn't fight with a
teacher. And he said that Auburey was prejudiced, hitting him
on account of prejudice. Auburey didn't hit him for prejudice.
Auburey hit him for calling him a hoodlum. And Auburey had
said, that teacher, the next time he hit him on the back, hit him
before the class, he was going to hit him back. So when he hit
Auburey on the back, Auburey started beating on him. I want
to give it to you straight. They sent him up right away for
fifteen days"—to the Detroit House of Correction. He was sentenced on March 10, 1965. "At Dehoco," Mrs. Pollard said, "he
had to fire the furnace every day."

13 | No More Trouble

"After Auburey got fifteen days," Mrs. Pollard told me, "he never got in no more trouble. He said, 'Momma, I can walk over things now.' Said, 'Momma, I don't want to get in no more trouble, I ain't about to go out there no more.' Whatever they did to him out there, he never did want to go back no more. He didn't bother Mr. Sunday no more, he didn't bother no teacher, ain't bothered a soul since."

14 | Little Brother, Don't Do That Way

Robert, the youngest Pollard boy, seemed to be getting in trouble a lot. Once a fur hat was stolen from a J. L. Hudson truck, and the police suspected Robert.

"I remember when the policemen came to the house," Thelma told me, "and they came in and searched the house, without a search warrant, too. They just came on in, there was about three or four cars, looked like somebody had really stole something, or somebody'd been murdered, you know. But I don't know, Robert, he didn't take nothing off none of them, you know. They'd tell him to shut up, and he'd say, 'I don't have to shut up in my own house.' "

"Robert shouted at the policemen," Mrs. Pollard said, " 'You don't talk to me that way in this house. This is my house. Don't you come in here swearing and yooping and yelling around. This is my house. You have no right in here without a warrant. Hit the door! Get out! I tell you, man, hit the door.' "

"So," Thelma said, "they was getting ready to hit Robert, and Auburey ran down the steps like a light. He was going to beat them up if they hit Robert. Auburey'd been nice enough to let them in the house. But the policemen didn't really search around much, because there was two white policemen, and they had known Auburey and Robert and me, and they came downstairs and said they had searched, but they hadn't really. They were pretty good friends. But the hat wasn't anywhere anyway."

"After the police left," Mrs. Pollard told me, "Auburey, he said, 'Little brother, don't do that way.' He said, 'You shouldn't ought to do no policeman that way.' "

15 | Welding All the Way Around

Of all the young men who witnessed the Algiers Motel incident, I have only been able to find that one, and that was Auburey Pollard, was touched at any point by the $231 million spent on anti-poverty programs in Detroit under the Cavanagh administration. Some time after his fight with Mr. Sunday, Auburey dropped out of school, and on October 10, 1965, he enrolled in the McNamara Skills Center, which operated under funds provided by the Manpower Development Training Act and was supervised by the Detroit Board of Education. "He took up welding," Mrs. Pollard said, "and so he learned to weld all the way around, he got 348 hours of welding. He made twenty dollars a week while he was learning it, so after he learned it real good he was a arc welder. He wanted to go into commercial art, but my husband didn't approve of it, because he said you couldn't make no money as a artist. But I think he could have made money. But his father didn't want him to, he wanted him to take up a trade, so he took up welding."

The Skills Center records show that Auburey did not complete the course but dropped out on January 28, 1966, to take a job with the T. L. Gersack Company. "They first put him in a little bitty small place," Mrs. Pollard said. "He didn't like that."

Mr. Pollard made a comment to me one day on anti-poverty programs. "It's just pitiful how the Negro, just all the Negroes in Detroit, and the ones with money and without, they do not understand that without one ball you cannot bounce. Don't look for no pity. No sympathy. Nobody going to give you that. Know what I mean? Patting you on the back, that ain't going to help you none. If I can't run, you can pat me all day, and hell, I'll still be sitting here. But if I make up my mind I want to run, seeing everybody else run, I'll get up and go right along with them. I might be a little slow. A friend of mine says, you know, he says, 'I might not be a racehorse but I'm a Shetland pony running on the racetrack with all the racehorses. I might be way back here, but I'm still running.' "

16 | Supposed to Be a Pretty Good Job

Employment records of the Ford Motor Company show that an Auburey Pollard was hired at the Rouge complex on October 20, 1966. "He was a arc welder at Ford's," Mrs. Pollard said to me. "Supposed to be a pretty good job. Sometimes his eyes were bothering him, because the first job they got for him, he burned his cuticles in his eyes, didn't have his mask right, probably. So he worked at Ford's on arc welding."

17 | Decide a Whole Lot of Things

Toward the end of his life, Auburey began to feel that he was something of an outsider with his friends; they were using him as a fighter, they didn't really like him. Part of the basis for this feeling may have been established in the fall of 1964, when all three of his best friends were sent as juvenile delinquents to the Boys' Training School, in Lansing. "They sent me up for B. and E.," Sortor told me, "Carl for B. and E., Lee for car theft. Me and Carl, we was in the same place. There was about thirty-six in a cottage; we wasn't in the same cottage, you know, his cottage was over further than mine, but we'd see each other when we come out to go to our details, used to talk to each other."

"At the Training School," Lee said to me, with a faint smile at his lips, "they showed you how you could get along without taking cars and without stealing and stuff like that. That you don't have to do anything like that. It was all right, though. You had a chance to study and decide a whole lot of things before you get out. I was office boy. I got out about a month before Carl, three weeks at the most. Sortor got out a week after I did."

18 | A Less Happy Circle

"I don't hate no policemans," Mr. Pollard said to me one day, speaking of the kind of justice black men and boys get in Detroit, "don't hate no judges, but if justice is going to be— when *I* do wrong, I gets fined, I suffer for it, and I don't expect any more. I could ask for leniency, but I really don't expect it, because I'm poor. But as far as the Negro, he lives in the ghettos, he doesn't know anything else but the ghettos, his parents teach him that because he comes up that way from a little small fellow, to get what you can—grab, quick! The Negro is looked upon as a minority group. Anything that he does, everybody see it. If you think I'm lying, go down to court tomorrow. You'll see how many—now"—and he began to count white suburbs on his fingers—"out in Dearborn, they got their own court; Birmingham, they got their own court; Redford, they got their own court. Murder, regardless to *what* it is, unless there's a case where they bring it downtown, but they keeps it out. What does this do with the Negro? It puts him in a circle, puts him in one little circle. And every one of them, he got to go down in front of Judge DeMascio, Judge Davenport, and the rest of them. It's a racket, that's all it is! It's the politicians. They work in a circle. You can see the money moving. You don't have to be blind unless you're stupid!"

19 | She Taught Him About Life

"This one time," Sortor told me, "I come out of the Training School, home leave, and I seen Auburey. He say he was staying with his older sister. I say, 'Come on, man! I know you ain't got no older sister.' It was this older woman; she had a place of her own."

I asked Mrs. Pollard later if she had liked the woman. "Like her? How could I like her? She's older than I am! Her son was a friend of Auburey's. She liked boys, she taught him about life. Auburey wasn't but seventeen years old, and she took him in, her own children sleeping in the house and she's sleeping with Auburey. Once when a boy of hers had a burst appendix, Auburey took him in his arms and carried him to the hospital. It was right then, while they was waiting for news from the hospital, that she took Auburey. Auburey told me he loved her, told me not for me to break it up. I didn't break it up. She's the one broke it up!"

"When she wanted to break it up," Sortor told me, "she had two men, one named Mac and another one, up to her flat waiting for him when he come in, they was going to beat Auburey up. But Auburey beat *them* up. They went down and made a complaint against Auburey, and he got taken down there, and they made him put up a peace bond"—a device, used by the Wayne County Prosecutor's Office, which has no legal force but is simply a warning to contentious persons to cease combat for a given time or face prosecution.

20 | Equal Friends

Sortor and Carl and Lee were back from Training School. "We was all equal friends," Sortor said. "Everybody liked the other guys. Whenever one of them got down to the police station, we'd go down and see what they got him for, and the police would say, 'Well, he got to go down to court for something,' so we'd leave him some cigarettes and candy. Carl and Lee had cars. But Lee's Bonneville was broke, so we'd drive around in Carl's—a '63 Grand Prix. We'd ride to the Twenty Grand, and go out to the White Castle, around there, go to after-hour parties. Sit around playing records, drinking a little beer. Where we was going, they used to know us, they was just a place where a guy liked to throw a little party, you know, after a dance."

21 | On Being Beaten Up

The Twenty Grand was the boys' favorite place. "It's one of the most popular spots as far as the Negro grass roots," Al Dunmore, managing editor of the Negro *Michigan Chronicle*, told me.

"They have a bowling alley there. They have a hall available for quantities of dances, plus most of the blues and rock-and-roll outfits, the second-line Motown artists—this is the stepping stone to the top white places, like the Roostertail and the Elmwood. It's a place where you can pick up a girl. You go in the door, and you sit at a table, and shortly after you'll be sitting by a girl."

One night at the Twenty Grand, Sortor told me, "some friend went up to Auburey and said I was going to shoot him, you know. So he came over there to see me before I'd shoot him, we was talking. When I first went in the Twenty Grand I seen him and went up to him and shook hands, walked around and talked for a little while, so I said, 'I'm going on over here on the other side of the floor, man.' He said, 'Okay, I'll see you around here.' I said, 'Okay.' And so I went over there and set down and talked with two or three girls, you know, then I seen Pratt and some more girls talking with Auburey, next thing I know he ran over there and hit me on the side of my head, see."

"Him and Sortor was fighting," Auburey's younger brother Tanner said, "and the police turned around, and Sortor got away some way. Sortor had said something, told everybody Auburey was going to kick his butt, or something like that, so Auburey went over there and started fighting with Sortor, and so everybody was standing around watching, and the police, they came over and they grabbed Auburey and they started beating him up, and then they grabbed Sortor, and the next thing I know they let Sortor go, and so I was standing there, watching them beat up Auburey, and so everybody was talking about, 'That's your brother, you know, why don't you go on and help?' And I say, 'No.' So finally I just walked up there, and I say, "That's my brother.' So the policeman turn and say, 'What? What?' I say, 'That's my brother.' So he turned around and hit me. So then some more policemen came over and started hitting me, and so we started fighting.

"There was so many polices, you know, they didn't beat me that bad, they just got in a couple of hits, but they was swinging so fast, you know, I was moving out the way, and they was hitting each other. I'd duck down like this, you know, and this one policeman's hand would just go on over and hit the other one. There were so many of them, you know how it is, hitting one person. There was so many policemen that they probably beat up they own self, beat up each other.

"And so anyway they took us down in the basement, to this little room. That's when they beat me up, when they took me down there. One of them was holding me, and another was talking about, 'Where do you get hitting me at?' I said, 'I didn't hit you.' And he say, 'Yes, you did.' Other one says, 'That's the one. That's the one hit you. Go ahead.' And then one policeman run up to you and hit you, and then another one run up to you and hit you. And then they'd hold you up, you know, and hit you in the stomach and stuff, you know, and hit you in the teeth, you know.

"This one big fat guy, he bashed my leg and my spine. And knots all over my head, broke my tooth off, and all that. I had a couple of cuts from the sticks.

"And so they asked, 'Anybody got to go to the hospital?' Took Auburey downstairs, too, they was beating him up, too. They put a big flash, like, a mark across his face. They let Auburey go. But I was beat up so bad they had to take me to the hospital, X-rayed my leg and my spine. They said it was just all bruised up, that's all. And they X-rayed my head.

"And so anyway, that morning that they let me go from the hospital, I went to court and asked the judge, 'Could you send me to a lawyer?' He said, 'No, if you got a lawyer, you'd have to have your lawyer right here.' So he said, 'Do you want to go to court or not? If you don't want to go to court, we'll just take you back to jail.' And so I told him, 'Yeah, I want to go to court.' Because it was my first time that I'd ever been in a courtroom, I didn't know nothing about courts, too much. So the judge, he asked me, 'What happened?' I told him that the polices jumped on me. So anyway the judge gave me a year's probation and a hundred-dollar fine. It was Schemanske"—the

Honorable Frank G. Schemanske, who will appear again here.

Tanner's date that night was a little blond white go-go girl named Lucy. In her version of the fight at the Twenty Grand, Tanner's mother told me, "Lucy ran out of there, and the police was after her. They tried to rape her, but she got in a cab and got away."

Following up on this accusation of attempted rape, I got this story from Lucy:

"When me and Tanner went in, we went there to have fun, you know. I paid my admission and Tanner paid his. And we went to dancing, and Auburey was there, and I danced once with Auburey, and then all of a sudden about an hour later there was some scandaling going on, you know, and I noticed there was two guys, you know, and it seemed like it looked like Auburey, but I wasn't sure. As far as I seen it, Tanner wasn't in it. What I did hear but I didn't see was that when Tanner tapped the guy on the shoulder to tell him something, you know, the policeman just turned around and whammed him. When the policeman did this, and there was a couple of policemen on Tanner, and I guess Tanner had to try to defend himself.

"And so after the fight was over with, a policeman came over to me, you know, after everything was quieted down, and he says, 'Where's the guy?' I says, 'What guy?' 'They says the guy that you came with.' I says, 'Why?' He says, 'He was fighting and he got away.' I says, 'Oh, really? I didn't know they was fighting. I didn't see him fighting. I thought it was somebody else.' I was just a little disgusted, you know, so I went around and talked for a while, you know, some other guy I danced with, I says, 'You know that guy I came in with?' He says, 'Yeah.' 'Did he leave, or what?' He said he didn't know. So I went around looking for Tanner. So I didn't see him, so I thought I might as well go. So I went, and some guy started following me, talking to me; it was an elderly guy around in his thirties, you know. I was going to catch the Grand River bus, it was about two blocks' distance, you know. So I walked across Fourteenth, just right across the street, and I started walking towards the first building, you know, and the guy kept begging me, you know, like if I would take a ride with him, saying all kinds of junk, you know, and I began to get jumpy-like, seems like he gave me the impression he would go *urph!* and pull me somewhere, you know. And so I started to walk back, so I crossed back to Warren, over back to the Twenty Grand parking lot, saying, you know, 'Okay, I'll take your ride,' because he did say his car was in the parking lot, you know. I thought I would just say that because I thought he would grab me. I was scared about that, you know. He's still walking. He started walking ahead of me, you know, and then he started talking to a couple policemen, and so I went into a telephone booth, and I was going to call a cab, but I seen a cab coming, so I jumped in the cab and went over to Tanner's house."

22 | They Thought He Was Big

"If anybody wanted to borrow some money from Auburey, you know," Tanner told me, "he'd loan it to them. When he was working, he'd loan me about twenty dollars, and my sister some money and my mother some money and my father some money, boy across the street some money, his friends some money."

"When Auburey used to have money," Thelma said to me, "when Auburey use to work at Ford's, he used to give one of his friends money to buy things, he used to give him money to get his hair did and get his clothes cleaned—and when the friend had money he wouldn't give Auburey a quarter. When Auburey used to get his whole pay, he used to make just about a hundred and twenty dollars a week, and him and his friends would split it up, and then when his friends would get paid, they would get long gone with their money, wouldn't give him a penny. I told him to stop hanging around with them."

"Auburey used to think the boys was plotting against him," Lee said to me once when I visited him in jail, speaking to me through the visitors' glass, "because sometimes we wanted him along and sometimes we wouldn't take him. A lot of people were scared of him, because when he drank he could really fight."

"All that crowd is heading for is trouble," Thelma said to me, in a fiercely maternal mood. "They think they're slick. I think, one thing, if Auburey never would have been with them, he'd have never been where he is now. What did he like about going with that crowd? They thought he was big, because he beat up everybody for them. He could fight real good, that's probably why they liked him. He'd do all the fighting, while they'd stand back and watch."

23 | Carl and Lee

One trouble was that the pairs of friends were diverging. Carl Cooper and Lee Forsythe were very close and daring; Auburey and Sortor were more on the cool side. Sortor, having shared the experience of a corrective institution with Carl and Lee, was fraternal with them in a way Auburey could not be.

Carl Cooper, whom, of course, I never met, because he was killed along with Auburey at the Algiers, was seventeen years old when he died. Like Lee, he was small of stature: five feet five inches tall, 122 pounds in weight. He apparently dressed with a fierce and iridescent bravado; as we have seen, he loved clothes so much that he wanted to take up the trade of tailoring. He was the brightest spirit, the craftiest, the funniest, the most charming of the friends. "I had to whip him one time," his step-father, Omar Gill, said to me. "One time. Once Carl got whipped. I told him then, I said, 'You act like a man, I'll treat you like a man. If you act like a child, I'll treat you like a child.' And I never had to bother him. He was a guy, just a good, good guy. He was a good guy, always had a pretty smile. I mean, you can't imagine until if you'd seen him, you would have just liked the guy. You know how you see people and you just like them right off? That's the way everybody was with him. On Sundays, you couldn't get into this house, with the young guys waiting to take him to the Twenty Grand. Just everybody came right here to see Carl. Boys, ladies, girls came to see Carl. That's what kind of guy he was."

"Me and Carl," Lee told me, "knew each other about ten years—from we was seven, eight years old. We was just everyday friends, sort of like brothers. We first got together over on Airport Road, used to stay over there, by the side of Grand River. After that we just sort of come up together. We was just like brothers. Like if I got in the House of Correction, Carl told me he slept to keep my time away faster. If one of us got in a little trouble, the other one was there to help. During the winter I guess I was getting in the most trouble—driving without a license, tickets, stuff like that. No serious trouble. Thirty dollars' fine to pay my ticket off, and eight days . . ."

The outside world treated Carl, to a large extent, not as a man but as a bothersome child, and he responded in kind. He managed to keep fairly steadily in trouble. He was arrested twice in the autumn of 1966 for driving without a license: thirty dollars, five days the first time; seventy-five dollars, ten days the second. A week before Christmas he was arrested for violation of the state narcotics laws—possession of marijuana; he was not tried for this until the following May. In February he was arrested in Highland Park for "Investigation of Disorderly Person"; nothing came of it. Toward the end of April he was arrested for driving without a license again; he failed to appear in court. On May 2, he was sentenced to sixty days in Dehoco on the drugs charge, and he was released just three weeks before the riots. Three days before them he was arrested in an alley south of Outer Drive and east of Kentucky on suspicion of Breaking and Entering; he fitted a complainant's description of a prowler in the back yard of 18300 Indiana, and he had on him a gold ring with three stones and a Benrus watch, which may have been his and may not have been.

"Once," Mrs. Gill said, "a colored police talked to Carl, and he said, 'The boy dresses nice and all,' he said, 'I don't understand it.' He said, 'Carl,' he said, 'why do you go out in the white neighborhoods?' Carl said, 'I go out there because they have everything,' he said, 'we have nothing.' And they made him see a psychiatrist, and he said there wasn't anything wrong with Carl, but he said if Carl got caught, and if he had a friend, said he never was going to involve a friend. Just may as well get used to that, you know. So a lot of things he got in trouble about, he just took the blame for it, you know. In fact, he had just been home a month on the day he got killed. He did sixty days in the House of Correction for narcotics, which was he had come from the barber shop, you see, and this other fellow had left the stuff in the car. He was trying to make a U-turn, trying to give the stuff back to the fellow soon as he realized it was there. The police stopped him, you know, for making an improper U-turn, and so when they got him to the station and told him to put everything out, he did, he put the bag up there, and it had marijuana in it. So he wouldn't tell on the other fellow. I tried to get him to tell, I said, 'This is really going to go hard on you now,' and had to get him out on bond and lawyer's fee and everything, you know, but still he wouldn't tell."

Lee Forsythe, who was two years older than Carl and almost exactly his size, walked, when he was "going around," with a bantam straightness in fine wild clothes, under a high and slick pompadour, his eyes wise, his speech understated and soft, an ironic smile of detachment and fearlessness covering every speech that might be understood as earnest. Friendship was the highest prize of life to Lee, and Carl, above all others, was the giver of the prize. Riding around, picking up girls—that was his higher education.

"We three, Carl and Sortor and me"—and so in the mind of at least one of the friends, Auburey *was* an outsider—"we didn't ever fight. Tell the truth, we never did fight. Carl was the youngest, but he was sort of like the big brother. He'd tell me and Sortor when we do wrong—he didn't *do* wrong, if you listen to him. After he come from Lansing, we used to rastle a lot, and we even got some girls to rastle"—the ironic smile. "Once we was rastling, and he went in the door the wrong way, and we had to take him to the hospital for that. Other than that, he was just an old happy guy." Even with the punishments of life, there was a great deal of laughing; if not pure freedom, at least intermittent wholehearted carefreedom.

"The House of Correction," Lee said to me, "that really make you want to drive without a license. You don't get the right amount of sleep; shoveling coal, you just don't like that. Since I was little, I couldn't shovel coal up into the burners. I had to go outside and throw it to fill up the cars. I worked midnights. They had all kinds of work—cow barnyard, dairy, kitchen."

Lee, who reached the tenth grade in high school—all three who had been to the Training School dropped out of public school after their release—had a job briefly with Ford and worked for a year pumping gas at a Standard station at Petoskey and Richton. He lived with his mother. At the conspiracy hearing he gave some extended testimony—during a passage when the defense lawyers were probing at the boys' sources of income, in an attempt to discredit them as pimps and criminals—that he supported himself as an artist, selling paintings to friends and "to the people in the neighborhood." I got to know Lee fairly well; he never mentioned art and never showed me a painting, and I honestly don't know whether this was truth or an elegant put-on, which might have occurred to Lee because of Auburey's unfulfilled talent.

24 | Michael

Michael Clark came late into the lives of the friends, and his was a disturbing influence—and, in the balance, most unsettling of all to Auburey. His presence broke the symmetry of the pairs.

Michael was a handsome and, by Thelma Pollard's standard, "slick" young man who said in court that he was twenty—though he lied so much under oath that I cannot assert that even that was true; an arrest report two weeks before the riot gave his age as eighteen. His style was bold, cocky, and elusive. When Michael dressed up in a dark suit, with a brightly striped cravat held in place by a tie pin, wearing at a calculated angle a white straw hat with a brim only an inch wide, he looked like many, many dollars; his eyes, the whites tinged with some of his hot blood, had a glint of scorn in them, and the left side of his mouth was slightly lifted, not quite in a sneer, for he was too charming to sneer, but in a dandy assertion of his worth.

Carl's mother told me once, "Michael, he was not actually one of the crowd. I think maybe Carl had been knowing Michael, but Michael had just started coming around." In court Michael claimed longer relationship with the boys than they said they had had with him. Carl and Lee were more attracted to Michael's daring ways than Auburey and Sortor were; all three of the others were somewhat jealous of Michael's hold on the man they considered their own stone champ, Carl; and Sortor's having shared the Training School time with Carl and Lee drew him more than Auburey into Michael's orbit.

A dropout from the eleventh grade of Chadsey High School, Michael had been working off and on for three years for an uncle, Robert Harris, "a painter and designer," as Michael testified. Early in 1967 he worked for two and a half months—earning, he testified, $225 a week—at the Chrysler Tank Arsenal, where he said his mother also worked ("I was putting a motor in the tanks . . . I was a tool man, rather"); he quit. Then he worked two months for Jones and Laughlin Steel Company ("I drove a high-low, and I used to clean out furnaces"); he was laid off. Two convictions were on his record, both in 1967: Carrying Concealed Weapon and Larceny from Building.

25 | Googy-Googy and Go-Go

Tanner Pollard married Lucy, the little white go-go girl, not long after the fight at the Twenty Grand.

Tanner was eighteen, Lucy was nineteen. Lucy's mother had

died in childbirth with her third baby when Lucy was about six; her father had brought her up. She and Tanner had met at a bus stop. "I was coming from downtown, you know," she told me, "and I always had to catch the bus like usually, so I catched the bus to Plymouth Road. At the bus stop where you catch the bus for Plymouth, Tanner asked me for my telephone number. And Tanner, he went to Plymouth Road with me, and he started calling me." Lucy had already then mothered a baby girl by a black man; at the time when she and Tanner met, the child was not living with her. When she married Tanner, she was able to have the child again; and not long afterward she gave birth to a daughter by Tanner, for whom Tanner made up a name, Palarena.

Tanner and Lucy rented a small house in a mixed (for they were mixed) neighborhood, and they lived there, in almost unimaginable slovenliness, with Lucy's two babies and her two teen-age brothers. A supermarket shopping cart sat parked eternally on their front path, and the yard was strewn with folded newspapers thrown by a newsboy and left to rot in rain and snow. Once in a while Tanner's mother, outraged beyond speech by the mess in the house, went in like a storm with powders and detergents; but it took only a few days for the litter on the floors to get deep again.

For a time both of them worked, Tanner as a waiter and busboy at a place called the Black Knight Supper Club, where he told them he was twenty-two; he looked it—tall, brown-skinned, with a narrow and mischievous face. As his father had told me, "he's always googy-googy," full of pranks and teasing. Once I sat down with him, his wife, and his mother, in a small eatery, and when a prim, elderly white waitress came to take our order, Tanner looked up with big eyes and asked, "Hey, got any fried rat today?" The woman almost fainted. At the end of our meal, Tanner picked up everyone's plates and licked them. "Awful hungry," he said, deadpan. His education left something to be desired. Once he asked me, "Where do you stay?" I said, "The Statler." "No," he said, "I mean home." "In

Connecticut," I said. "Where's that at?" he asked me. "Is that in Indiana?"

Lucy worked from place to place, nights, as a go-go girl, earning five or ten dollars a job, in small night spots in the northwest part of town. "I have a lot of guys following me, see," she told me. "You know, they think that since I'm white that I'm supposed to be doing something for Tanner, because he's colored, and they're jealous, you know. So they telling Tanner, 'Here you got a white girl, why don't you put her out there.' Stuff like that. They're always following me."

Between their two jobs, Tanner and Lucy saved up enough money to buy a car—"an old Cadillac," Tanner told me. "It was filthy, been setting out there, you know, had mud all in the seats, real dirty all over. But I cleaned it up and shined it up till it didn't look too bad, you know." It cost $595, plus another $150 for a new (secondhand) engine.

26 | Big Brother

"Chaney was Auburey's hero," Mrs. Pollard told me. "He was all wrapped up in Chaney, called him Big Brother. When Chaney left, Auburey adopted Chaney's best friend, Bobby Harris, as his new brother; when Ford laid Auburey off, Bobby helped him get his compensation. He was closer to Sortor after Chaney left, too. Chaney used to make every one of the other kids do chores around the house; he assigned the work, and they done the work. When Chaney left, Auburey, he took over. He cleaned my whatnots in the picture window on the glass shelves, washed the woodwork, painted around. He kind of did it for Chaney."

27 | On Money and Justice

In the country where Auburey and his friends and brothers lived, there were (and there still are) two perceptions, black and white, of justice. This is such a crucial fact—crucial to all racial violence, central to the Algiers Motel incident—that I shall ask you to get acquainted, at some length, with the most wounded and bitter spirit in the Pollard family, Auburey's "Little Brother," Robert, who articulated to me all that need be said about the black perception. I visited Robert in prison; we sat in a pew in the prison chapel, and he talked.

Things had gone badly for Robert for a long, long time. He was in a hurting place in the family: at the bottom of a totem pole of brothers, and with a baby sister who was the cynosure of all.

School authorities had reported him as "uncooperative." The B. and E. with Auburey took place when Robert was nine. Two years later he was taken in for another breaking-in; two years after that, for Robbery Not Armed. When he was fourteen, he was arrested for violation of a knife ordinance, for larceny from the mails, and for theft. At fifteen, he was taken for breaking a bus window, and for halting traffic in a residential street and shouting obscenities. Once he was found unconscious on a street—drugged, his mother thought, and "in the hospital he woke up abusive," she told me, "called the nurses 'white bitches' and the doctors all kinds of 'bastards.'"

Robert had just turned sixteen when, one May evening, he was charged with stealing seven dollars from a twelve-year-old newsboy. He was found guilty and sentenced to from three to ten years in the Michigan State Reformatory, which is really a prison.

"Robert was beat up so bad when they took him in," Mrs. Pollard told me, "that the polices told me he tried to commit suicide. When I saw Robert, he told me, he said, 'Momma, I didn't try to kill myself. They tried to kill *me*.'"

"Justice," Robert Pollard said to me in the prison chapel, "is a way of keeping a person from getting any more than he's got. Railroading is just sending a person to prison, it's taking advantage of a person. They take advantage of a person when a person knows that he don't have anything. This is what they take advantage of, see."

Perhaps I should say here that Robert, a short, stocky youth, the blackest-skinned of the Pollard brothers, talked to me in the presence of Tanner, who, with their mother, had vouched for me, and he spoke in a low but strong voice with sustained and absolute conviction. By the time I saw Robert, I had had quite a little experience both of being put on and of being trusted; I was convinced that Robert was telling me things as he saw them.

"Actually the crime they got me for, actually I didn't do it, see. First they had me on another charge, something that I didn't do, one of my friends did it, but the man said I did it; this was a larceny from a house. So then I went to court on it, and while I was in court on that one, they arrested me in court on this other one. They said I had robbed somebody. They arrested me, the man jumped on me up there in 1300 Beaubien, when I was in Recorder's Court. They took me out of court and took me upstairs and jumped me.

"My lawyer, he tricked me, see. He told me to cop out, told me to tell them that I did it, and he'd get me a probation. And I did this, and I ended up with three to ten. I plan on getting my money back from him when I get out, anyway. He owes me two hundred and forty-some dollars. The judge asked me did anybody promise me anything, I told him no. And that was wrong of me to tell a lie to the judge, because that just made my time more harder. They didn't find no knife on me, they didn't catch me with no money on me, they didn't catch me on the scene, or nothing. They just arrested me in court and put it on me."

28 | Paying Off

"They don't have no type of justice in court," Robert said, "because there's a whole lot of peoples up here that's railroaded. They're railroaded paying off the judges with money. If you can pay off so much money, they get your time cut, see. Every judge down there would do that. Money, it sings. If you got enough money you can do just about anything you want to do in the world. You can buy the judge, you can buy the lawyer, you can buy the prosecutor. This is happening every day. Railroading people. They give them so much time for something that ain't worth it. Like this guy, he was sitting in a car with a white broad. Now, he wasn't doing nothing wrong, and they give him three to ten. But he had a state lawyer, they throwed a state lawyer on him, see, and state lawyers, they get paid sixty dollars, see, that's in court costs, see, there's a whole lot to it, see. It actually ain't nothing but a racket, you know, just like I go out there and I steal a whole truckful of TV's, and I sell them, all, every one of them I got, and I get good prices for them—it's the same way as down there in court, see. You got the money, you can buy your time. But all I had was two hundred and forty-some dollars, and court costs cost some sixty dollars, I think. Justice is all connected with money. I don't think it. I know it. If you talk with any convict in here, he can tell you, he done paid off. There's some convicts in here done paid out five thousand dollars to just get two years, but they could have had life. It's many convicts in here would tell you that."

Then he added: "The railroading, it's worse for colored, because there's a lot of prejudice. Mostly be down to the court they's white."

29 | Prejudice

"If it had been the other way around down there at the Algiers," he said to me, "colored policemen killing white boys, I don't think they'd get off! Because there's so many white peoples that's prejudiced. I would say the policemens are prejudiced. Because they have called me names. I have been in McGraw Station, and a man throwed a sandwich on the floor, throwed it down there and say, 'Git it, Dirt.' They have called me all types of names. 'Black boy.' They have throwed black coffee on me. I was cussing at them, and stuff; I was calling him names— 'Peckerwood,' like that, and one of them come and throwed black coffee on me, partly in my face and partly on my shirt, and he say, 'Shut up, black boy,' just like that. McGraw Station.

They were questioning me about a two-hundred-and-fifty-dollar mink hat, it come off a J. L. Hudson truck. I don't actually know who took it off the truck. The man say I had taken it off, but he had me mistaken. I was talking about, 'You all are always trying to get somebody.' They been after me a long time, too. Since I was eight. Because I used to get in a whole lot of trouble. They knew my name, because I'd been down there so many times. One detective, he was questioning me down there, he was kind of fat and heavy-set, he told me that he wish he could have caught me breaking in that house, he would have shot me. This was when I was sixteen. I used to come down to the station on little misdemeanors, he used to read off my record to me, tell me what I had been doing and all like that. It says in the law book that they're not supposed to look back on your juvenile record.

"I could be waltzing down the street, and the guy, he'll pick me up and take me down to the station, trying to say I snatched somebody's purse or trying to say I B.-and-E.'d some place, and tell me, 'Bobby, you want to tell us about it, you know you pulled that B. and E.' So I say, 'What you talking about, man, I ain't pulled no B. and E.' He say, 'Aw, come on! You know, kid, you pulled that B. and E.'

"You know, they pass out sandwiches in the morning before you go to court, and they passed out some baloney sandwiches, and they supposed to set them up in the bars, or other than that down on the bench, and he throwed it, and he said, 'Git it, Dirt.' I was waiting to go to court about a knife."

30 | You Don't Actually Have No Freedom

"Money, that's what makes the world keep going," Robert said to me. "Money. Without no money, wouldn't nobody—if you didn't know nothing about no money or wonderful things to have or anything, you wouldn't care nothing about no money; you wouldn't want nothing. You'd be doing just like peoples in Africa, or somewhere, sitting up and eating dead things and going round, don't want nothing but a old house or something, just a shelter to keep the rain off of you. Go round and kill wild animals and eat them, you know; you're free to kill what animals you want.

"But here, it's against the law to kill animals. You kill a animal and eat him, you'll go to jail for serving that kind of animal.

"Everything have a law to it, see. Every time you walk out a door, anywhere you walk, you breaks a law. See, because they got so many laws. Actually if people really look at it you don't actually have no freedom. Because anything you do, you've broken a law. I mean the least little thing, you know. You can't even spit on the sidewalk; if you spit on the sidewalk, that's a ticket. They done covered the earth with cement and you can't spit on it.

"If people got a better job and was making more money, and they got in trouble or something, then they'll worry about something like spitting on the sidewalk, see, but a person that never had anything, they don't even let it bother them. I mean, he cares that he's in jail, he cares about his freedom, see, just like a wild animal running out there in the woods or something, you know, you lock him up, he's going to want to get out, although he don't have anything, he still want to get out.

"Something that you were never taught and raised up to, you know—what I'm trying to say: What you want to know won't hurt you. What you don't know, you don't want it."

31 | Anti-Poverty Programs

"As long as there's money in the world," Robert said, "won't hardly anything will change. The *people* won't change. The buildings and the cars and the clothes and stuff, and shoes would change, and different products, and trucks and boats and stuff like that would change, but the people wouldn't change. If you can bring them more money, they'll take it.

"In a certain extent, there's always going to be somebody over you. All peoples are not the same. Somebody's always going to have a little bit more than you. Somebody else is always going to have a little bit more than *that* person, and over and over and over, see. Like it might be this little boy's got a penny right here, and this other boy might be a little bigger, he's got two cents, or they might be the same size, two cents, and three and four and five and six, and all up to a thousand dollars.

"People is very evil against other people. It's just like your next-door neighbor. Okay, you got a '65 Cadillac, and you been living good all the time, and your next-door neighbor, he sees, and you been having yours about two or three years, and he's going to try and do better than you is, see, he going to get him a '67 or '68. Because he have always been better than you, and he want to keep on.

"Just read history. You can see this, see, because ever since the world has been here, ever since money has been discovered, people always had more money than other peoples, see."

32 | How It Works

"What would be the best thing to do is to see if I'm really telling the truth. Just have a person picked up for a certain thing and tell him to just sit in the bullpen with a whole lot of prisoners downtown and watch lawyers come by and say, 'Will you cop out to a certain sentence? Would you cop out to ten years? I can get you two to ten.' And a guy, he'll say, 'Well, yes, how much would this cost me?' And he'll say, 'Well, it might cost you four hundred dollars.' And the guy say, 'Well, okay,' he'll say, 'you get me off and I'll give you the money.' 'Okay.' The lawyer takes the money, he'll go to the judge, he'll pay the judge maybe two hundred in cash right there, and he'll pay the prosecutor a hundred, and then he'll keep the rest; a lawyer's always going to keep something for hisself. And then you go in court. Now sometimes they pay the jury off, too, see. The jury gets paid, too. This is just a front to make society, sitting out there, you know, make this man seem like he's not guilty. That's if he's got money. But if you don't have no money, they'll just railroad you."

33 | Prospects for the Future

"This is not me. I'm just saying what happens to some people, and, I know, most people. They are very cold-hearted after they been here. Some people get out there, and they don't care about nobody. And sometimes when they do come back, they come back with a real sentence. Maybe like the first time they been up here, maybe they got two years, maybe one, or three or something; then they'll come back with maybe life or something like that, or twenty-five, or fifty, or natural life, or something like that. There are quite a few lifers here. Quite a few guys with twenty-five to fifty, ten to twenty. I know some guys got the same time I got, and they just thinking, most of them say, when they do come back, they'll be doing life or twenty-five years or something. That's what just about all of them say when they're leaving. They say if they do go out there and do wrong, they're going to do something big, and bring them back lifers, because it ain't worth it for that little stuff."

34 | Laid Off

During the winter, early in 1967, Auburey was shifted from welding to laboring at Ford. "He had to do labor work," Mrs. Pollard told me. "They change him up, you know. When he started doing the laboring part, it gave him sinus from the dust, so he got sick for a while." Ford records show that he took a medical leave, beginning March 1, 1967; his employment was terminated on April 12, 1967, because he had not notified the company of his whereabouts or of his intention to return to work.

Thelma was a bit disenchanted about his quitting. "You know how boys get," she said, "after they work for a while. They don't want to work any more. Especially Ford's—they give you a lot of compensation and stuff."

But something more complicated was at work. "When he

was at Ford's," Mrs. Pollard told me, "Auburey gave his father money to put down the payments on Chaney's car; it was a '63 Catalina. Sixty-seven dollars a week, but for some reason his father didn't make the payments. This was a big hurt to Auburey. A big change took place in him after that."

35 | The Last Family Party

"Thelma," Mrs. Pollard told me, "works for a lawyer. He taught her how to file his cases for him, and she types for him, and he's very nice to her. Because she's awful young, because he give her the job when she was fifteen years old, because she was coming out of high school."

One evening after supper Thelma gave me some of her views.

On the Vietnam war: "That's foolishness. I think the United States should take care of their own. They're having a war between themselves. I think they should take care of themselves first."

On what should be done at home: "Let everybody be equal. Let everybody get justice, you know. Like policemen, they do something to somebody and won't get any time for it, but let somebody do something to them! I think the police force is prejudiced—against people altogether. They think they know everything, that everything they say is right. They could have made a mistake, too. Some of them just get on there because they like to shoot. Most of them just like to wear that uniform, make them think they're big. Lots of times they just stop you for the fun of it. I try to stay out of their way. And a lot of time white policemen, they'll stop colored people for the fun of it. If they see a white person doing something wrong, they let them go. It's more colored people that's got criminal records than white people, and white people do just as much dirt as the colored people do."

On integration as against separation: "I think everybody is equal, you know. Shouldn't nobody be better than anybody else. All the schools should be the same, and I think all the neighborhoods should be the same, too. If people have got enough money to buy a certain house, they should be able to buy it. All the schools should be integrated. I think the races should have more social experience and everything together, they should communicate more, you know."

Thelma's graduation was the occasion for the Pollards' last family party. Chaney sent money from Vietnam for a new dress and a tiara with rhinestones in it. Auburey cleaned up the house from top to bottom.

36 | Away from Home

Early in June, Carl, Lee, and Michael all took rooms at the Algiers. Carl was in A-14 on the third floor, Michael next to him in A-13, and Lee was downstairs in A-5. "We just decided we wanted to stay around down there," Sortor, who, with Auburey, often slept in one or another of these rooms at the motel, told me. "You know, we'd go to the Twenty Grand, pick up a lot of girls, you know, didn't want to bring them to our house, you know, so we went on down there." "Maybe," Mr. Gill said to me one day, "they figured they could do more away from home."

37 | The Only One

Report on 1 ARREST V.S.N.L. [Violation State Narcotics Laws], 1:00 AM, 7-11-67, MICHAEL CLARK, N/18 . . . :

"Rec. r. r. to above place man with a gun. Talked to the guard Norwood Jackson n/48 . . . Stated that four Negros had gun. At this point the males came down and we talked to them and they stated that they were visiting the def in room A-13. The def came up to us and stated that these men were visiting him and then he turned and went back into the building. I & Patr. St. Onge followed him and as I approached the third floor I heard the trash recepticle being pushed then the def entered apt

A-13. I looked in the recipticle and found a piece of foil paper containing suspected marijuana held on evidence tag #681042. The def denise putting it in there but he was the only one in the hall way.

"Narcotics were taken to Bureau by St. Onge in A.M."

As it happened, two of the three officers who arrested Michael were Jerome Olshove, who was destined to be killed the night before the incident at the Algiers, and Roy St. Onge, who was to hold the shotgun that would cause Olshove's death.

After this, Michael moved into A-14 with Carl. The reason he moved, he testified, was that the arresting officers had kicked in the door of A-13, and the door had not been fixed when Michael came back from jail. Michael and Carl paid $13.60 a day for A-14, according to Michael's testimony; actually neither of their names appeared on the motel registry, because the room had been signed for "by a young lady by the name of Sandra," whose last name Michael testified that he did not know. After that, when Auburey and Sortor spent the night, they usually stayed downstairs with Lee.

I V

Confession

12

Could You Get
My Statement Back?

Monday, July 31

1 | Report for Questioning

Five days had passed since the nightmare at the Algiers. The story had broken—rather discreetly in the *Free Press* the night before, then with screeching headlines in the *News* on this Monday morning, July 31. On the basis of the accusations of Witness Greene in the *News*, a dangerous finger seemed to point at Warrant Officer Thomas, the man who had raised the alarm of snipers in the first place.

On the Monday morning the Homicide Bureau sent orders to the Thirteenth Precinct that all police officers who had been present at the Algiers on the night of the incident, and indeed any who knew anything about what had happened there, should report that day at 1300 Beaubien Street for questioning. By about noon, seven men from the Thirteenth Precinct had assembled at Homicide, accompanied by a superior officer from Thirteen, Lieutenant Gerald Hallmark.

Each man was directed to write down everything he had done and seen that night.

2 | It Was All Over With

"I Patrolman Ronald August Badge #116 Assigned to the 13th Precinct was designated to Patrol Task Force #2—East of Woodward, South of Highland Park, North of E Grand Blvd, and West of the Grand trunk Railroad. Our task force was dispatched approx 12:15 AM 7-26-67 by our Sgt in charge Sgt Victor Wells that at Woodward and Euclid 'the Army is under heavy fire.'

"When Task force #2 arrived at Woodward and Euclid I observed Many State Police, and National Guard South at Virginia Park and Woodward. We then took cover with Task force Number 2 that consisted of One Scout Car and 3 Army Jeeps. The Army Jeeps had 12 to 15 men dispatched with us. The Patrolman in our unit were Patr David Senak, Patr Robert Paille, and myself.

"On arrival we then deployed our selves around the Algiers Motel Manor, and then entered the Premises. Guardsmen and Police had Several men and two white girls against the wall on the first floor.

"There were Two Negroes wounded in the room to left of Lobby, and One Wounded Negro to the right of the lobby. Many Guardsmen and Police left saying it was all over with. I then went outside to call for a Wagon Patrol to convey everyone to station and Hospital. Radio responded that one would be on the way.

"We were waiting for the wagon to appear when More shots could be heard fired outside and Several guardsmen ran in and asked for our assistance. We then all ran out side and took cover where Sniper fire was reported West of us about the middle of the block down Virginia Park. We then received a Radio Message regarding our relief, and to call the station this was about

1:30 AM 7-26-67. As of this time the Wagon Patrol had not appeared at the scene."

"(Signed:) Ronald W. August"

At the foot of August's statement appear these lines written in a different hand:

"Q. Did you fire inside the bldg?
"A. No
"Q. Was any prisoners taken out of the house?
"A. No
"Q. Did you see a Guard Commissioned Officer on t!.e premises?
"A. No."

3 | There Was Shooting Down the Street

Synopsis of Statement taken from Patrolman Robert Norman Paille Assigned to #13 Precinct:

"Patr. Robert Norman Paille 32/W/M wrote a statement at the Homicide Bureau on July 31, 1967, he stated that on July 26, 1967 he was assigned to Scout Car 13-11 and Task Force #2, he was accompanied by Patr. Ronald August and David Senak. He stated that on Wednesday, July 26, 1967, about 12:15 AM they received a radio run to Woodward & Euclid, that 'Army was under heavy fire.' Patr. Paille stated he was in the last Jeep which was one of three (3) jeeps, following a Scout car.

"Upon arriving at the scene Patr. Paille observed that everyone had taken cover, he hid behind a jeep. Patr. Paille saw men rushing the Motel Manor and he followed, entering through a door at N.E. corner of the Motel. Paille stated he saw a body lying on the floor. He then rushed to the second and third floors and assisted in searching for snipers and guns. Paille then returned to the first floor and heard some of the Guardsmen say there was shooting down the street. He investigated and found no one. Paille said he thought he saw some State Police officers at this time.

"Paille then returned to the Motel and was told by his fellow officers that a wagon had been called to pick up the bodies. Paille said that at this time, part of their convoy had left for another trouble area. Paille said that he and his two fellow officers then left the scene."

4 | Can We Go?

After the officers had finished their writing, Lieutenant Hallmark wanted to leave. "I figured," he testified in the murder hearing, "that the statements were through, and I was ready to go back . . . but I asked several of the other officers—I don't know which ones—'Can we go? Did anybody tell us that we had to stay?' And they said, 'Yes, they told us we had to stay.' But they just said, 'they,' and I don't know who 'they' was."

The men sat around talking for nearly an hour. "I think I was sitting alongside of Riley," Lieutenant Hallmark testified, "but I wouldn't really be sure, because I was reading the paper." One wonders what the effect of the presence of that day's newspaper in the room—with its big headlines, its exposure, its conjuring up of phrases—*that nigger didn't even kick*—may have been on what happened in the next few minutes.

5 | Two Dead Men

Synopsis of Statement, Paille:
"At 1:30 PM, Det. Sgt. Clifton Casey then asked Paille how many bodies he had seen in the building. Paille answered one dead in a room in the NE corner of the building and one dead in the room on the first floor on the North side of the building. Casey asked, when you left the building where were the other occupants of the building. Paille answered they were lined up against the wall, approximately four (4) men and two (2) females. Casey asked, what were you armed with. Paille answered a 30-30, a 357 mag, and a service revolver. . . ."

6 | Conference

In the Homicide bullpen Ronald August approached Hallmark, who, as he read the paper, was surrounded by detectives and by the other officers from the Thirteenth, and asked if he could speak with the lieutenant alone. They went out in the hall. August asked, according to Hallmark's testimony, "Could you get my statement back? I would like to change it. I would like to make a new statement."

7 | In the Corridor

Synopsis of Statement made by Lieutenant Gerald Hallmark, Assigned to Precinct #13:

"On July 31, 1967, Lt. Hallmark reported to the Homicide Bureau in company with the following officers: Patrs. Paul Rehn, Edward Riley, Gerald Kiss, and William Jones. Patrs Ronald August, David Senak, and Robert Paille also reported to the Homicide Bureau, for the purpose of being questioned regarding their activities on Wednesday, July 26, at the Algiers Manor Motel. Lt. Hallmark reported that at approximately 2:00 PM, Patr. Ronald August asked if he could speak to him in private and they stepped into a corridor just outside the Homicide Bureau office where Patr. August stated he had shot one of the men at the Algiers Motel and asked if he could get his original statement back. A few minutes later Patr. Paille approached Lt. Hallmark and stated 'I shot one of the men.' Lt. Hallmark asked Patr. Paille if he knew who shot the third man and he replied 'No.' Lt. Hallmark then asked Patr. Paille what part Patr. Senak had in the shooting, he answered, 'We shot almost simultaneously at the man.' "

8 | Silence

David Senak kept his mouth shut.

9 | Suspension

Lieutenant Hallmark consulted, immediately after the conferences in the corridor, with his inspector, and he then suspended August and Paille from the police force—"somewhere," he testified, "around two fifteen or two thirty; sowewhere around there."

10 | Pause

There is no record of further questioning of August, Paille, or Senak until four o'clock—nearly two hours after the two confessions.

11 | Lawyer

Synopsis of Statement, Paille:

"On the same date at 4 PM Det. Sgt. Casey attempted to question Paille further. Paille requested that he be allowed to consult an attorney before answering any questions."

From what happened later, it must be assumed that Paille called Attorney Norman Lippitt, counsel for the Detroit Police Officers' Association.

12 | My Rights Under the Law

At 4:05 p.m., Lieutenant Elmer Reed, in the presence of Detective Sergeant Robert Everett, read to Ronald August a form published by the Detroit Police Department, "DPD 342-B, Constitutional Rights Certificate of Notification":

"I understand that I have a right to remain silent, and I do not have to answer any questions put to me or make any statement. Any statement I make or anything I say can be used against me in a Court of Law. I have the right to have an attorney (lawyer) present before answering any questions or making any statement. If I cannot afford an attorney (lawyer), one will be appointed for me by the Court prior to any questioning. And I can decide at any time to exercise my rights and not make any statement. I understand these are my rights under the law, and I have not been threatened or promised anything, and I now agree to answer any questions put to me or make any statement."

The detectives took the new statement August had said he wanted to make.

13 | The Tragic Part

Statement of Ronald August . . . in the presence of Elmer Reed and Robert Everett, Inspector's Office, Special Investigation Bureau:

" . . . On the morning of the 26th around 12:25 a.m. we received a run that the Army was under heavy fire at Euclid and Wood-ward. Upon arriving at Woodward and Euclid we saw Army personnel at Virginia Park and Woodward at the Algiers Motel. We left our vehicle on Woodward Avenue and took cover just west of Woodward Avenue behind a brick wall, a gateway to Virginia Park. I then approached the Algiers Motel manor, which I believe is 51 Virginia Park, and went inside.

"I then went inside the main entrance and then observed a colored wounded man on the right side of the lobby. He was laying on his stomach in a pool of blood, and to the left of the lobby just past the stairway going upstairs I observed this man sitting or laying in a pool of blood.

"I then went upstairs and looked in all the rooms and found no one and I found no weapons. I returned downstairs and I circled the manor outside and found no weapons. I returned to Woodward Avenue and brought the scout car back to 51 Virginia Park. I then called Radio and informed Radio that we had wounded men and prisoners. I then returned inside the Algier Manor and watched the people standing against the wall. I then took the two white girls into a room which was the first doorway to the left of the hall as you entered and I questioned them about the shooting from upstairs. They said they heard shots but did not know who was shooting at us. I also asked the girls where they were from and they stated Columbus, Ohio. I asked the girls who they were with and they told me the colored man just discharged from the Army. They told me his name but I do not recall it. It may have been Miller or it may have been Green.

"I left the girls in the room and called the man they said they were with. He said the girls had been with him since last Friday. One girl, with red hair, had a cut on the left side of her head in the hairline, and I told her as soon as help came she could go to the hospital. I also told her she would be all right. She then stated, 'Why did they hit me?' I told her everyone is excited and I did not know who hit her.

"I then told the two girls and the man Green or Miller to go back in the lobby with the rest of the people against the wall and when the wagon came we would convey them to the station and the hospital.

"Now comes the tragic part. One fellow on the wall stated he wanted to see an officer in the other room. I don't know if it was Green or Miller, I don't know his name.

"We went into the room left of the lobby and he stated he did not know who shot at us and he pleaded to let him and his friends go. I told him everyone was going in when the transportation arrived. He says, 'You are not going to shoot me, are you?' and I says, 'No, I never shot a man in all my life and I have no reason to shoot you.'

"He then grabbed my shotgun and pushed me on the bed and I screamed, 'Get back.' We both stood up from the bed and then he let go of the gun and I pulled the trigger. The safety was on and the gun did not fire. I released the safety and he reached for the shotgun again and I pushed him away and fired one shot that struck him, I believe, in the right side. That's all, except that the wagon never came. I didn't want to shoot him. I wanted to put him back out there with the rest of them but he just wanted that gun and he wouldn't let go."

"At this time," the synopsis says, "Attorney Norman Lippitt entered the room and requested that the interrogation cease."

14 | I Believe State Police . . .

Synopsis of Statement taken from Patrolman David Senak Assigned to #13 Precinct:

"On July 31, 1967, at 4:10 PM, Det. Lt. Alfred Pare advised Patr. Senak of his constitutional rights and Senak made the following statement. 'On Wednesday, July 26, 1967, I reported for duty at 12 Noon and was assigned to Task Force #2 comprised of Patr. Paille, Patr. August and myself, together with about 12 to 15 National Guardsmen. We had one Scout Car (Myself and Patr. August along with two guardsmen) and three jeeps. Two jeeps contained all guardsmen and the last jeep contained guardsmen and Patr. Paille. At 12:15 AM we received a radio run to assist guardsmen at Euclid and Woodward: "Guardsmen under fire." We were at Woodland and Cameron and proceeded to the scene.' Quest: What did you see when you arrived at the scene of the run? Ans: 'I saw local, State Police and other guardsmen advancing on the Manor from Virginia Park.' Quest: Were these officers and guardsmen shooting at the manor? Ans: 'Yes.' Quest: Do you know if there were any shots coming from the Manor. Ans: 'Not for sure.' Quest: Where did you park your vehicles? Ans: 'On Woodward Avenue in front of the island at Virgina Park.' Quest: Could you see other police vehicles or U.S. Army jeeps? Ans: 'I saw some State Police cars on Euclid at Woodward, and jeeps all around the area.' Quest: After you got out of your vehicles what did you do? Ans: 'We separated and went toward the back of the Manor House. I took cover by the edge of the main part of the motel. I believe State Police broke open the rear door of the Manor House and then I watched the roof of the Manor House as I approached the back door and went in.' Quest: Where did you go when you went into the Manor House? Ans: 'I went to the second floor with another police officer (white and in uniform) and a guardsman.' Quest: What kind of weapon did you have? Ans: 'An 8-mm. Mauser (my own).' Quest: Did you try to gain entrance to all the rooms? Ans: 'Yes, all but one.' Quest: How did you get into that room? Stop, 4:53 PM, Attorney Norman Lippitt entered and questioning ceased."

V

The Algiers
Motel Incident

13

The Snipers

1 | Hot Dogs

After the crap game broke up in Lee's room, Carl and Lee wandered out to the pool in the main part of the motel, and Auburey and Sortor lay around A-5 watching television.

Papa's Delicate Condition, starring Jackie Gleason and Glynis Johns, with a song in it, "Call Me Irresponsible," which had won an Academy Award, had begun at nine, and the serial "I Spy" had come on later on another channel, and then all channels showed news of the turmoil outside in the city's streets; after that, *Lives of the Bengal Lancers* and the "Tonight Show" came on—all frequently interrupted by commercials and news bulletins.

This room of Lee's was at the back of the annex; a pair of French doors opened from it onto a wooden back porch with steps down to the motel parking lot. Two double beds stood on wall-to-wall carpeting. The television set was in a corner of the room, against the outer wall and to the left of the French doors, and a refrigerator-stove stood across from it, near a connecting door to room A-2, through which one had to go to get to the front hallway of the annex and to the stairs to the upper floors. The rooms were smartly furnished and clean; they must have given the young men, whose homes were crowded and cluttered, a sense of luxury—of living almost within the commercials they kept seeing on the tube.

Carl and Lee brought the two hungry white girls, Juli and Karen, into the room. Sortor turned the television set off, and one by one the boys turned on transistor radios. "They had about three radio sets going at the same time," Juli testified. She said she had known Carl casually before this but got to know Lee for the first time that night, and she and Karen now also met "two fellows that I didn't know"—Auburey and Sortor.

Lee had a cache of foodstuffs. "We bought them at the store," Sortor told me. "They was in there before the riot broke out, you know; we had kept a icebox full of food." Mr. Gill told me that when he went to the motel after the shootings to get Carl's clothes, "I saw Lee had quite a bit of food, canned food and hot dogs and things."

Lee and the girls cooked some hot dogs. The meal took about twenty minutes.

Carl, whose room was upstairs, "had a record player," Juli testified, "and asked us if we wanted to listen to some records." The girls decided they would like to do that, and they went with Carl and Lee up to A-14.

Sortor cooked some more hot dogs for Auburey and himself. He burned them, he testified, and opened the French doors onto the back porch to let out the smoke. At some point he turned the television set back on—loudly enough so that he and Auburey did not hear what happened upstairs in Carl's room a few minutes later.

2 | A Toy

When the two couples reached A-14, they found Michael there; the girls knew him. Carl started up some music on his record player.

"We were sitting around listening to records," Juli testified in the conspiracy hearing. "Everyone, everybody was just sitting around talking and listening to records. And," she added, "that's all."

Attorney Lippitt, cross-examining her, asked: "That's all?"
"Uh-huh."
"Come on, your memory is better than that, isn't it?"
Juli made no response to that question.

They listened to music, she said, "approximately ten minutes, fifteen." Then, according to the synopsis of a statement Karen made to the police, "Carl Cooper pulled a pistol out from under the bed. Cooper and Forsythe were playing with it. They had blanks in it and Cooper shot it twice."

"During this time," Juli told the police, "Carl Cooper fired a gold-and-silver blank pistol toward Lee Forsythe; Lee ran out as though frightened." "He shot it once," Juli testified later, " . . . toward the door . . . Lee Forsythe was standing quite close. . . . He didn't fire *at* Forsythe; he fired at the direction that he was in. He wasn't intentionally meaning to shoot Lee."

Juli described the pistol as "a pellet gun or something, just looked like a plastic gun to me. . . . Silver or gold, one or the other. . . . a toy, a blank pistol or something. . . . It wasn't a real gun."

"Could it," Prosecutor Weiswasser asked her, "fire a fatal shot, as far as you could see?"
"No."

3 | Three Days, a Week, Three Weeks

Michael Clark, who had spent time in prison for carrying a concealed weapon, could not be expected to wish it known, even during hearings weeks later, that a weapon might have been in in his possession, or even in his room, on the evening of the incident. Like all his friends, he was cynical to the soles of his feet about the judicial process; an oath in court meant nothing to him except as a factor in a larger danger. Fear of jail made most of the boys crafty; Michael was either less intimidated or less subtle than they, for he was blatant in his disregard for truth and even consistency in his testimony. His lies, which grew bolder, more disdainful, and more ironic with the passage of time, as well as the more cautious evasions and untruths of the other boys, confused even Prosecutor Weiswasser, who was supposed to be on their side; to them, he was just a prosecutor, a familiar enemy, and they were suspicious of his help.

"Clark stated," according to the detectives' synopsis of their interview with him, "he overheard Sortor tell a police officer that Clark had the pistol. When Clark was questioned, he denied having a pistol because three days previous, he had given the pistol to his brother-in-law."

By the time of the murder hearing, a fortnight after this interview, the three days had grown into a week. In the conspiracy hearing, later still, Michael testified, "Look, I say that my brother-in-law had a pistol over there in the Motel about three weeks before all this happened, and he came and got it about three weeks before it happened. . . . It was a starter pistol."

Michael did not want it thought that he had even touched the pistol three weeks before the night of the killings.

"And he left it with you, didn't he?" Attorney Kohl asked him.

"No, he didn't leave it with me."

"Who did he leave it with?"

"I didn't know anything about the thing until I found it up under the pillow."

"Until you found it *what?*"

"It was up under the pillow."

"What pillow, sir?"

"The pillow on my bed."

"The pillow on your bed?"

"Yeah."

"What did you do with it?"

"I recognized it. I recognized the gun. I knew whose it was."

"What did you do with it?"

"I didn't; Carl took . . . the pistol from under my pillow . . . and he hid it."

Michael would not admit that a starter pistol had been shot, as the girls said it had, in the annex on the night of the killings.

"Now," Attorney Kohl asked him, "is there anything else that took place, as you sit here under oath—let me rephrase that question: Was there any shooting in that motel that night?"

"Not to my knowledge, no."

4 | A Gun of Any Kind

Sortor and Lee also denied under oath that there had been any starter pistol there that night.

"Before the police or military personnel started firing," Weiswasser asked, "had there been any shots from within, from inside the Algiers Manor?"

"No."

"Or annex?"

"No, no shots in there."

And later Weiswasser asked, "Did you see anyone in that motel that night with a gun of any kind in his hand outside of police officers?"

"No," Sortor said, "I didn't."

"Did you at any time see any person," the prosecutor asked Lee, "at any time while you were in the Motel that night other than a police officer or soldier or a trooper with a gun?"

"Nope."

And later: "And up in that room on that night Carl Cooper shot the blank pistol, didn't he?"

"Not while I was there, no. . . . I saw a blank cap pistol earlier that day," Lee said. "I didn't see any gun that night."

5 | Green Hornet

During the first stages of my relationship with these young witnesses, when they must still have thought of me as a detective-like person, they kept putting me on; and they denied to me, too, the presence or firing of the starter pistol.

"They said there was a starter gun they had there," Lee said to me one day, "and in court they said that it was fired at me. Earlier that day my little brother had come over, and he had a little Green Hornet gun, but he took that with him. It sounded just like a cap gun, but it looked real."

And Sortor said to me on another day, "Wasn't no starter pistol. I don't want to shit you or anything, but there wasn't no starter pistol in there."

6 | Mocking the Police

Late one morning several weeks later, I was sitting in the back room of Sortor's home with him and with a friend of his, whose right hand was wrapped in bandages, at a table covered with laundry, and Sortor was drinking wine, and a record player was going full blast in the front room, and we talked awhile about Auburey. Then I asked Sortor what had tripped off the episode at the Algiers that night.

He looked me straight in the eyes and said, "I know but I ain't telling."

Perhaps it was that I did not press him, or perhaps it was simply that much time had passed since the night when he had lost his two friends and the danger seemed somewhat remote at last, or perhaps it was the wine—whatever it was that made him decide that silence no longer mattered, he suddenly leaned back in his chair and said, "Them girls didn't even know what happened down there. Me and Auburey was downstairs, eating, sitting there, and we were looking at TV. See, Carl was somebody who always had to be having fun. He come running downstairs, him and Michael, just trying to scare us, you know. They was mocking the polices that come in there in the morning to search us down, you know, hollering at us to put our hands up, and scaring us. He shot it twice. Michael said, 'Look out!' you know. They was only two blanks in the gun. Lee stayed upstairs. See, me and Auburey didn't know it was a starter gun at first, and we was scared at first, you know. They was laughing at us. Shot one straight out and one at the floor, you know."

It is quite possible that Sortor was putting me on again this time, all the way, but I do not think he was. I do believe he left something out of an essentially true story: something about one of those who may have been shooting craps, and was wearing a yellow shirt, and who may not have gone home when the others went.

Sortor pushed his hat forward on his head, as he finished the account, and looked at me as if to say, "That's it." But then he gave his friend a flicker of a look of wisdom and shared secret amusement. I could not begrudge their sharing and asked no more, as I supposed there was a good reason—perhaps loyalty—for the distortion of the record, if there had been one.

As they had watched television in A-5, Sortor and Auburey—and perhaps a lingering friend in a yellow shirt—had not heard Carl fire the starter pistol at Lee upstairs. Something Sortor mumbled to me once, then quickly corrected, led me to think that Carl might have chased him or Auburey or their friend right out onto the back porch, or that Carl (or perhaps another; perhaps the friend in the yellow shirt had also handled the gun) might have made some kind of demonstration out there on the back porch.

7 | A Neighbor's View

Synopsis of Statement taken from Willie Harris, 36/M/N, 47 W. Euclid:

"Willie Harris states that on Tuesday night, July 25, 1967, does not know what time, he heard a shot fired in the rear of his home. Harris investigated and observed a Negro man standing on the lower left rear porch of the Algiers Manor Motel, and saw the man fire a shot in the direction of Woodward and Euclid; it appeared that the man had a revolver.

"Harris stated that after the second shot, he observed a man who looked like a private guard fire a shot at the Manor Motel. Harris heard several shots after this. He described the Negro man as wearing a yellow shirt and dark trousers."

8 | Army Under Heavy Fire

Were the shots of a blank pistol the sound of "snipers" that had caused Warrant Officer Thomas to call high command and tell them that he and his men were being fired upon; that caused the alarm that brought the police that killed the boys—"Army under heavy fire," two cops had quoted their dispatcher as saying? I have not been able to find any other plausible explanation. Not one of the scores of witnesses has ever said, in court or to me or to anyone else I have been able to trace, that he saw real snipers at or near the Algiers that night.

What greater—or more bitter—irony could there be than that the three boys at the Algiers may have been executed as snipers because one of them, satirizing the uniformed men who had made them all laugh in the midst of their fear during the search that morning, had been playing with a pistol designed to start foot races, from which it was not even possible to shoot bullets?

Except, of course, that as it turned out the boys were not executed as snipers at all. They were executed for being thought to be pimps, for being considered punks, for making out with white girls, for being in some vague way killers of a white cop named Jerry Olshove, for running riot—for being, after all and all, black young men and part of the black rage of the time.

14

A Game of Chess

1 | A Guy in a Yellow Shirt

Warrant Officer Thomas was amazed by how fast the police came in response to his alarm of snipers.

"Jeez, it semed like I just walked out of the building," he testified, "and they were coming. I don't think any more—I ran out of the building and I believe I was across the street in the wash-rack area or pretty close to that area when the police cars were coming down the street . . . I believe I was at the garage area or the wash-rack area. I believe that was where I was standing. . . . I was under the assumption they were coming because I called them. . . . I had another man with me, Seaglan."

One of the private policemen—not Dismukes, Thomas testified, but another—"went in behind the gas station, between the gas station and the wash rack there. . . . I heard a shotgun blast—what to me was a shotgun blast or what sounded like a shotgun blast. . . . About this time the police were coming down Euclid. . . . I can't truthfully say whether or not the police were already there or they were coming down the street. It was real close."

"One of my men," Melvin Dismukes told me, "went around between the car wash and the parking lot there, and he found a boy crouched down behind a car. He had on a yellow shirt and green pants."

From Report: Riot Duty in Detroit, State Trooper Stan Lutz, 829, Paw Paw Post 51:
"Upon arriving at the scene of the shooting incident, officers made contact with other riot personnel. The first one contacted by undersigned officer was a Negro Civil Defense officer [private guard]. He advised that he fired a warning shot over the head of the subject in the alley just prior to this officer seeing him walk out of the alley."

Thomas, testifying:
"Approximately at this time the prisoner came out of the alley or out of the back yard or out of the Algiers area. I'll put it that way. . . . The private guard brought a man out of the alleyway. I assumed he came from the alley."

From Synopsis of Statement made by Corporal Hubert C. Rosema, Michigan State Police, Paw Paw Post:
"Corp. Rosema states he observed an unknown Negro male about 20 yrs old coming from the alley next to the car wash, his hands above his head, holding sun glasses. Negro man was searched and informed Rosema he had just left an apartment where he had been playing chess and was on his way home which was four houses from the car wash."

Thomas:
"Well, it's pretty hard to describe him. All I can say is he had a bright-colored shirt on. That's about it. He had been surrounded and I asked him who was in there, and he said two of his buddies and two white girls."

Testimony of State Trooper John M. Fonger, Houghton Lake Post:

"There was a colored man coming from the building, walking. I can't say he was coming from the building. He was walking down by the Shell gas station which is right there. I believe it's a Shell gas station." (It was, in fact, a Standard station. This detail matters only as one of a thousand exemplifications in this narrative of the thesis of Leo Tolstoy in *War and Peace* that history has to contend with the phenomenon that after a battle there are as many versions of the battle as there were participants in it. This is especially true, as we shall see later, where the factors of guilt and personal danger enter into the history. Justice, as well as history, has to contend with this variance, and we shall see that the white man's justice, in a Northern city just as much as in Mississippi, almost invariably prefers the unreliable testimony of whites to the unreliable testimony of blacks.) "He was walking down there and he was stopped, being it was after curfew. He was asked where he was going. He said he was going home after playing chess."

Thomas:

The private guard "said he had seen two guys either go into, or in the back of, the annex there at the Algiers. . . . He said, 'Be careful.' He said, 'They went in there,' or, 'They were in there,' and he said, 'They were awfully young-looking.' That was the statement. . . .

"I believe the other private policeman told Seaglan, or asked Seaglan, to watch him, to hold him in other words. . . .

"And then we tried to get one of the policemen to take the prisoner and nobody wanted to take him. I asked a couple of them if they wanted him, and they said, 'No,' and the one state trooper told him to take off."

To Ladd Neuman, Thomas reported this order in more pungent terms: "The guy said, 'Well, boy, you can get your ass going. Take off.' "

Trooper Lutz was stuck with the prisoner. "This subject," Lutz wrote in his report, "was approached by undersigned and two other unidentified officers and was searched for any weapons. While searching the subject, other shots were heard from the rear of the car wash building, this officer could not determine where they came from, as the view was blocked by the car wash building. The subject was ordered to lay down on the ground and undersigned officer guarded him while the other officers took cover. Undersigned officer and the subject taken from the alley were inside the car wash building in one of the open driveways for protection from gunfire."

Thomas:
"At this time they started shooting. It was quite a few shots. Some of them were at street lights."

"Trooper Davies stated "—to the Detroit police—" he fired 4-5 shots at a light in the rear of the car wash. . . . "

"Rosema stated he was carrying a 30 cal. Carbine and had fired 3 shots at a street light near the car wash."

Thomas: "Then I attempted to put out the street light."
Prosecutor: "Did you succeed in putting out that street light?"
Thomas: "No, but I believe my sergeant did."

Thomas:
"The group began shooting in the direction of the annex."

"It was like a war," Thomas testified. "I mean this is a fact. I am not hiding anything. This is war. I mean, there was shooting, there was all kinds of shooting. I imagine there was two hundred rounds shot within a ten- or fifteen-minute period."

15

Man, They're Going
to Shoot

1 | A Shot Came Through There

After the byplay with the starter pistol Carl and Michael went back upstairs, and Auburey and Sortor remained in A-5. Sortor testified that he closed the French doors and went over to the stove. "About two minutes later, then," he said, "a shot came through there." This was undoubtedly the shot fired by the private guard over the head of the man in the yellow shirt as he crouched behind a car in the parking lot, very near the French doors. "It sounded like it came in the room, you know," Sortor testified, "so we ran upstairs. . . . Auburey jumped up and he said, 'Somebody's shooting,' so we ran, we ran upstairs."

2 | Somebody Playing the Fool

Since about midnight, Roderick, Fred, and Larry, the three members of the Dramatics still at the Algiers, had been sitting out, to keep cool, Larry in his underwear and all three in stock-inged feet, on the separate back porch that could be reached by a single door from room A-3. They heard a couple of shots, which they all agreed came from upstairs—presumably the first shots of the starter pistol. "We didn't think anything of it," Roderick told me, "just figured it was somebody playing the fool." But the reports apparently made them a bit nervous, because they went inside, closed the door, and sprawled on the beds. The phone rang. Fred Temple answered, and it was Larry's girl friend of about a year, Glenda Tucker, a singer in a group called the Fabulettes; she asked for Larry, and Larry began chatting with her.

3 | Looking out the Window

Auburey and Sortor rushed into A-14. "And Auburey said, 'Somebody's shooting,' " Sortor testified, "and they said, 'You just playing.' " The boys upstairs had evidently taken the private guard's warning shot as another round from the blank gun, which must have remained downstairs (it was never found); and they now took Auburey's and Sortor's excited announcement as just more pranking.

But those two, Lee said to me, "told us that the police had surrounded the building. So we looked out the window"—the lights were on and the curtains were open, but the windows were closed, as the room had air conditioning—"and see a state trooper's car in a back alley, and this guy told us to get back from the window. The car was over on Euclid."

"We seen this here guy coming," Sortor told me, not naming the man in the yellow shirt to me (none of the friends ever named him), "that's when everybody was looking out the window, when this guy was coming out the side, and they told him to put his hands up and took him on somewhere. He came on across, you know, and we say, 'Man, they going to shoot that guy,' you know, so he throwed up his hands."

"We seen an officer sneaking up side of the wall there . . . "

Sortor testified. "I don't know if it was a police officer or what, but I seen somebody sneaking, you know. Because, you know, he was all cropped down like this, you know. He had his rifle." "It was a shotgun," Michael testified.

"I saw a boy," Michael said in court. "He was, well, he was down in the back in the parking lot, and he was, he was walking north towards the police car, and he had his hands up. He had an orange shirt. And let's see; I told Carl, me and Carl was looking at him, and then I don't know if he got in the police car or what, but anyway we came—let's see, we came back away from the window, and then that's when Carl said, 'It's getting hot in here. Why don't you cut the air conditioner on?' And I went back to the window and I was cutting the air conditioner on and I looked down and this is when I saw the officer down in the parking lot."

4 | To See What Was Happening

"And so at that time," Lee testified, "I went back down to my room to see what was going on. . . . And my back door was open"—either Sortor had not closed it, as he thought, or Lee reopened it, presumably to see what was happening outside to the man in the yellow shirt—"and I heard them, they told me to get away from the door. . . . Somebody hollered in and said, 'Get away from that door.' So I got away from the door and run back upstairs. And before I could get upstairs—"

5 | A Dropped Phone

"I was, you know, talking on the phone . . . " Larry testified. "I was, you know, like sitting on the floor and then a few minutes later I heard some shooting, you know, it sounded like shotguns or something." He asked Glenda if she heard the shots, and Glenda said she did.

"I heard," Roderick told me, "a policeman outside say, 'Shoot the windows out.' "

Larry said to Glenda, "Wait a minute"; he wanted to get some trousers on, he told her. He dropped the headpiece of the phone and left it on the bed.

"Then," Roderick said, "they did shoot a window out, and we thought all the windows would be shot out, so we laid on the floor."

6 | Up into the Window

"As I was cutting the air conditioner up," Michael testified, "I looked out the window and then this officer shot up into the window . . . where I was. And after I saw—I heard a shot, so I fell on the floor. . . . "

"A shot came through the closed window," Karen told Allen Early. "You could not open the windows. Everyone hit the floor and no one was hit. Then everyone crawled out the door."

7 | Glass Shattering

As Lee ran up to the second floor on his way back to Carl's room, he heard several shots outside and glass shattering on the third floor. "When I got up to A-14," he testified, "everybody was outside in the hall lying down."

16

How to Attack a Building

1 | A Little Tear Gas

"You hear a lot of times," Auburey Pollard's father said to me one night long after the killings, "some guy that went berserk over in this neighborhood, he's got a shotgun. The police don't do nothing, they stay outside, and that's where they might shoot a little tear gas, and a lot of the time they don't shoot tear gas, do they? Huh? They plead him out, don't they? So then why would they want to kill three youngsters like that? It's nuts! It's nuts! And I'll always say it's nuts."

2 | Riot Plan

Granting that the third night of the Detroit uprising might not have been thought by the exhausted policemen a suitable time to plead with men they believed to be snipers to come out of a building, Mr. Pollard's outburst made me wonder exactly what the police had been trained to do under these circumstances.

The *Riot Control Plan* of the Detroit Police Department has this to say, under the heading "Attacking a Building":

235

"1. When rioters or snipers are barricaded in a building, chemical agents should be used (either grenade or gas gun projector) through windows or doors." On the same page, the instructions say, "The use of tear gas is an effective and humane method of riot control," and a diagram is provided, entitled, "Driving Barricaded Persons Into the Open with Minimum Casualty Risks," and suggesting, "Blocking the retreat with gas first, and then gassing the room where the resisting person, or persons, are located, is the surest way to safely accomplish the objective."

"2. Troops should be instructed to avoid 'bunching up' if sniper fire from buildings or rooftops is encountered.

"3. Cover, if available, should be taken and a selected small group (5 to 7 men) should be detached as an assault force. These officers shall be equipped with automatic weapons, rifles, shotguns, and gas, and shall advance under cover of a support unit. Unnecessary or indiscriminate gunfire should be avoided and consideration should be given to employment of a police rifle marksman for counter fire if the location of the sniper is definitely established. This action should be closely controlled and supervised.

"4. Should armor vehicles be available, consideration may be given to their employment as a covering force in the assault phase of the operation.

"5. Maximum emphasis should be placed on all units involved in any disorder to closely observe all rooftops and windows from which sniper or fire bomb action might emanate."

17

Everybody Downstairs!

1 | Too Much Shooting

"So," Michael testified, as to what happened after the first shot broke the window of A-14, "I fell on the floor and then I came—we all came out of the room. And they was, we could still hear shooting into the bedroom, and they was shooting into the building. And so everybody came out into the hall, and let's see, Carl Cooper and Lee—let's see, Carl Cooper, Lee Forsythe, and the two girls, they went downstairs; and James Sortor, Auburey Pollard, and myself, we stayed upstairs because we heard too much shooting, and we wasn't going down there. . . . We was right there by the stairs, because just as we was getting ready to go down the stairs, Auburey, he went into . . . a linen closet in the hall, because they was doing a whole bunch of shooting downstairs and he was scared to go down there. . . . And then we—no; Sortor went in the closet with Auburey, and then I told them to come out of the closet. . . ."

"I know when I got in the closet," Sortor testified, "then Auburey came in the closet. Then Michael . . . he came in and he said, 'Get out of that closet, man, because, you know, they're coming around here and if they see us in there, they think we're doing something wrong or something.' "

"And then they came back out," Michael testified, "and sat on the floor with me, we was all, us three was sitting on the floor, down on the floor." According to the others, they were lying down. "And after a while we started hearing someone kicking in doors. We heard the doors kicked in, and then we heard a bunch of shooting. And then they was going all the way down the hallway doing that to every door. And then when they got up to the second floor, we started hollering down there and telling them that we was up on the third floor."

"We hollered," Sortor testified, "saying, 'We're up here, don't shoot.' "

"And one officer," Michael went on, "somebody hollered up there and told us to stay up there. And then when they got through searching the second floor, one of them told us to come down. . . . They said, 'Put your hands in the air and come down.' That's what we did."

"And so we were going to stay up there," Sortor told me, "until they come up there and get us, you know, so when we see them coming up, we started hollering, 'We ain't did nothing.' So they told us to come on down, and so they started to beating us with them rifles and stuff."

"Clark stated," according to the synopsis of what Michael told the police, "that there was a lot of shooting and glass breaking. He heard someone yell from downstairs, 'He's dead,' and also heard someone yell, 'Everyone come down.' "

2 | One Man and Two Ladies

"When I left A-14," Juli testified, "I went to A-7 on the second floor, Karen and I did, because I didn't know where else to go."

In that room, Robert Greene, the Vietnam veteran, was in

bed asleep; he had slept through all the noise up to this point, he later said. Both Greene and the girls testified that they had become acquainted in the motel.

"Everybody ran so I just told Karen we would go down on the second floor. Everybody was in a scuffle. . . . A lot of people upsetting things and screaming and yelling and stuff like that. . . . We knocked on the door and he let us in and told him, you know, there was a bunch of confusion and that, and we heard the police go up to the third floor. He said, 'Well, just sit quiet,' you know. 'Be calm.' And he opened the door, and when he heard the police come down on the second floor, he hollered, 'We are in A-7. Don't shoot.' "

"Police came in and went to the third floor," Karen had reported, according to Allen Early's notes. "Could hear the police say, 'They're up here.' Heard them knock down all the doors and went into the rooms and called them names and asked, 'Where did you hide the gun?' Heard things being pushed around or scuffling. Doesn't remember if she heard shots. Could hear the boys pleading. . . ."

"I didn't know anything about any shooting," Greene told Prosecutor Eggleton, "until the two girls came up to my room hollering, 'Let me in. Please let me in. They're shooting up the place.' . . . As soon as I got up and opened the door I heard firing upstairs and downstairs. I told them to come in, put their hands on top of their heads. I turned on all the lights, opened my door, and a couple of seconds later a police officer, he came up and poked a gun in the door and said, 'Was anyone in here?' I said, 'Yes, one man and two ladies.' He said, 'Put your hands on top of your head and sit on the bed.' I said, 'We already have done it.' "

"In a few minutes," Juli told the police "a police officer came in the room carrying a rifle or shotgun. He was six feet, hundred and ninety, white, looking wild. The policeman shot through the closet and asked if anyone was in the closet or bathroom." In her testimony, Juli said, "He looks around, he shoots—I thought he shot in the closet—but he did shoot in the bathroom. And after he shot in the bathroom, he said, 'Is anybody in there?' and he immediately turned to us and said, 'Stand up with your hands up.' Well, we already had our hands up, and he came charging at me with his gun and hit me on the side and knocked me down. And two more ran in and did the same to Karen and Robert Greene. Well, I jumped back up and he immediately took that long end, the metal end of the gun . . . and hit me in the head. And so then they, you know, took us downstairs and put us up against the wall . . . with our faces against the wall." Juli identified Robert Paille as the man who had struck her.

"One peered in the door," Early's notes on Karen report, "and looked into the open closet door and shot in there and then shot through the wall into the bathroom and then asked if anyone was in there. As he came in he told them to put their hands up and all three put their hands up. The 3 were sitting on the bed with their hands up when the first officer came in. He told them to stand up. After he shot, a couple more (two she thinks) came into the room. Told them to keep their hands up then got behind them and beat all three of them down. Told them to get up and get downstairs. . . . Juli had blood running down her face. . . . Made them stand up against the wall in the lobby. As they were coming down the steps she saw Carl lying in A-2 with blood all over him. . . ."

From David Senak's statement to Homicide:
"Quest: Where did you go when you went into the Manor House?

"Ans: 'I went to the second floor with another police officer (white and in uniform) and a guardsman.' "

3 | I Saw Him

"And when we came down," Michael testified, "I saw him . . . this one right here, Paille . . . he had a shotgun pointed at my face, and he told me, he told me and Auburey and Sortor to keep on down to the first floor. And when we got down to the first floor I saw Carl Cooper . . . right across from the stairs on the first floor. . . . He was laying down, he was on the floor and I kind of hesitated because I was going over to him, and that's when Dismukes, he hit me in the back . . . with the barrel of the rifle. Then he told me to get against the wall. . . ." Elsewhere Michael testified that Senak "pushed me up against the wall."

4 | Already Killed One

"I started down towards my room," Lee testified, ". . . but I didn't make it to the first floor. . . . There was some more shooting downstairs, so I ran into A-9 . . . —coming up the stairs on the left-hand side. . . . I was alone in there, and then I lay down on the floor and I heard some more shooting. . . . And then I heard the police come in and ordered the people downstairs and as I got up, getting ready to go out towards the door, I saw him kick into A-7 and took the two girls and another fellow downstairs. . . . That was on the same floor, and I could see them shooting into the room. . . . I stayed in A-9 . . . and still I hears some more shooting. Then one of the officers come to the room I was in and asked me to come on. Before he come out he took his gun and went to shoot it but it didn't go off, and he told me to get downstairs, and as I was leaving out the door he hit me on the back of the head. Going down the stairs a trooper hit me. I got beat all the way down the stairs. When I was still upstairs this one fellow shouted to me, 'Get your black ass down here, I already killed one of them.' That was on the way down the stairs, because I—I was the last one down—because I had stopped and hesitated because I had seen what looked like Carl, and when I stopped, then he came over and pointed the gun at my head and said to get over in the line, he'd killed one of us already."

18

Phone Calls

1 | Watch Out

Glenda Tucker, Larry Reed's girl friend, was left hanging on the telephone. According to the police synopsis of her account, "Reed said, 'Wait a minute,' that he wanted to put on his trousers. She did not hear any shootings from inside the building. She hung up when Reed failed to return to the phone and called back to the motel clerk. The clerk told her there was trouble in that part of the motel and she could not connect her."

Miss Gilmore, the clerk, told the police, "After the [first phase of the] shooting stopped, a girl called, and Clara Gilmore answered the phone at the switchboard. The girl asked if anyone had been shot. She said she had been talking to her boy friend, Cleveland Reed, in room A-3. Miss Gilmore picked up the phone to A-3, and the line was open. She listened and heard someone yell, 'Get your hands up.' A few seconds later, someone yelled, 'Watch out, he's got the back of the gun,' then she heard several shots. She then pulled the plug."

2 | Quiet over Here

"I called back over there about twelve," Mrs. Gill, Carl Cooper's mother, told me, "and talked to the girl on the switchboard, and she said she couldn't accept any calls and I said, 'Well, why?'— you know. And she said, 'I just can't accept any calls right now. Soon as I get a line clear.' And I said, 'Well, what's going on?' And she said, 'Nothing. It's quiet over here.' So that was a puzzle to me, you know. Like I say, I was nervous for some reason."

Carl was already dead.

19

Enter and Exit: State Police

1 | Deployment

Outside the building, the sequence of events had been this:

Warrant Officer Thomas had called in his alarm, and foolish horseplay with a blank pistol had been escalated into a dispatcher's phrase: "Army under heavy fire."

Task Force #36 of Kiefer Command, a scout car and three jeeps manned by August, Paille, Senak, and several Guardsmen, had responded promptly and had swung into Woodward from the east and had parked in front of the main part of the Algiers; the men had deployed to surround the annex, starting from the screening walls at Woodward and Virginia Park.

At almost the same time, three state-police cars, which had come under gunfire a few blocks to the west, had swung eastward onto Euclid and had been stopped by one or more of Thomas's men on the corner of Woodward by the Great Lakes Building and had been informed of the supposed sniping; the troopers had not heard the broadcast alarm. Their deployment, somewhat delayed by the encounter with the man in the yellow shirt, had mostly been concentrated to the back of the annex, in the parking lot.

2 | A Zigzag Approach

"The way we were operating, it's a standard operation," Trooper John M. Fonger testified at the conspiracy hearing, "one man watched the car, so this left three men watching the cars and the rest deployed towards where we were instructed the shots had come from. . . . Ran around a house that's right next to the Shell gas station, ran up to a tree, and from there worked over to what I believe is a brick wall. . . . I was crouching, running through the parking lot in a zigzag pattern . . . because I had been shot at previously and I didn't want to take a chance." In his report to his superiors, Trooper Fonger wrote that this wall "was at the back of a parking lot of the building in mention. From there this officer followed two Detroit City Policemen and one State Trooper up to a set of stairs that led to a door on the left rear of the building." The two city policemen must have been Paille and Senak, who by their own accounts entered the annex by this door; August went in the front door on the Virginia Park side.

"We had seen a person in this room prior to this . . ." Fonger testified, "standing by the door. . . . I saw a person standing, look out, and duck back. . . . He never came outside. What he was doing is looking out the door." This was evidently Lee Forsythe, who, as we have seen, had gone down to check his room and had been warned away from the door by someone outside.

3 | We Are Going Inside

"I remember," Warrant Officer Thomas testified, "one policeman—or there was a group of policemen going into the building. One yelled, 'Hold your fire please. We are going inside.' And this was at the back side of the house. I assumed it was a house. At this time I didn't know it was the annex of the Algiers. I remember one policeman having a difficult time breaking a window. He hit at it three times. The third time he broke it."

4 | Followers

Since the deduction probably has to be made that Carl Cooper was killed when he rushed downstairs, apparently trying to escape outdoors through Lee's apartment, only to run headlong into the first wave of the assault, the crucial question becomes: Who were the first uniformed men to enter the French doors at the back?

It was clearly not modesty that impelled all those witnesses who admittedly went inside the back way to characterize themselves as followers, not leaders; they all say they saw the body in A-5 already lying there as they entered. In these moments rival services seem to have deferred to each other with unusual generosity.

From Paille's statement to the detectives: "Patr. Paille saw men rushing the Motel Manor and he followed, entering through a door at the N.E. corner of the Motel. Paille stated that he saw a body lying on the floor."

From Senak's statement: "I believe State Police broke open the rear door of the Manor House and then I watched the roof of the Manor House as I approached the back door and went in."

Trooper Fonger, like other state troopers in their testimony and reports, speaks of his having followed in the train of Detroit policemen.

5 | Appeared Like He'd Been Shot

"When we got to the back door," Trooper Fonger testified, "I hollered, 'Come on out, we won't shoot.' Well, we received no reply to this, so we went into the door. I believe there's two doors, which weren't locked"—causing wonder why the window had had to be broken. "We went in. Just as we got inside the door we heard some shots to the exact number, I believe, possibly three and one, but I can't state that for sure. . . . We went into a room. There was a bed to the left, a closet to the front, and a door to the right. I saw a television going to the right. . . . We checked this room initially to make sure there wasn't any snipers in this room."

"The door," Fonger wrote in his report, "was opened by a Detroit City policeman. This officer then followed another City policeman into the room. In the room a subject was observed lying face down, with blood and other parts of the inside of his body on the floor by his stomach, arm, and face."

"He was lying," Fonger testified, "with his head facing . . . away from the door. That's about the only way I can describe it. I can't remember as far as south, north, east, or west. But he appeared like he'd been shot. There was quite a bit of matter lying around him and it would appear coagulated blood." This phrase led to a theory, which we shall see unfold, that Cooper was killed some time earlier by black criminals, not by policemen at all; the theory came to nothing in the end. Coagulation, at any rate, served to emphasize Fonger's followership. "I would say was body to it. In other words, it wasn't blood," Fonger went on to explicate. "The blood, it was enlarged. . . . It was either lung tissue or body tissue and blood, or else it was coagulated blood. . . . I couldn't say how fast it takes blood to coagulate, but it had to sit there some time. . . . As far as turning the man over to see if he was still bleeding, we did not do this. Somebody felt for his pulse and couldn't find one. . . . There was also a spent red shotgun shell laying on the floor. This would be to the victim's feet or who was supposed to be the victim." (I cannot help commenting that racism tiptoes its guilty way through quiet phrases like that last one.) "His head was facing a door. We opened this door and . . . we then went into the hall or lobby, but anyway, all I can recall is it had a marble floor"—actually, a black-and-white-checked composition-tile floor. "I also noticed what would appear to be dry blood on the floor, a couple dry blood spots on the floor. . . . It would appear to be dried blood. . . . Ketchup could also appear to be dried blood. . . . I saw a brown stain on the floor which I associated with blood, but this is going back—well, to the medical, I cannot testify that it's blood on the floor. . . .

"Before we went into the hall, we heard some other shots which sounded like to our right or the back of the building. . . ." One line of speculation followed by the investigators associates these shots with the death of Fred Temple in room A-3; the timing of this death is not agreed upon by various witnesses. "We went into the hall. There was a few people out in the hall going back and forth in the rooms and coming out. They were dressed in light-blue shirts, dark-blue pants, and were wearing helmets"—uniform, during the uprising, of the Detroit police.

"At this time," Fonger wrote in his report, "a Detroit Officer came out of the room followed by another unloading a nickel covered pistol, and saying, 'That one tried for my gun.' It is not clear to this officer if these men were City Policemen, or private policemen, as they were not wearing a badge or other identifying items." It had, however, been clear to Fonger, in the darkness at the back door, that Detroit policemen preceded him into the building.

"There were two officers that came out," Fonger testified, "and one of them had a nickel-plated revolver and he was taking the shells out of the gun and he said, 'That one tried for my gun,' . . . or, 'That one had a gun.' We then went into the room and there was a Negro male lying against the bed with numerous holes in him—or I should say—I'll have to clarify that also. He was bleeding from the front in numerous spots. His eyes were open."

"It appeared to this officer," Fonger wrote, "that this subject was still alive, as it appeared as he was breathing. . . .

"This officer then went back into the hall and observed two

officers dressed as those described above, drag a Negro male with black pants and a black piece of material over his hair out of a room, and put him against a wall of the hall. Another Negro male, with only his under shorts, was then dragged out and also placed against the wall. . . . A remark was made that they should pray."

"We checked the room which would be to the front," Fonger testified, "to the west, which would be probably the southwest corner . . . We checked this room for snipers. We checked the closet, we checked the bathroom. We came out of the room."

"Shortly after this," he wrote, "two white females were thrown down the stairs, one with a large cut on her cheek. They were told to get against the wall and pray. Other Negroes were also brought down from upstairs and placed against the wall."

"I was out by the front of the hall," he testified, "the front of the building. I walked out to see where I was, and I leaned over and I looked at a sign that said 'Algiers' on the front of the building, and I walked back in. . . . And as I was walking through, a subject was taken into the bedroom and was struck. I saw one blow. That was all I saw. . . . He was a Negro. . . . I was making my way to the back of the building. . . . I walked out the same way I came in."

"At this time," Fonger reported, "this officer felt the situation was completely out of control, and started outside to get Cpl. C. ROSEMA, who was in charge of this officer. As this officer was going outside a Negro was taken into a room by a large Negro officer and was being beaten."

"At this time," Trooper P. A. Martin, also present, reported, "Cpl. C. Rosema came into the room and advised this officer, undersigned, that we were leaving immediately as he didn't like what he had seen there."

"The corporal who was in charge of my unit," Fonger testified, "said that . . . we would leave because there was somebody else handling the matter, and we were to be relieved anyway. . . . So we got the rest of our unit and we left."

6 | Walkout

Of all the chapters in this narrative, this may have been the most inglorious. Law-enforcement officers of the State of Michigan, having seen actions by policemen of the City of Detroit that were "out of control," were evacuated by a commander "as he didn't like what he had seen there." Faced with the evident need for strong measures to prevent the crimes of that scene from being carried farther, the state troopers simply washed their hands of the whole nasty business and walked out.

20

Conduct Becoming
an Officer

1 | Courteous but Firm

How had Ronald August, Robert Paille, David Senak, and the other Detroit police officers at the Algiers during the incident been trained to behave in these circumstances?

The *Riot Control Plan* of the Detroit Police Department, in a chapter entitled "Guide Lines for the Individual Officer," gives these instructions:

"Maximum effectiveness will result if the officers at the scene are able to gain and hold the respect of the rioting element. This respect will be attained by a thoroughly professional approach to the problem. . . .

"Conduct: Courteous but firm. Policemen must maintain a completely neutral attitude at the scene of a disorder and completely avoid fraternization with either element. He should strenuously avoid the use of insulting terms and names. Expressions which may be used casually without thought of offending are nevertheless offensive to members of minority groups and invariably antagonize the person or group to whom they are addressed. . . .

"Listen to and take command from your superior officers. . . .

" 'Hand-to-hand' fighting or individual combat must be avoided as far as possible. . . .

"Never at any time should a single officer attempt to handle one rioter. The idea of individual heroic police action is not only unnecessary, it may be positively damaging and foolhardy. . . .

"Don't be prejudicial or guilty of unnecessary or rough handling of persons involved. Use only that force which is necessary to maintain order, effect the arrest, and protect oneself from bodily harm.

"The officer assigned to crowd control must always act in such a manner as to insure impartial enforcement of the law, and afford to all citizens the rights guaranteed to them by the Constitution and the legislative statutes."

21

Up and Down the Line

1 | Butt-Stroking

In the hallway, milling, cuffing, and calling out commands, the uniformed men drove the occupants of the annex against the east wall. "They made us stand," Roderick Davis told me, "with our legs and arms spread, our hands up against the wall." "Had us spread-eagle," Robert Greene told Prosecutor Eggleton.

When he first arrived in the line, Roderick told me, he heard a voice say, "We're going to kill all you black niggers off one at a time."

The hallway was sparsely furnished. At the north end a small wooden office desk stood catercorner next to a large mirror centered on the north wall. Along the west wall were the entrance to A-3, where the Dramatics had been staying, the stairway, the door to A-4, and, close to the front wall, some overstuffed chairs, one yellow and one blue, with a low table between them. Over the chairs was a painting—"On the Beach," by Margaret Keane, according to a prim little brass plaque on the frame—a portrait of a slender blonde in a white shirt open quite far down the front.

253

Victims were now ranged along the east wall, Lee Forsythe first, next to the door to A-2, within which Carl's body lay. I am not certain of the order in line, but from what I have been able to piece together I think Fred Temple and Larry Reed may have been next—if, indeed, Fred ever reached the line at all; Michael Clark was surely next. Beyond him stood a sentimental Victorian fountain, consisting of two large plaster shells, cupped upward, the smaller one above markedly scalloped and containing a fat little boy-girl in bloomers pouring air from a waterless amphora. To the right of this bad recommendation for purity, standing with raised hands against wallpaper of dogwood blooms and leaves, were James Sortor, Auburey Pollard, Robert Greene, the two white girls, and Roderick Davis, I believe.

"They started butt-stroking us on the back and shoulder blade . . ." Robert Greene told Eggleton. "They were trying to make us say that did we know who was shooting in the building. . . . And one of the police officers said, 'I'm gonna kill you all.' Then he turned to the two white girls, and he said, 'We have two nigger lovers here.' . . . So he started hitting . . . with a weapon; this was with a shotgun. Butt of his shotgun. . . . He started going up and down the line hitting. One police officer pulled out his blackjack. He beat one colored guy down to the floor. Then beat him back up. He said, 'Who's firing in this building?' I said, 'I don't know, 'cause I was sleeping in the bed by eight thirty. I didn't know anything about it until the girls come upstairs, knocking on my door.' He was going up and down the line."

"It was two more officers," Michael testified, "they was going up and down the line, hitting everyone with their rifles and things, and they kept on asking about a gun, and when they got to me, they asked me had I seen a gun. I told them, 'No,' then they hit me, then they went down the line and started hitting everybody else."

"And there was another officer there," Michael testified on a different occasion, "he was going up and down the line beating everybody and asking where was the pistol at that was shooting at him. So everybody kept saying they didn't know nothing about no shooting and hadn't seen no shooting and hadn't seen no pistol. . . . They was beating us, and then while our hands was on the wall, they would come by and hit us on our fingers and everything and kick us and hit us in our head. . . .

"They would ask us a question, and then before they would get the answer they would hit us. . . . I was hit in my side, in my back, I was kicked, I was hit in the head. . . ."

Early's notes of Karen Malloy's story: "Told Michael to take the rag off his head and started to beat him and he started to fall down. Policeman said, 'Don't fall down or we'll shoot you.' "

"This guy Senak was the one doing most of the beating," Lee told me. "After the officer told me to get in the line," he testified, "first he pointed to the body and asked me what did I see, and I told him I seen a dead man. And he hit me with a pistol and told me I didn't see anything." Lee identified Senak as the man who pistol-whipped him. "It was quite a few of them there," he testified. "They was just going down the line. One came down and then another came down and started beating us."

"I seen," Sortor testified, telling of joining the line, "a few of-ficers hitting the ones up against the wall. . . . It wasn't all of them hitting at the same time. . . . All of them didn't hit me. . . . A few of them hollered out different things, you know, what they should do, you know." Sortor testified that Senak was the one who had put him up against the wall. "This officer, he was walking back and forth hitting us in the head and everything." As to how he saw anything at all, Sortor said, "You got your face sort of slanted to the side, you know. You weren't going to turn all the way around with them beating you in the head."

"I had only my underwear on," Larry Reed told me. "They wouldn't even let me put my pants on."

One of the officers, Michael testified, "went over to Auburey

Pollard, he got him off the wall. And then August"—Michael's identifications, as we shall see, were not always accurate—"and Paille started beating him right there, right by the wall. And Auburey fell, and one of the police officers had a shotgun and he hit him with it, and the shotgun broke. . . ."

"Pulled Auburey out the line," Sortor told me, "and just bust him in the head with the gun, and he said, 'This nigger made me break my shotgun. . . .' "

"And then," Michael testified, "Auburey said, 'I'm sorry that I broke the gun.' And then . . . they started beating him some more."

"They took twenty or thirty dollars out of my pocket," Roderick Davis told me. "Reached in my pocket and took it out."

"The policeman who first entered room A-7," Karen told the police—and elsewhere she identified that man as Paille—"walked up and down the line hitting people in the ribs and asking who had the gun and who was the sniper."

Sortor testified that Dismukes "came in about the time they was beating us." Another time he testified that Dismukes hit him with a stick on the back of his head behind the right ear. "He just struck me with the stick and asked me where, where was the gun. . . . On my shoulder, you know, when I went down, he hit me across my shoulder. . . . When I went down, when I fell down to my knees, then he hit me across my shoulder, told me to get back up by the wall."

22

Just in Time to Pray

1 | Enter (?) Charles Moore

Charles Moore told me that in the middle of that night he drove his Cadillac, crumpled in front from the collisions with the police car the previous Sunday, from his home in the northwest, down the Lodge Expressway; he got off at Pallister, made his way up two blocks to Virginia Park—"they wasn't bothering anybody in the curfew"—and drove into the Algiers parking lot by the driveway between the annex and the main part of the motel. "As I was coming in between there," he said to me, "a policeman stopped me. He had a shotgun. This was about when Dismukes started firing—way I figured after when I heard about it all. They took me in the building and put me in the line. Going in there I saw a body lying on the floor."

No one of all the witnesses, inside the annex or out, reported having seen any such person that night as Charles Moore; no policeman, Guardsman, or trooper told in court or in reports that he had seen a car pull into the Algiers parking lot or that he had taken a black man inside the building. Considering the number of men who remarked on the presence of the captive in the yellow shirt—he was taken at just about the time when Moore said he drove up—this lack of corroboration is especially notable. But Moore told me and others an extraordinarily circumstantial story.

Moore told a reporter from the *Free Press* that he drove to the Algiers intending to visit his friend Adams in the motel proper; he said he also knew Shirley Williams, the man who had had been living in A-1, whose tape recorder had been taken out by the police that morning, and Eli ("Bubba") Carter, the protector of the two white girls.

" 'Turn around and face that wall,' " Moore told me the police commanded, " 'and don't look in back of you.' " "Everybody was so scared," he told the *Free Press* reporter, "begging them not to kill them. I was scared, too. They kept saying they were going to kill all of us." "People were shouting, 'I ain't done nothing,' " he told me. "Pleading for their lives. And then they said to pray. 'Pray out good and loud.' "

2 | Oh, Lord, Please

Charles Moore told me he shouted out over and over, "Oh, Lord, *please* help me to get out of this alive."

Larry Reed told me he recited the Lord's Prayer at the top of his voice.

Roderick Davis, at the command "Start praying out loud," called out first the Lord's Prayer, he told me, then "Now I Lay Me Down to Sleep," then the Twenty-third Psalm. His voice was deep and strong: "The Lord is my shepherd, I shall not want . . ."

He told me: "One of the policemen said, 'He's *really* praying,' and they all started laughing."

23

Enter Warrant Officer Thomas

1 | Too Much Paperwork

Of all those who protested their reluctance to enter the annex and their tardiness in doing so, Warrant Officer Thomas was the most fervent.

"It wasn't but a matter of a short time," he testified, "that the policeman came back out of the building. . . . The State Policeman walked back to the car and asked one policeman how many were shot, and I believe the statement was two or three, to that effect. When one State Trooper came back to the police car I heard him call his dispatcher and state that there was one dead and one was still kicking and to send an ambulance. . . .

"The one prisoner that we had, I tried to pawn him off. I had no reason to keep a prisoner. I had no place for him. I asked one of the policemen, I believe it was a State Trooper, what he wanted to do with the prisoner. He said—he made the statement, 'I don't want him. There is too much paper work to him.' "

"We interrogated the prisoner," Thomas testified another time. "In fact, the one State Trooper searched him, and he told him to take off. He asked him where he lived, and he was clean. He said take off. I asked him if he wasn't going to arrest him. He said, 'There is too much paper work involved.' That was the statement I got from the State Trooper. . . . And he told him to make it, and the guy wouldn't—he said he wasn't going to run, he was afraid of getting shot."

2 | We Left the Scene

"I was directed to stay with the patrol cars," Trooper Robert Mickelsen told the Detroit detectives, "as a guard and radio communications, as the others dashed across the street. A short time later, someone yelled to call for an ambulance, which I requested by radio. The other officers returned to the patrol car shortly, and we left the scene before the ambulance arrived." (It never did.)

3 | The Building Was Safe

"I went back into the Great Lakes Building," Thomas testified, "and I called my battalion commander, Colonel Dryden, and reported there had been a shooting, and we assumed, or I assumed, that one was dead and one was wounded critically, to this effect. And he referred me to the Sergeant-Major, and they were pretty busy. This was at the high command post. And the Sergeant-Major said, 'Go over and check it out.' All right. So I hung up there and called the president of Great Lakes Insurance Company, Mr. Gaillard, and reported to him that there had been a shooting in the area, but as far as I was concerned the building was still safe; that there was no damage done to the building." This extraordinary latter phone call—announcing, in effect, that the property of the Great Lakes Insurance Company had not been damaged by Carl Cooper's blank pistol, but that, indeed, this same Cooper and possibly one other had already given their lives for having threatened the property, if only with noise—was, at the very least, an ironic realization of the perception of the black population of Detroit, that law-enforcement officers were out in force during the rebellion in order to protect not human rights and human life but material property, store goods, buildings, capital investment. This perception intensified the rage and gave the spur to stealing and burning.

"I went out front asking one of the men to go with me. I had several volunteers— . . . I had two volunteers, and I picked Henson. . . ."

"I can give you the time the phone call was put through," Thomas offered in the conspiracy hearing. "The phone call came through to the battalion commander, I believe, at ten minutes to one. This was 0050 hours." But chronology was always a pesky jumble to Thomas. In the Dismukes trial, he testified that he had called Mr. Gaillard first and the command post afterward.

4 | Check the Annex

"Warrant Officer Thomas then returned to the Great Lakes Building," the synopsis of Thomas's statement to the Detroit police said, "and called the Battalion Commander, Lt. Colonel Dryden, informing him of the incident and reported no National Guard casualties. He was referred to Sgt. Major Kazup, who requested Warrant Officer Thomas to check the Annex and see what the situation was. In company with Pfc. Henson, Warrant Officer Thomas entered the front door, saw private watchman Dismukes, several Army personnel (About 5) and two Detroit Police officers, (One of the Detroit officers he recognized from an earlier incident) and 5 or 6 Negro men and 2 white girls lined up facing the wall on the east side of the lobby. One of the officers were beating one of the Negro men over the head with a pistol and then a blackjack. One of the girls was already bloody."

"To give you an idea of time," Thomas testified, "I don't

know how long it takes for blood to dry on a person—the blood on the girl had already started drying. It was already dry. How long this takes, I don't know, but I estimate it between fifteen, twenty, maybe thirty minutes after the original entry into the building."

5 | Reluctance

Attorney Lippitt: "How did you feel about this building?"
Thomas: "I didn't want to go in there."
Lippitt: "Were you frightened when you walked in there?"
Thomas: "I would say I was."

6 | Pretty Rough

"I think I seen this Dismukes first," Thomas testified, "He was one of the first ones. . . . I believe I asked him how many was dead. . . . And I'm pretty sure of this. This is not really accurate. I think he said there was two dead. . . . There were two policemen. . . . They were questioning them, treating them pretty rough. . . ." Thomas, under examination, identified Senak as one who was hitting those in the line ". . . with a pistol. . . . It looked like a slap jack. I mean, he could have hit them with his hands, too. . . . I attempted to search one of the front rooms and also I . . . saw a shotgun with a broken stock on a chair in the hall."

"Warrant Officer Thomas looked in room A-2," the synopsis reported, "and saw a Negro man whom he had seen on the street earlier in the night lying in the doorway apparently dead. In room A-3 was another Negro man propped by the bed. He also appeared to be dead. He saw no one else in the room. Thomas and Dismukes searched the second floor, found no weapons."

"I walked up the stairs into the hallway and came back down," he testified. "It looked to me at the time it had been pretty thoroughly searched . . . because the beds were all turned over and stuff was laying out on the floor and pretty well scattered around." Thomas returned to the hallway.

7 | Confidence

"Then this warrant officer," Robert Greene told Eggleton, "that's when he came into the picture. . . . He said, 'I know how to handle these niggers.' "

24

Interrogations

1 | About a Gun

Now began a new phase of the incident—a series of individual interrogations. Foreshadowing the gruesome "game" to come, the officers began to take people from the line, one by one, into rooms, for what might have been called—and might strictly not —questionings.

A warning should be posted, at this point, as to chronology. There was so much confusion in the hallway, with so many uniformed men acting independently, spontaneously, and dangerously, that the record is unclear; memories of officers and witnesses alike were shaded or distorted later by guilt, fear, and bewilderment. We have seen how some have tried to emphasize the lateness of their entry into the annex. I am continuously aware that my reliance in this narrative on the statements of witnesses tends to fragment the story; it is not so much written as listened to, in bits and pieces. The sequence of these fragments follows, as far as it is possible to follow, my sense of the run of the actual events, but I must emphasize that I cannot vouch for many minor and some major points of chronology.

Lee Forsythe, I am quite sure, was first to be taken. He was at the head of the line, and several witnesses agreed that he went first. He testified that Paille took him into room A-4, the door to which was more or less across from the fountain in the hallway. This room, with a large bay window looking out, by day, on the elm-lined avenue of Virginia Park, contained a double bed, a kitchenette against the wall opposite the bay window, and a television set by the window across from the foot of the bed.

"He was going up and down the line," Robert Greene, the veteran, said of one of the officers. "Two boys were standing there, and they were living on the top floor. So one of the guys said, 'I was up in my room, but I don't know who was shooting. All I heard was bullets coming through the window upstairs.' So then he said, 'This guy here, he was in the window.' So he took this guy here in the other room, A-2"—if Greene was referring to Lee, I believe he got the room number wrong—"and they talked to him a little bit. . . . You could hear blows being thrown."

Lee told me how Paille "started questioning us, asking us where the gun was. And I kept telling him I didn't know, so he pulled me out of the line and took me into A-4, I think it was, and began beating me and tried to make me tell where the gun was. I was the first one in the line. The biggest one was the one took me in the room, Paille. I remember him from the dimple on his chin. When he took me in the room, he told me he was going to find out where the gun was. 'You black bastards, you been giving us a whole lot of trouble.' "

"He just asked me about a gun," Lee testified. "I told him I didn't know anything about a gun. . . . He knocked me on the bed. . . ."

"And then," he told me, "he just picked me up and put me back in the line."

2 | A Further Search

Sortor was next. He told me about what happened on the line after Paille brought Lee back out. "So he said, he asked us which ones he brought from the third floor. So Michael and Auburey said he brought them from the third floor. I didn't say nothing. So he started beating us, so he pulled Michael, to tell him who the other one was, or he was going to kill him, you know. Michael told him it was me. Then Paille said he was going to kill me. So he took me in this room, busting me on my head. He hit and tripped me, so I fell on the floor, you know. So I got up, you know. He pulled the trigger right"—cocked his pistol, in other words—"and he say he should blow my head off. He was going to blow it off if I didn't tell him where the gun was. He held his gun to my head and he said, 'I'm going to give you a count of three.' But I said I hadn't seen no gun."

"I could hear them beating Sortor," Michael testified.

"They told us a wagon was coming," Lee told me, "so Sortor pretended to go find a gun, to pass the time till the wagon came."

"He said," Sorter told me, " 'You go on with me to find this gun.' I told him I didn't know where no gun was. So he took me upstairs, and around the rooms, looking for a gun."

"An officer forced Sortor to accompany him," the police synopsis on Sortor said, "while he searched Apts 5 and 14, and another apartment with a fire escape, for the gun."

"And when I went upstairs I looked into a few rooms," Sortor testified. "He told me to look around up under the beds and stuff upstairs where I was on the third floor."

"He told me to pull some of the beds loose and stuff," Sortor told me, "made me look in the closets, pull some of the clothes out. So he brought me back on downstairs, told me to get up against the wall."

"And when he come back," Lee told me, "they started beating us again."

3 | Pleading for Mercy

For some reason Auburey seemed to attract more blows than anyone else. Roderick Davis, who stood not far from Auburey in the line, told me that Auburey had begun to weep as he begged for his life after the officer broke the gunstock over his head.

"They come and got Auburey," Michael testified, "and they beat Auburey all the way from the wall all the way in there and beat him some more. . . . He was still telling him he hadn't seen no gun and that he hadn't did anything."

"He got another guy," Greene said to Prosecutor Eggleton, apparently, in the sequence, speaking of Auburey, "and took him in there. You could hear blows being thrown also. Then he said, 'No, I don't know anything about it.' And he pleaded for mercy. Then they brought him back and put him against the wall."

4 | Sea Change

Up to this point all the physical and mental torture in the hallway and the rooms had been in the guise of a search for a sniper's weapon. It was now that a final sea change toward horror occurred, spreading subtly from the loins of some of the men of law and order.

"They took the girls into A-4," Robert Greene told Eggleton. "That's the room right across the hall. You could hear blows being thrown and you could hear the girls screaming. And then he called me in there. I had my hands up when I went into the room. He told me to put my hands down to my side."

"Greene was then called in," the synopsis of Greene's statement to the police said, "and saw that Juli was bleeding about the forehead, a mattress on the floor was bloody, and Karen's clothing had been torn. Greene was questioned as to his relationship to the girls."

"He started asking questions," Greene told Eggleton, "and asked whether I had intercourse with any of the girls. I told him, "No." Then he asked me what I was doing there. I told him, 'I just got discharged. I came here looking for a job. I arrived here Friday.' And told him what was what, the reason I was there. Then he said, 'Okay,' and told me to move out. Prior to me going out, I noticed one of the girls' clothes was ripped."

"Questioned them one at a time," Karen Malloy told Allen Early. "Who had the gun, who was the sniper, whose camera was it, did they live there? Pushed her out the door and ripped her dress from the back. Pushed her back up against the wall."

5 | New Language

"So I came out from A-4," Greene told Eggleton. "This warrant officer, he spoke up then. I told him that I'd like to go back in the service. He told me, 'We don't need niggers in the Army, like you.' . . . So I didn't say any more, and I received another blow. And I was struck behind the head. . . . This was with a rifle butt."

Then, according to an account given to me by Charles Moore, a policeman approached Greene and began to rant at the black man who had been discovered with two white girls in his bedroom. Since Moore could not name the speaker, we must guess—and we can guess—which officer would have used language of the sort Moore reported; which officer had begun to dominate action that was shaded now toward some unthinkable finality.

The officer said to Greene, "You sure you're not one of these black-ass nigger pimps?"

Greene, an ex-paratrooper, a veteran of Vietnam, reached in a pocket and pulled out papers warranting his honorable discharge, and held them up for the officer to see. "I just got out of the service," he said.

The officer hit him and said, "We're going to kill all you black-ass nigger pimps and throw you in the river. We're going to fill up the Detroit River with all you pimps and whores."

25

The Knife Game

1 | Defend Yourself

"Threw a knife," Early's notes on Karen's story said, "and told him, 'Here, defend yourself.' The knife landed on the floor. Cop told him he'd kill him if he picked it up. Cop told him to pick it up."

"So they kept on going up and down the line," Greene told Eggleton. "So they tried to make this youth pick up a knife. He told him, 'Pick it up so I can blow your goddam head off.' . . . The boy wouldn't pick up the knife. He said, 'I said, pick it up.' The boy picked it up and dropped it immediately."

"Then they took me off the wall," Michael testified, "and one of them told me to pick up a knife off the floor, and I told him that I wasn't going to pick it up. So then they made me pick it up . . . and he hit me, and then he . . . hit me again, and oh, he told me he could shoot me right then and say that I tried to kill him. I told him, 'Yeah,' so he told me to drop the knife, so I dropped the knife, and he told me to turn around and get back against the wall, and I got back up against the wall."

"The policeman dropped a knife," Roderick said to me, "and he said, 'Pick it up.' The boy said, 'I won't do it.' The policeman beat him till he slid down the wall slowly and picked it up. The police said, 'Now defend yourself.' The boy dropped the knife back on the floor and said, 'You might as well kill me.'"

2 | Stab Me

"So then," Michael testified, "they called Auburey Pollard off the wall and told him to do the same thing. . . . And they told Auburey to do the same thing, but he started—he wasn't going to do it, then they started beating him. Then they made him pick the knife up, and they started beating him again, and they told him to drop the knife. When he put the knife down, they took him and put him back up against the wall and were still beating him. Then they came down to Lee. . . ."

Roderick Davis told this part to a reporter from the *News*: "'Pick the knife up.' 'No.' 'If you don't, we're going to kill you.' So the boy reached down . . . and picked the knife up and the police told him to stab him with it. The boy started crying and said, 'No,' and dropped the knife. That's when another policeman hit me in the head and told me to keep my face toward the wall."

26

Skin Show

1 | All of Them Pulled

"One of the officers," Lee told me, "he said, 'We're going to get rid of all you pimps and whores.' They asked the girls did they want to die first or watch us die."

"Questioned them up against the wall," Early's notes said, "& ripped all K's clothes off & half of Juli's. Policeman said, 'Hey, you broads, do you want to die first or see the others & then go?'"

"One of the policemen," Roderick said to me, "told the girls to take off their clothes. Senak pulled them out to the center of the room. Tore one of them's dress off—hooked it with the thing on the end of his gun—and made the other one pull her dress off. He said, 'Why you got to fuck them? What's wrong with us, you nigger lovers?'"

Sortor testified in court that both girls had their dresses torn. "I seen one, had her clothes—uh—off. . . . I seen the officers pull them off. . . . The policemen . . . and some Army mens. . . . All of them pulled, pulled her clothes off her." The girl, Sortor testified, wound up naked except "just her panties."

"The officers," the police synopsis on Sortor said, "had pulled their clothes off and all they had on were their panties."

2 | Watchers' Feast

The girls were returned to the wall. "The girls' dresses were torn from behind," Dismukes told me. "The dress had fallen off one and was lying around her feet. The other was holding hers up in front."

A handful of airborne troops, "men in green uniforms," Juli testified, "came in as a group after they had ripped our clothes off." "The soldiers came in," Karen told Early, "and everyone stood around as if they were waiting for something."

The police synopsis of the statement of Wayne Henson, who had entered with Thomas and never advanced beyond the front doorway, said "Henson observed . . . 4-5 airborne police watching."

"When they'd stripped the girls down," Sortor said to me, "they told me and Lee and them to look at them. Said, 'Ain't you ashamed?'"

The men in uniform who were not hitting people at the wall, Sortor testified, were "just standing back. Just standing there laughing, you know, all like that."

27

The Death Game

1 | One at a Time

"Then," Lee said to me, "they started killing us one by one."

"They were going to shoot us," Michael testified, "one at a time."

2 | It Was All Right

"One of the Detroit officers," Thomas told the police, "pulled the 'big man' "—Roderick Davis—"out of the line and took him in A-4." In court Thomas was more explicit. "Officer Senak," he testified, "took the first man out of the line . . . into the front room, one to the left in front." "When they went in," Greene told Eggleton, "he closed the door." Roderick Davis said to me, "They told me, 'Lie on the floor face down, and if you make a move or say a word we'll kill you.' " "I followed them to the doorway," Warrant Officer Thomas testified, "and Officer Senak told the man to lay on the floor and he fired a round through the wall. I seen him point the gun to the other direction. He

273

didn't shoot him. He scared him. . . . He winked at me. He didn't say nothing." "I thought," Roderick testified, "he shot in the floor because I felt like vibration reaction by my feet." "In the floor or through a chair or something," Roderick said to me.

Attorney Kohl: "Now, you were in a room with David Senak when he took a prisoner in there?"
Warrant Officer Thomas: "Yes, sir."
Kohl: "And is it not true that he told the man to lie down on the floor? He fired a shot but he didn't shoot at the man, did he?"
Thomas: "Definitely not."
Senak fired, Thomas testified, "right in the corner."

"He looked at me," Thomas testified, "and winked, indicating it was all right. . . . When we took the first man in I realized what he was doing. And it was better than letting these people be beaten; seriously. I felt somebody was going to really get hurt seriously, and I felt this was the best thing at the time."

"Then," Roderick told me, "they said, 'Don't budge an inch or you'll be dead.' " And the men left him alone in the room.

3 | Want to Kill One?

"The warrant officer," Greene told Eggleton, "came out, and the policeman asked the other officer, 'Did he kill him?' And the officer said, 'Yes.' " This was for the ears of the people in the line.

"This officer . . ." the Thomas synopsis said, "asked Thomas if he wanted to kill one. Thomas said, 'Yes,' and took one of the men"—Michael Clark—"into A-4 and fired a rifle shot into the ceiling, forcing the man to remain in the room."

"I also took one person into that front room," Thomas testified. ". . . I used my M-1 rifle. . . . I also told the man to lay on the floor, and fired a round through the ceiling . . . toward the corner so that anybody upstairs wouldn't get hit. I didn't think there was anybody upstairs around at the corner of the house."

"Let's see," Michael testified, "August"—once again he seems to err; even Senak's lawyer placed Senak in this role—"told the soldier to shoot me or something. Anyway, the soldier told me to lay down. Then he shot. I think he shot out the window or in the hall somewhere. Then he told me just to lay there and be quiet. And he said if I make any noise, he going to come back and shoot me for real."

4 | Announcement

"Clark and an unknown man were taken into room A-4," the Sortor synopsis says of this first phase of the death game, "shots were heard, and the officers returned, saying, 'We killed those two.'" Telling me the story, Sortor said, "And so they said they were going to kill us, you know. They said they were going to kill us niggers, you know, so they picked Michael and this other guy out, so they said they were going to kill these two niggers, so they took them in this room in there, we heard two shots, so the police come out, so he said, 'I killed them two mother-fuckers.'"

Karen told the detectives "she believed the police killed Michael Clark." From the synopsis of Juli Hysell's statement: "They . . . made Hysell believe Clark was dead."

5 | Rational, Reasonable Explanation

Thomas testified, "Immediately after the officer shot into the wall, into the floor, or corner, or wherever you want to call it, and laid the man down, they"—the people against the wall—"thought this man had been shot and they were willing to talk. . . . I believe it was one of the girls—I wouldn't swear to it—said, 'Why don't you tell him about the gun? Carl is dead any-way.' And this is one of the statements I specifically heard to this effect."

"One boy spoke up," Juli testified, "and said that the boy

that was dead was the one that had the pistol, and that's the only thing that was said to my knowledge about the pistol."

"One of the persons" Karen told Allen Early, "who had been in A-2 & come up to A-4 said, 'Go on and tell them anything because they've already killed him.' This was with reference to the blank pistol. This other person then said, 'The guy in there on the floor' (referring to Carl in A-2) 'had a blank pistol.' Policeman said, 'Why didn't you tell us that before we killed the other guy?' "

Having elicited from Juli, in the conspiracy hearing, an estimate that the ordeal in the hallway had been going on for about twenty minutes before this first mention of the starter pistol, Attorney Kohl asked her, "Now, if in fact there was simply a blank pistol that had been fired, will you advise this Court, please, what rational, reasonable explanation there could be for not telling the police who would have the gun and who had done what for a period of twenty minutes?"

Juli answered: "Because everybody was scared."

6 | Next?

Karen told Early, "The talking policeman then said, 'Who shall we get next?' "

28

The Death Game
Played Out

1   I   Want One?

"Then the first officer," the Thomas synopsis said, "asked the officer with the OCD type helmet (who was dark complx w/m), 'Do you want to kill one now?' He said, 'Yes,' and the first officer gave the shotgun to the second officer, who took a Negro youth from the line. . . ."

"He said it," Thomas testified, "loud enough for everybody to hear in the room, 'Do you want to shoot one?'—or to this effect."

Thomas testified that August had not been particularly active along the line-up. "Patrolman August," he said, "was very refined. He didn't say anything that I can recall." But it was August to whom Senak now turned; Thomas testified that Senak handed his shotgun to August and told him "to take a man into the back room or into a room."

"Then the guy next to me," Greene told Eggleton, "they took him to A-4. The officer told him not to take him to A-4.

He said, 'Take him to another room.' And he took him to A-5, I think it was A-5, that's the back room there." (It was A-3.)

"The game was going on," Thomas testified, "and I said, 'You can't kill any more in here. There are too many now.' And that is when I believe the other policeman handed Patrolman August the gun."

2 | A Thing to Scare People With

Assistant Prosecutor Avery Weiswasser asked Thomas: "Did Senak hand a gun to August?"

"Yes, sir."

"What did he say when he handed him the gun?"

"To the effect this was a game. I mean, this is a thing to scare people with."

But in other testimony Thomas said, "I can't recall what was said. I know there was a conversation. I won't deny this. The idea was to give the impression that these people were being shot."

Yet again Weiswasser asked, "Did you know if anybody bothered to tell August it was only a game?"

"No, sir," Thomas replied.

3 | Don't Shoot

From the Michael Clark synopsis: "Clark then heard someone take Pollard into Apt. #A-2 and heard Pollard yell, 'Don't shoot. Don't shoot.' He then heard a gunshot."

From the Lee Forsythe synopsis: "Forsythe stated he heard Pollard yell, 'Don't shoot,' and a door slam, Forsythe believes in room A-3. A few seconds later, Forsythe heard a shot fired."

4 | A Brush of Clothing

"Then I believe Officer August took this man to the rear of the room," Thomas, who followed August into the room, testified, "and I heard a shot. And Officer August had his back to me. I seen a brush of clothing, and I heard something fall. At this time I got scared."

"Did I see him fall? . . ." Thomas asked himself in testimony. "I won't say that. I seen movement. Officer August was standing between myself and him, and I seen a flash of clothing, what I thought was a flash."

Prosecutor Weiswasser asked at one point: "Did you hear any struggle going on prior to that time?"

"No," Thomas answered, "I can't say I did."

"I want to be honest with you," Thomas testified later on. "I have seen the pictures of the room after the two bodies were discovered in there. And I believe the man that Officer August took back there had a shirt on, dark gray shirt. And the pictures don't show this. And this is why I was confused on this point. You can see something or think you see something and think about it, and you don't know if you've seen it or not. And I thought I seen that flash of clothing. And it looked like a gray shirt."

5 | Announcement

From the James Sortor synopsis: "A shot was heard and an officer returned, saying, 'That one didn't kick.' "

From the Robert Greene synopsis: "Then a shot was heard and the Warrant Officer returned, saying, 'That nigger didn't even kick.' "

Sortor said to me, "Auburey didn't lose his temper in that room; he was too scared. I figure if he would have lost his temper, he would have lost it when they was hitting him with the rifle. It was too quick for him to be in there tussling with the guy. It was too quick. He went in there, I heard the shot, and the guy came out, and he said, 'That one didn't even kick.' "

6 | Strictly Their Business

"At this time," Thomas had said, "I got scared. . . . It scared me. I was scared. I will be honest with you. . . . As far as the conversation goes, I believe I told the policeman that this was strictly their business, and I called Henson, who was outside at this time. And there was more shooting in the street. In fact, more shooting, and I told him we were going to leave. . . ."

29

Out

1 | Exodus

Warrant Officer Thomas was not alone in his impulse to flee after the murder of Auburey Pollard in the game that he, Thomas, had so blithely joined. The hallway was virtually clear of uniformed men in a very short time. Convenient firing was heard not far away; all but a handful ran to do their duty.

"And then some more shooting started down the block there," Greene told Eggleton. "All of them rushed out of the Manor house there and ran down the block. Two policemen were left there."

"And then I heard some more shooting from outside," Michael, who was still lying on the floor in A-4 at the time of which he was speaking, testified. "And then some of the officers and all of them went outside because I heard—let's see, the soldier told me, he say, 'That's another one of your friends out there shooting at us.'"

"I remember," Sortor testified, "that I heard officers say they were shooting down the street, and some of them ran out—ran out of there, and that's when the officer—when they left, this officer went into this room and got Michael and them up, and they told us we could leave."

2 | Solicitude

Despite the sudden fear he said he had felt, Warrant Officer Thomas did not, after all, leave. He was soon to be found in room A-4 again, with Patrolman August, the naked girl, and the half-naked girl. "These two," Karen (the one who had lost all her clothes but her panties) told Early, "were very nice."

"They then took K and J into a room (A-4)," Early's notes said. " 'What was the trouble?' They said they didn't know and they didn't ask them any more. These two were very nice. Thought Juli should go to the hospital. . . . The cop asked them if they had any robes. J & K said, 'No.' Told them to get out and get a robe."

According to the Thomas synopsis, "Warrant Officer Thomas was then asked to escort the girls to the Algiers Motel next door; as he was leaving he was joined by private watchman Dismukes and Pfc. Henson."

"I believe," Thomas testified, "it was Officer Senak that asked me to escort the women back to the motel room, their own motel room. . . . Myself, Henson, and Mr. Dismukes escorted these women back. . . . Henson, myself, and Mr. Dismukes went to the girls' room, and when they opened the door there was a colored fellow laying on the bed, and Mr. Dismukes approached him and shook the bed and woke him up. He was sleeping. And I held him at, you know, in custody more or less until Mr. Dismukes went in and checked the girl's cut on her head because she was bleeding so severely that, to see if she needed medical attention right away. I asked Mr. Dismukes to do this. And he went over and he said, 'Well, it look like it will take a couple of stitches.' " (Juli had seven stitches; she also testified she suffered a slight concussion and developed a black eye.) "So I warned the girls, I told them to stay in the room until after five-thirty,

until after the curfew lifted . . . and then came out because they
are liable to get in trouble if they come out of the motel. I was
satisfied that the girls did not need medical attention right away
because she had almost stopped bleeding."

3 | Get the Hell Out

"And this police," Greene told Eggleton, "he told us . . . "Get
out of here, because I don't want to see you get killed like the
rest of them.' So we started out the back way. The two girls,
they went out the front. . . . I told them I wasn't going out
there on the street. So he said, 'You better get the hell out of
here if you want to live.' And I went through A-2, where the
guy was lying in a pool of blood. I went over to the office and
stayed there until the next morning."

"They told us to get out fast," Charles Moore said to a reporter from the *Free Press*. "Said, 'We're going to come back
and kill all you niggers.'"

"Paille," Sortor told me, "went in the room and told Michael
and this guy"—Roderick—"to come out of there, they can go.
Asked us, did we like policemen? We say, 'Yeah!' The guy says,
where we live at? I told him I lived in Joy Road, gave a wrong
address. Said we could go. They just told us to keep on going,
don't come back. This one guy asked could he go back and get
his pants or shoes, one. That's all I remember. I was trying to
get on out."

Roderick, who had been left lying on the floor in A-4, said
to me, "A policeman told me to get off the floor and get out in
the hallway. He said to leave out; he said, 'Start walking in the
direction you're going with your hands above your head, and
if you look back, we'll kill you, because we'll be following you
all the way home.' Fred Temple asked could he go back to the
room and get his shoes and shirt. I passed him. Larry was just
ahead of me. They told Fred it would be all right to go and get
his stuff. I was too scared to go for my shoes, I just kept on
walking in my socks. Out through the back rooms. Almost
stepped on a body. That really scared me, because I hadn't seen

it before, see, and they shot in the floor by me in the room there, so I didn't think they were *really* killing people."

Both Roderick Davis and Larry Reed said under oath in court that they had seen Fred Temple in the hallway at the very end. This was Roderick's testimony:

Q. When did you last see Temple?
A. In the line as we were going out the room—out the building.
Q. Beg pardon?
A. I saw him in the hallway as we were going out the building.
Q. Do you know where he was going?
A. I believe he was supposed to have been going out like the rest of us were.
Q. Did he go out like the rest of you did?
A. No.
Q. Did you hear him talk to anybody about permission to go to his room?
A. Yes.
Q. Well, what did he say, what did you hear him say?
A. Could he go back and get his belongings or clothes or shoes, one.
Q. Did anybody go back there with him?
A. I don't know. We were walking out.

Prosecutor Weiswasser questioned Larry Reed on the same point:

Q. When was the last time you saw Fred Temple?
A. The last time I saw him was when we were at the hotel, just before I left, when the police let us go.
Q. Do you know where he was going?
A. The last I saw him I heard him ask about some shoes, and I never did see him after that again.

"We went out side," Sortor testified. "Some more officers, they stopped us over there. . . . And then they asked us where we was coming from. We said, 'The motel.' And they said, 'Who let you all go?' And we said, 'Them police officers over there.'"

VI

Aftermath

30

A Matter for Investigation

1 | Puzzles

And so we find ourselves back again at the beginning of this book. The harrowing incident is over; the witnesses are scattering. Robert Greene goes to the motel office and spends the rest of the night there; Charles Moore gets in his car and drives home—so he says. Michael goes to the Mount Royal and calls Carl's parents to tell them Carl has been killed. Rod and Larry, washed by the light of a locomotive, fall in the hands of the Hamtramck police. Lee and Sortor run to Carl's house and collapse there, panting out the story. . . .

Gradually, as the hours and days pass, a stench rises, and the Algiers Motel incident becomes a matter for investigation. By midday on Monday, July 31, five days after the incident, the newspapers have broken the story; the *News* has bannered Robert Greene's accusations that a National Guard warrant officer was the principal killer; and perhaps it is the shock of the publicity that impels Ronald August and Robert Paille to confess, during the day, that their hands held guns that killed, or helped to kill, two of the three victims, Auburey Pollard and Fred Temple.

It is by now, on Monday, July 31, clear that the killings in the Algiers were not executions of snipers, looters, or arsonists caught red-handed in felonious crimes in the heat of a riot, but rather that they were murders embellished by racist abuse, indiscriminate vengeance, sexual jealousy, voyeurism, wanton blood-letting, and sadistic physical and mental tortures characterized by the tormentors as "a game." Yet, in detail, much that is puzzling remains (and please do not expect all that is still mystifying to be cleared up in this book, for it will not be): Who killed Carl Cooper? Did more than one man kill Cooper? What was the role of David Senak, whom Paille, in his confession, implicated? What was the extent of Warrant Officer Thomas's actual guilt? What did Dismukes do? Were the state troopers blameless of crimes they would not curb? When and how, and under the muzzles of how many guns, was Fred Temple killed? Was Temple killed, as Carl Cooper apparently was, during the first wild rush into the building, or was his murder the last inning of the death game?

2 | Show-ups

That evening Carl Cooper's stepfather, Omar Gill, took Sortor, Lee, and Michael to police headquarters for show-ups. Though the detectives had garnered two confessions, they wanted corroborating witnesses and a lead to Carl Cooper's killer. Karen and Julie were also on hand. Against a wall under bright lights a row of white men—members of the Detroit police force who had been in or near the Algiers that night—stood in civilian clothes, and each witness was given about three minutes alone in the room to pick out the beaters and shooters. After all the witnesses had gone through, another line-up followed, of Guardsmen who had been around the motel that night. The show-ups were not a success. Michael and Sortor both identified Paille as one who had bullied them, and Sortor made one misidentification; otherwise all drew blanks. In court later the defense lawyers would try to make much of the failures of identification during these show-ups.

"When they went to the line-up," Omar Gill told me, "they were afraid. After Lee talked to the FBI man downtown, this is what he said to Lee, he said, 'Now you stay close to home because we don't know what might happen.' Now, why would the FBI man say that?"

"To know the terror," Eddie Temple, Fred's brother, said to me, "that they had installed in them at this point! I'm surprised that they could recognize any one of them, because these boys were just terrified. You talked to them and they were in a different world."

"The girls, of course, were very frightened," Leon Atchison of Congressman Conyers's office said to me. "They would not go down to the Prosecutor's Office unaccompanied. They didn't want to go down there by themselves. So that the Prosecutor's Office, in order to get in touch with the girls, had to call us, and then we would get in touch with the girls and take them down. They said they wanted to girls to come over and look at a line-up. So we went over about ten thirty in the evening, Coleman Young, myself, and the two girls.

"One thing that really struck me: When we got in the elevator, we were the first on the elevator, then about six National Guardsmen and several police officers crowded on the elevator, and the girls' reaction was just fantastic. If they could have gone through the back wall of the elevator they would have done it; they were just cringing and shivering, until the men got off at a floor before we got off.

"Then we got up to the Prosecutor's Office and turned the girls over, and we sat there in the lobby to wait for them, and we wondered why it took so long, you know, for them in the line-up. We were there about two hours, which made us rather suspicious.

"During that time two plain-clothes officers came over and

said they wanted to question the girls before we took them back, about another matter. The Senator and I objected to that; we said that we brought them over specifically to look at a line-up, and we would not want them questioned without Nathan Conyers, their attorney. They were a little bit upset at that. So we told them that we just wouldn't permit them to question the girls at twelve o'clock at night without any attorney or preparation. And they continued to stall, seemingly, with bringing the girls back to us.

"Finally Juli's parent showed up, her mother, her father, and an aunt who lives in Detroit. The mother was crying and the father was very upset. They asked her such questions as, 'Do you know what you're mixed up in now?' And, 'Why didn't you call us? You know you're in a lot of trouble.' And, 'We're going to take you back home.' Juli is a very headstrong girl, and she was insisting that she was not going back home with them. She said, 'I'm eighteen years old, and you can't tell me what to do any more, and I'm not going back home with you.'

"We were standing there waiting to take them back to the Algiers, where they were still staying, and the father said, 'You might as well go ahead, because she's going to stay with us, she's not going back with you.' And then they tried to talk to the other girl, into going with them also, and she just walked away from them; she said she was not going back. Then Juli broke down in tears, and went into hysterics, said they were treating her like a baby, insisting that she would not go with them. But the father became very insistent and asked us to leave, so we left with the other girl and took her back to the Algiers. Strangely enough they were still staying there. They figured that would be the last place anybody would look for them. One weekend they did go to Canada because they were frightened, and they just left a number where some of their friends could get in touch with them, so if anything urgent came up we could get ahold of them. They were very, very frightened and it seemed that after that, the whole movement on the part of the Police Department was to portray them as prostitutes, so as to destroy their credibility as witnesses. My view on that is: Whether they were prostitutes or not, I don't think that that has any bearing on what they saw and what they did in fact experience."

3 | Lawanda Schettler's Vision

At eleven thirty that Monday night, while the show-ups were still in progress, a woman named Lawanda Schettler called the Homicide Bureau and said she had something to tell about the Algiers shootings. An hour later Detectives Edward Hay and Robert Hislop visited Mrs. Schettler at her home, an apartment in a six-story building at 150 West Euclid, close to the Algiers.

"She stated," the two men reported, "that shortly after midnight, early Wednesday morning, she parked her car in front of and across the street from the Manor House Motel. She started toward the side door of a house across the street from the Manor. She intended to get some beer at this house.

"As she was walking to the side door, she saw two (2) Negro men carrying shotguns or rifles, walk up the front steps of the Manor House. Two white girls were sitting on the front porch. They both got up and stepped aside, as if frightened. She heard the door open with a loud noise, as if kicked open, and then heard a loud voice saying, 'Man, you held out on us.' This statement was immediately followed by several shots from inside the Manor House.

"Lawanda Schettler ran to her car and went home."

Here was a lead that the detectives could not but welcome. Coupled with the word "coagulated," which soon appeared in the formal report of one of the state troopers—not in Fonger's, as it happened, but in another man's—Mrs. Schettler's story led to hopes of establishing that Carl Cooper's death had been a separate occurrence from the others; that he had been killed, half an hour or so before the "sniping incident" had begun, by black criminal confederates of his, avenging some sort of hold-out, or settling a grudge.

Mrs. Schettler, a firm-figured white woman of forty years, who keeps a long-haired cat and sometimes goes barefoot, at home, with white polish on her toenails, likes Hamm's beer, and it was this predilection, she told Ladd Neuman some time after these events, that made her a chance "witness" of the Algiers affair. With her husband Chuck, a lanky worker at Chrysler who wears his hair in a crew cut, and with several other residents of their building, she had been riot-watching that evening from the flat roof of the apartment house. The beer ran out. She was thirsty. "I decided to be a good Samaritan," Mrs. Schettler told Neuman; she offered to go to a blind pig, about which she knew, on Virginia Park directly across from the Algiers, to replenish the supply. She descended to her car shortly after midnight, drove east on Euclid to Woodward and then south one block—passing, on Woodward, a National Guard (she thought) jeep with four men in it, which did not challenge her, even though this was long after the curfew hour—and into Virginia Park, where she pulled to the curb across the street from the annex. Turning the corner, she had looked at the porch of the annex and had seen there, she said, "two gals sitting on the step." She had noticed them, she told Neuman, because there was "a bright outside light on and a record-player blasting." She was an alert witness; she observed, even while driving, that one was a blonde, the other a brunette. She parked her car and got out, and as she walked to the door of the blind pig, she looked back and saw that another car had driven in behind her and had stopped in front of the annex. Two black men got out—"they were young, say twenty-three, twenty-five"; another exact observation, considering the distance and darkness. They approached the porch of the annex, carrying long guns tight against their hips, with the barrels aligned vertically with their legs, whether rifles or shotguns she could not say; but, she told Neuman, "I saw guns with barrels on them." When she saw the guns she started back toward her car.

As the two men stepped up to the porch, the girls, Mrs. Schettler said, arose and ran to either side. "What stood out," she told Neuman, "was—as I was getting to the car, walking—was that I have a daughter, you see, and if that was my daughter with all that paint and makeup, well . . ." As she boarded her car, she heard "this door banged, sounded like it was kicked open," then the holding-out line was shouted, two gun blasts followed, a man screamed, and "by the time I got to the end of the block I could hear a girl screaming." On her return home, she did not tell her husband where she had been. "I was terrified, and I came back without any beer, damn it."

Mrs. Schettler told Neuman that though she did not want to get involved, nevertheless her conscience bothered her, and she brooded for several days and lost sleep by night; finally, reading in the papers that policemen had been arrested, she consulted her priest and with his blessing called the detectives. (The only trouble with this part of the story is that the policemen had not been arrested when she called Homicide.) As she unfolded her tale to Neuman, with her husband kibitzing, she and he began dropping, with increasing frequency, first names of friends of theirs on the police force. Mr. Schettler, an avid fire-watcher and amateur crimefighter who claims to have broken up a couple of muggings, commented on a visit paid his wife by the FBI, following up on her information: "I'm sick and tired of these bleeding hearts talking about civil rights. What about the rights of decent citizens?"

The Police Department took up Lawanda Schettler's story with high hopes. Somewhere they dug up a rumor that "a contract had been out for the life of Carl Cooper," who, according to one report, had knocked over a dope pad and had stolen drugs and jewelry. Detroit sleuths, I was told by Assistant Prosecutor James Garber, were dispatched all the way to New Jersey, Minnesota, and Louisiana, in attempts to run down leads on the story told by the lady who was out during Warrant Officer Thomas's war looking for a bottle of beer. "All of which," Prosecutor Garber told me, "came to a blah ending."

4 | I Was Going to Get Railroaded

Up to this time and for the next few days, the finger remained very much on Warrant Officer Thomas in spite of the two confessions—and perhaps even partly because of them, in the sense that the Police Department would understandably have liked the onus for the Algiers mess to be at least shared with another service, the National Guard. This urge for Togetherness was similar to the gallantry with which each of three services gave credit to others for first entry into the annex during the assault on the building. On this occasion, Robert Greene's accusations against Warrant Officer Thomas gave apparent substance to the desire for common cause. By the same token, Thomas's wish was very strong indeed that the Police Department alone would be willing to take the blame; yet he also wanted to be fair and loyal to fellow men-in-whatever-uniform, and not be a tattletale. The conflicts in him were so unsettling as almost to transform him—had not the issues been so deadly—into a comic figure.

In the conspiracy hearing, Attorney Kohl illuminated by a line of questioning Mr. Thomas's agony of those first days after the Greene accusations.

Q. Going back to the events in question, do you recall being interrogated yourself on a number of occasions because of the contention that an unidentified warrant officer had allegedly killed one or more people at the Motel?

A. Yes, sir, that was in the paper. . . .

Q. All right. And this inquiry shortly was directed in your direction, towards you, wasn't it?

A. Yes, sir.

Q. And after which time there was substantial, considerable interrogation of you by various authorities?

A. Yes, sir.

Q. This was true not only locally but on a Federal level?

A. Yes, sir. . . .

Q. Do you know how many statements have been taken from you?

A. Not offhand. I mean, there was quite a few of them, I know. There was one to my counsel. There was two to the FBI.

There was two to the Police Department. One was to Officer Casey and one was to Schlachter. I have been questioned several times by these people.

THE COURT: By whom?

A. By these people. The FBI—

THE COURT: Oh.

A. —and the Homicide. Also during the lie-detector test there was a lot of questions asked there. Every once in a while somebody would call up a question and call me. It was several times, I mean, ten, fifteen times.

Q. And did the time come when you were asked if you would testify against any of the Defendants here involved today, Detroit Police Officers?

A. That was confusing. . . .

Q. Were you advised that they were considering pressing charges against you? Were you advised of that?

A. I was advised that they were trying to pin the two murders on me. In fact, when I talked to Mr. Kaier of the FBI, I was pretty well shook, because I was under the impression that they were trying to hang these murders on me.

Q. That was just about what he told you, wasn't it?

A. I asked him—I figured I was going to get railroaded. I figured I had had it, and I asked him how many years do you get for each murder.

Q. And it was after that that there was further discussions and you were asked to testify against the Police Officers here?

A. I was confused on this. This, to me, is very distasteful.

Q. Yes.

A. Because these people—you got to take into consideration I called these people. I mean, we worked together out there on the riot and it is hard, because you hate to see anybody lose their job, maybe even have a jail sentence out of something like this. I have very little taste for this, but anyway—

Q. Well, did there come a time when you were told, "Well, we are not going to press charges against you, but we want you to testify"?

A. I will be honest with you; I don't know who I was a witness
    for on the first deal up until the day I was brought into
    Court. I didn't know I was for, for sure, whether I was for
    the Prosecutor or the defense. . . .

Thomas was asked by the Detroit detectives to take a lie-
detector test, and he did. "I could hear the needle, you know,"
he told Ladd Neuman. "And out of the side of my eye, I thought
I could see it move. I couldn't see them, of course. They were
watching through a two-way mirror or something. Boy, there
was one question! They asked me if I'd had a shotgun any time
that day. I know that damned needle pegged when he asked it.
And I even remarked about it. But I guess it's the way you
recover."

On Tuesday, Thomas and Wayne Henson were called in for a
show-up of Detroit police officers, and Thomas took the pre-
caution of getting his commanding officer, Lieutenant Colonel
Howard Dryden, to accompany them. Colonel Dryden did not
have the spirit of Togetherness. He thought that his men were
treated in a hostile manner by the detectives, and that Thomas
was rushed through the line much too fast. "They took us
through in about thirty-three seconds!" he told Neuman. He
threatened to leave, taking his troops with him; then they did
pull out. All three went back the next afternoon for a repeat
performance, with guarantees that the procedure would be more
dignified.

From the police summary:
"On August 1, 1967, at 6:20 PM, Warrant Officer Theodore
Thomas viewed police officers and identified PATROLMAN DAVID
SENAK as one who did the beating of the persons in the line-up.

"On August 1, 1967, at 6:25 PM, Pfc. Wayne Henson viewed
police officers and identified PATROLMAN DAVID SENAK as the officer who questioned the people in the line-up in the lobby of
the Manor House.

"On August 2, 1967, at 2:50 PM, Warrant Officer Theodore

Thomas viewed police officers and identified PATROLMAN RONALD AUGUST as the officer who shot a man, and also identified PATROLMAN DAVID SENAK as the officer who did the questioning and the beating."

5 | One Half-Solved and One Unsolved

On August 2, Detective Schlachter requested from Wayne County Prosecutor William Cahalan warrants for the arrests of Ronald August for the murder of Auburey Pollard and of Robert Paille for the murder of Fred Temple.

Of the three murders, one was half-solved and another was unsolved.

The Pollard case seemed fairly clear-cut; Pollard had been killed by one man at the climax of the killing game, and August, after looking at photographs of the victims, had said he was that man; Thomas, who had witnessed the killing, had also indentified August as the killer. That case was solved.

As to the killing of Carl Cooper, there were no leads but Lawanda Schettler's beery tale. The weight of the evidence, as time passed, indicated that Cooper had run downstairs from A-14 with an apparent intent of escaping through the back door and had run into the first officers to enter the building—but who had they been?

When had the death of Fred Temple take place? Had he been killed without ever leaving room A-3 and without ever having been on the line in the hallway, as the testimony of Thomas and state troopers who said they had seen his body in that room some time before the end of the game would urge; or was he killed last, as the testimony of Temple's best friends, Roderick Davis and Larry Reed, who kept insisting that they had seen him on the line in the hall at the very end, asking permission to go back and get his shoes, would argue? Those who gave the former testimony would have had a motive of trying to prove that Temple's death had taken place *before* their entry into the building or after their departure from it.

There are some hints that Thomas and some of the state

troopers may have seen more than their sworn testimony would suggest they saw; that Thomas may have been in the building earlier and some of the state troopers longer than their testimony made it appear. These hints further suggest that the second body they said they saw may have been Pollard's rather than Temple's.

Here are two such hints:

In his report Trooper P. A. Martin, describing Carl Cooper's body, as if at the time of the troopers' entry into the building, wrote, "Lying beside his left hand was a knife, commonly known by this officer as a Toad Stabber." But Juli Hysell told Stephen Schlesinger, a Harvard law student who was gathering material for an article, "I saw one of the policemen place a knife next to Carl Cooper's body—the same one which had been used to threaten Clark." If Juli was telling the truth, and if her observation was correct, the knife did not appear beside Cooper's body until after part of the game had been played; some troopers may have witnessed the second killing, or at least been present in the annex when it took place.

By his own account Thomas did witness one of the killings—that of Auburey Pollard, at the climax of the game. In the Dismukes trial, Prosecutor Weiswasser gave Thomas a scare by asking him if he had not, in his telephone call to Sergeant-Major Kazup at the command center, said he had reason to think a policeman had murdered a prisoner. (Kazup, in a statement to the police, had reported, "Thomas said he realized a police officer had murdered a prisoner," and that this was a "bad business.") "I did make that statement," Thomas admitted. But in all his testimony to that point, Thomas had tried to make it seem that his call to Colonel Dryden and Kazup had taken place before he had entered the annex. After this, one had to conclude either that Thomas had called after he had been in the building or that some state troopers had witnessed a murder and told him about it.

It is hard for me to believe that Fred Temple's two close friends could have been mistaken about seeing him in the line at the end. It could be suggested that they were lying—that they had seen their friend shot early in the incident and that they had agreed upon a fabrication in terror of the consequences of telling the truth; but in view of the willingness, and even determination, of all the black witnesses to take risks in their testimony on the Algiers case, this possibility seems remote to me. At the very least, there was some fishiness about the chronologies offered by Thomas and the troopers.

An easily solved problem: Whose word would be worth more, in the long run, to a white judge and a white jury in a court of law? That of uniformed white men, or that of black youths hanging around a place like the Algiers Motel and of a white girl who would consort with such as they?

6 | No Pistol Was Found

Prosecutor Cahalan, knowing that David Senak had been implicated in one of the killings by Paille's confession, had no corroborating evidence. He did know that Senak had helped to kill Joseph Chandler as he vaulted over a back-yard fence on the second day of the disturbance; and now another report was in, describing another killing by Senak on the Friday of the riot:

"At 10:45 p.m., Fri., July 28, 1967, Scout 13-5 (a 5-man car) received a radio run to 570 E. Kirby, 'man with a gun.' . . .

"From the investigation and interviews, it appears that PAL-MER GRAY, Jr., the deceased, had gone to 570 E. Kirby, Apt. #2, where he became involved in an argument over money with his father, PALMER GRAY, Sr. They went outside and tussled, and the deceased became enraged and threw bricks and rocks through the windows of Apartment #2. The deceased then left and returned later, armed with a small cal. black gun and threatened to kill everyone there. ELLEN GREYS called the police and the deceased left the apartment.

"The officers arrived at the scene and were told what had happened and went to 5341 St. Antoine, where PATROLMAN SENAK and Patrolmen Carroll and Alcorn went to the rear of the building. While they were in the alley, Patrolman Evans, who was in the front of the building, saw a Negro male, later identified as PALMER GRAY, Jr., armed with a rifle, run across St. Antoine. Patr. Evans yelled this information to the officers, and Patrolmen Carroll and Alcorn ran toward Kirby to intercept this man. PATROLMAN SENAK ran in an aisleway between the buildings, and as he reached the sidewalk at St. Antoine, he saw PALMER GRAY, Jr., on the sidewalk in front of 5341 St. Antoine with a rifle in his hands.

"The deceased pointed the rifle at PATROLMAN SENAK, and the officer ordered him to drop the rifle, which he did. The deceased then whirled and ran up the stairs at 5341 St. Antoine, ignoring the officer's orders to halt. PATROLMAN SENAK then fired one shot from his revolver (a Smith & Wesson 6-shot. 41 Cal. Magnum Revolver, Serial #69073, personally owned and Department-approved) into the wall as the deceased turned the corner on the stairway.

"The deceased ran to the top of the stairs on the 3rd floor, with PATROLMAN SENAK in pursuit. At this time, PATROLMAN SENAK ordered the deceased to raise his hands. Instead, the deceased ran back down the stairs toward the officer and reached into his pocket as if to draw a gun. The officer, being previously apprized by witnesses at 570 E. Kirby that the man had threatened them with a small dark-colored hand gun, feared the deceased was about to draw his gun, and fired one shot from his revolver, fatally wounding the deceased as described. No hand gun or other weapon was found on the deceased's person or in the immediate area at this time."

Prosecutor Cahalan, who ruled Gray's death not to have been riot-connected, now knew that of 4,400 policemen who had been out during the uprising in which there had been forty-three riot-connected deaths and this other one, a single policeman had had a hand in two killings, had been implicated in a third, and had been in the near presence of two others.

7 | One Night in Jail

On July 7, August and Paille were arraigned.

"They held us," Paille, who in his time on the force had taken a good number of citizens to jail, told me, "for one night in the county prison. It was the most awkward night of my life. During that time there, I tell you, it really was something. We were confined to an area there, isolated, and—we were both together—and jeez, it was, you know, it was almost unbreathable in that place, it was all closed and no windows or anything. It was hot in there, it was in the summertime, you see, and all night there you couldn't sleep, because, you know, it was just a bumpy little old mattress and everything else there, you know. I had to kind of position myself in one position there, if I'd rolled over either way I'd have fallen on the floor, and in the middle of the night, they had some guy out there, he was mopping the floors there, and I put a hanger against the door just in case somebody came along and tried to steal my wallet, which I had on my person, and he knocked the hanger over there, and he turned the light on, so right away I saw who he was, and he just left. But it seemed that all night there everybody was flushing the toilet all at one time, you know. And it was, you know, unbearably hot and everything else there, and just the thought of being in prison, all closed off from the world and everything else there. Unbearable!

"They held us for one night in the jail, and then the next day we went back to court, and they had looked into their logs and so forth there and found that on previous occasions they had released prisoners for this charge, murder, that they had us on at the time, and then they released us from that day on, on a bond, five-thousand-dollar bond, two sureties."

31

First Man in Court

1 | Alacrity

Actually the first man to have been brought to the threshold of punishment was Melvin Dismukes, the Negro private guard.

On Sunday evening, July 30, a show-up was staged at police headquarters, at which Sortor, Michael, Clara Gilmore, and two others viewed a number of black men, including the four private guards who had been at the Algiers on the night of the incident. Sortor identified Dismukes "as the person who beat him and others while lined up in the lobby of the Manor House"; and Michael picked Dismukes out, too.

Attorney Nicholas Smith, who took Dismukes's case because he was counsel for St. John's Episcopal Church, of which Dismukes's father was sexton, objected later to the treatment Dismukes received at the hands of the police on the evening of the show-up. Dismukes, according to Smith, had gone in voluntarily to see what help he could be and heard himself being told to fall in for a show-up. Smith was not present; Dismukes was told he was being represented by a lawyer named Seymore Posner, a member of the so-called Clinton Street Bar, which consists of hangers-around who seek appointments from judges. Smith based his objection on a Supreme Court decision in 1966, in *Wade vs. California,* in which the Court ruled that a show-up is a critical part of a proceeding and that denial of counsel at a show-up is a denial of due process; Smith argued that Dismukes was, in effect, denied his own counsel.

After the show-up, the police took Dismukes to the Fifteenth Precinct lock-up and held him for the night. Learning of this the next morning, Smith requested that Dismukes be brought at once to Recorder's Court, and Smith went there and waited all morning for his appearance. It was almost noon before Dismukes was brought in, saying that he had been told by detectives in the meantime that his attorney had granted permission for his subjection to a polygraph test; he had submitted to it. Smith, while acknowledging that, if asked, he would have given permission for a lie-detector test, said that whoever told Dismukes that the permission had been obtained simply lied.

Before August and Paille had been arrested, Dismukes was arraigned before Judge Samuel H. Olsen of Recorder's Court, charged with felonious assault. He pleaded not guilty. The very next day, on August 4, a pretrial examination was held. Sortor was the only witness. He testified that Dismukes had beaten him with "a stick, blackjack, you know, one of them long sticks like a club. . . . He just struck me with the stick and asked me where, where was the gun." Sortor told of Dismukes's having driven him to his knees and then having hit again "across my shoulder." Michael Clark had also been brought to testify, but Judge Olsen decided he had heard enough to bind Dismukes over for trial.

Two of the families of the victims of the murders at the Algiers asked me the same question, in effect: Why was the first man to be picked out at a show-up, why was the first man to be arrested for all that happened at the Algiers, why was the only man involved in the case to be charged with felonious assault, why was the first man to be bound over for trial, why was the first man to be taken into court in a hearing—why was this man a black man? What was it about the system of justice that produced this singular alacrity?

32

Logical to Be Nervous

1 | If We Can't Get Justice

For Mrs. Pollard, who had herself been hospitalized for a month in 1963 with a nervous breakdown after a brother of hers was murdered, her son Chaney's mental collapse after seeing Auburey's body at Wilson's Funeral Home was, both as an echo and in itself, deeply painful, and the pain was compounded when she took Chaney to the United States Public Health Service Hospital and was unable to get psychiatric care for him.

"Tell you how dirty Detroit is," she said to me, "the Veterans, with knowing he'd been in Vietnam for twelve months over there, they wouldn't even give him no psychiatric care or no nerve pills for his nerves after I told them that he was having a nervous breakdown on account of seeing his brother like he was, because they was so close together; see, Chaney was twenty-one and Auburey would have been twenty that Friday. Doctor said it was logical for him to be nervous; he said he'd be nervous, too, if his brother had got killed like his did, see. Only thing they told me to do was take him out of Detroit, to make him feel better. They just put that writing on a paper, but they didn't give him nothing.

"So I took him to Cleveland, to my sister in Cleveland, Daisy Hamilton. We was there about a week.

"So I put my boy up in the plane; he was supposed to go back to Vietnam. When I put him in that plane in Cleveland I knew he'd never make it.

"The way I heard it, some newspapermen went up in the plane to interview him, he had some scratches that was from being over there, he thought that one of those men wanted to kill him like they killed his brother. What did he do? Thought he had to defend himself and got in a ruckus. They jumped him and put him off the plane and put him in the hospital. He wasn't supposed to be up there, he was a sick man in the beginning, they shouldn't even have let him get on that plane. They had to lower the plane in California.

"Since this happened I got one letter from him, wasn't nothing on there, didn't even tell me where he was. So I was suspicious then; it was from Oakland, California, then it had a Red Cross on it, but other than that, getting a letter from him, I didn't hear nothing.

"You know how I found out? I kept worrying the Red Cross, and finally he begin to come to hisself and he called where I used to live at, and he talked to my mother-in-law, and my mother-in-law didn't even get the hospital number, I had to get it through the Red Cross. That's how I found out he was sick. And they been having him down there and treating him. United States Naval Hospital, 49B Ward, that's in Oakland, California. I even wrote his commanding officer and didn't get no letter, expecting that he had got back, because he was supposed to go right back to Vietnam. I don't even want him back over there, I don't know what he's going to fight for. If we can't get justice in the United States, that boy laying them land mines and booby traps over there, building roads, him thinking a lot of his commanding officer, I don't want him back over there, them murdering my son like they did. I don't know what kind

of justice the United States got, but they sure ain't got none.
That's the way I feel about it. So you can write that in writing.
I want it out. I want to let them know how they killed Auburey.
Just because two white girls sitting on the bed there with six
or seven boys. How in the hell they know who they was with?
Why'd they have to pick *him* and kill him? I asked the girls.
They said, 'Mrs. Pollard, we never went to bed with Auburey.
He was a good boy.' And they said to them white women, called
them nigger lovers and like they was a dog. Tell you what:
They wasn't doing it for my son. It's a hurting feeling. They
couldn't have did that if they'd gone into a white hotel and
there'd been some of them colored women sitting down there
with some white men; they'd have walked out the door. And
ain't no colored man going to go in no white hotel and go up
like that and shoot and get set free. This is what hurts so bad."

33

Senak's Peninsula

1 | Crime and Punishment

Although, because of insufficiency of evidence, David Senak was not arrested with the others, he had been suspended from the police force on July 31 on the basis of what Robert Paille and others had said about his role in the incident.

"After that," Senak told me, "I spent a lot of time on Belle Isle"—the city-owned island park in the Detroit River. "Just reading. I had a special peninsula over there. There was a tree on the end of it. I'd just go over there almost every day, and take a couple of books along and read. I was reading a series of books, *The Art of Clear Thinking* and *The Art of Clear Writing, Clear Reading;* I like law materials; I read some books on cross-examination. I got involved with novels. *Crime and Punishment.* I started *An American Tragedy* again, second time I started it and didn't finish it. That went on till it got cold. Till one day I came over to the island, and they chopped my peninsula down. This girl used to come out there with me, every once in a while when she had a day off, and we were going out there one day, and we came along and I was looking for my landmark, the tree, and the thing wasn't there. Couple of hundred feet down there was this big DPW truck, and they had this big tree in the back. It was because of erosion, it was undermining the roots of the tree, and it was going to fall into the water eventually, so they figured they'd just cut it down. I don't know what kind of tree it was, it was just a shade tree; but it was a nice spot. I was really upset at the time. I wasn't upset because of the circumstances of my suspension, because every time I saw August I tried to comfort him, in the fact that we were innocent—that's beside the point—I was despondent because of the fact that I wasn't on the job. I was no longer in a scout car. And to this day when I see the scout cars, you know, I get upset."

34

These Are Not Little Boys

1 | People vs. Policemen

On August 14, in Recorder's Court, the city bench that handles, in the first instance, criminal trials in Detroit, and which is all too symbolically situated next door to Police Headquarters, Judge Robert E. DeMascio began the pretrial examination in *The People of the State of Michigan vs. Ronald August and Robert Paille.*

That morning fifty-five policemen crowded into the heavy oak benches at the rear of Judge DeMascio's courtroom in a demonstration of support for the two accused men. Also present were members of the families of the murdered men and a number of other black spectators.

The hearing began with a little fuss over furniture.

THE COURT: I don't know whose idea it was to switch these tables around, but I like this court room looking the same way every time. Was there some reason for switching them around? No one asked the Court to do it.

MR. LIPPITT: I made no such request, Your Honor.

THE COURT: Well, switch them back. I think if we settle things at the beginning, we'll be all right at the end.

2 | Whispers

Judge DeMascio, who wanted things just so, was a forty-five-year-old married man with three children. Born in Coraopolis, Pennsylvania, he moved to Detroit with his family as a child; graduated from Eastern High School and majored in government at the College of Applied Sciences, Wayne State University, from which he graduated in 1943; then earned a bachelor-of-laws degree at Wayne Law School. He served briefly in the Navy. From 1954 to 1962 he was on the staff of the U.S. Attorney's office, and for the last two of those years was an Assistant Attorney in charge of the criminal division; he cracked down on pornography and successfully prosecuted a case involving obscene literature in the mails. Running as a Republican, he was defeated in campaigns for a judgeship in Common Pleas in 1961 and for Wayne County Prosecutor in 1962; in the latter election he accused two opponents of carrying on a campaign of rumor and gossip on the issue of race relations, saying that the two men "hope to win support on their whispered views and images in relation to Negro citizens." One of the candidates, he said, was "spending all his energies to wooing and winning the Negro vote"; DeMascio called on Democrats to cross over to him in protest against this tactic.

3 | Witnesses

After the tables were rearranged, and after an agreement had been made that all witnesses who had been called would be sequestered from the courtroom before testifying and from other witnesses afterward, the hearing proper got under way.

Auburey Pollard's father and Fred Temple's brother Eddie were called first and second, to testify on identification of the bodies, and Clara Raven, the Medical Examiner from the morgue, described the wounds.

Then Michael Clark came on. Prosecutor Weiswasser elicited from him an account of what he had seen in the annex, parts of which we have already come across; Michael was rather subdued and had to be told to speak up. He put it on the record under oath that Ronald August and Robert Paille had taken him into room A-4 when the death game began, whereas, as we have seen, David Senak and Theodore Thomas actually presided over that phase of the proceedings. With his obvious contempt for the judicial system, Michael Clark in all hearings simply named whoever was in sight as his tormentors. Occasionally he became peppery, particularly while being cross-examined by Attorney Lippitt.

Q. Who was in Room A-4 with you at the time you heard Pollard being taken to A-3?

A. There was another fellow in there, but I couldn't see his face because he was laying down.

Q. Were there any soldiers or policemen in room A-4 with you at that time?

A. If I'm looking at the floor I cannot see who's in there.

Q. Did you hear any soldiers or policemen standing over you or near you when you were lying on the floor in room A-4?

A. That soldier was still there because he hadn't moved.

Q. Could you see him?

A. I could see his shoes, yeah.

Roderick Davis followed. He testified to having heard shooting "upstairs," which reinforced the idea that there might actually have been snipers in the annex; then Larry Reed testified briefly. Both Davis and Reed said that they had seen Fred Temple in the line at the very end, as they were leaving. But Trooper John Fonger, who came next, testified to having seen a body, which must have been Temple's, in A-3, during the supposedly short stay of the state police in the annex, earlier.

Detective Lyle Thayer testified that Homicide's first word of the incident had come from the morgue, not from the public.

4 | Rights

The crux of the hearing came on the second day, when Prosecutor Weiswasser put Detective James Cowie, who had taken Ronald August's first written statement on July 31, on the stand.

The issue was drawn by Attorney Lippitt as he objected to the admission of that statement as evidence: "A police officer is in a very peculiar position when there are criminal implications involved in a report that he may have to make to superior officers or to any other commanding officer in the Police Department."

Put another way, the question was whether August and Paille should have been informed of their constitutional rights before being asked to make out a report of their activities at a scene where murders had apparently been committed.

Put yet a third way, the question might have been: How could the Detroit Homicide Bureau, which was in the business of investigating murders, have made such a blunder as to fail to inform a man, even a man on the force, of his constitutional rights before asking him to make a statement that might incriminate him?

"If Your Honor please," Weiswasser tried to argue, "these were police officers sophisticated in the knowledge of their constitutional rights, having been trained in this and in what they should tell people."

But Judge DeMascio wanted to defer his ruling until he had heard testimony from Detective Cowie's superiors.

5 | Confused

While the higher-ups were being assembled, Weiswasser put on Warrant Officer Thomas, who was confused, as we have seen, as to whether he was on the side of the People or on the side of the police; at times he was confused period—especially when the defense lawyer made him squirm with discomfort at ratting on a uniformed colleague.

Q. You saw the flash before you heard the gunshot, I think I heard you say?

A. I can't say for sure.

Q. You don't know which came first?

A. It is pretty confusing.

And again:

Q. You said before, when I cross-examined you, that you were confused and didn't know what point of time these things happened. Are you confused?

A. Yes, sir.

Q. Thank you.

A. I can't—

Q. Thank you.

Despite his muddle, Thomas told of having seen August shoot Auburey Pollard; at least, when all that he said was stitched together, it amounted to that.

After Thomas, Weiswasser introduced Detectives Schwaller, Schlachter, and Cowie again, in an effort to get the officers' various statements, and especially the confessions, on the record.

6 | All They Had to Do

MR. LIPPITT: I think what is crystal clear here, Your Honor, is that these men were under an intolerable situation. They were under this duress, which we say is inherent, and for that reason they wanted to change their statement. They had no other choice; they had no other choice.

MR. WEISWASSER: All right. All they had to do was keep quiet. If they kept quiet, they wouldn't be here today.

7 | No Less

After lunch that day, Judge DeMascio delivered himself of the key ruling, under which, in the end, Robert Paille was set free:

"There is not only the crime of homicide that could have come out of this investigation, but other crimes. And this complaint and warrant maybe could have resulted in naming one,

two, or maybe more. So I think at the time he owed an obligation to these two citizens in advising them in giving any kind of
statement that they had a right to remain silent; that they had a
right to consult counsel; and anything that they said could be
used against them in a court of law.

"That would be so if there was any other person. If it was
a regular, ordinary citizen, this Court would feel compelled to
make the same ruling, to rule that the police would have to advise an ordinary citizen that in this discussion or interview,
'Whatever you say might be used against you.'

"I don't think these two defendants, because they are police
officers, have any right to expect anything more; but they have
a right under the Constitution not to settle for anything less.

"I therefore rule that the statement is inadmissible."

8 | Parable

COURT: I know a little boy who lied to his mother, and he went
to tell his father, and his father clobbered him one, and he
thought he was going to his father to soothe his conscience,
and maybe his mother should have told him, 'Son, don't
say anything if you have to lie.' I don't know, Mr. Weiswasser, but I know this: That these men were not advised
of the Constitutional rights in the first instance.

MR. WEISWASSER: There is only one thing—one thing wrong
with Your Honor's example. These are not little boys.

9 | Foregone Conclusion

After the setback on the constitutional issue, there was not much
Prosecutor Weiswasser could do. He put Lieutenant Hallmark,
the man to whom August and Paille confessed, on the stand on
the second and third days, in a prolonged struggle to introduce
the confessions, but it was clear from the start that the same issue
would thwart him; and it did.

Only when he came to August's final statement, taken after

August had at last been informed of his rights by the Homicide Bureau, was he allowed to introduce a document. And this was the statement in which August had wrapped a claim of self-defense around himself.

10 | What's Funny?

David Senak appeared briefly as a witness on the third day. He declared under oath that he had not seen August or Paille fire a weapon inside the annex, and:

Q. Did you at any time fire a weapon inside the Manor House?

A. Inside?

Q. Inside. At any person?

A. No.

"When we were in court," Mrs. Gill told me, speaking of Senak, "he was sitting there bantering, you know, and when we went down to have coffee he was down there laughing, you know, just standing there grinning, and I said, 'Now, what's funny?' And then Mrs. Pollard went up and got a newspaper reporter, just to show him how he was acting down there, and he just stood there and laughed at them, as if to say that you can't win, or something, and then during court, that's what he was doing, sitting up there grinning, you know, like a person that don't have 'em all. And he's only twenty-five years old."

11 | We Felt Pretty Confident

By the fourth day, when the court assembled to hear Judge DeMascio's decision, the atmosphere surrounding the hearing—essentially the growing anger of the black onlookers at the realization that an old, old story was going to be told again—grew tense.

"The last day of the murder hearings," Paille told me, "Snick was all over the room, that's a Negro organization, and we had a rumor that they were going to kill us that day, so I told August, I says, 'If there's any shooting over here, just dive down there, and I'll get over you,' and that there. Try to conceal him and that. And, you know, we'd stay out of the line of fire and all. But it happens that about fifty policemen showed up that day, too, so we felt pretty confident we'd get out of there okay. But the Muslims were there, Snick was there."

12 | Decision

Judge DeMascio's decision was that, failing the presence of the statements he had ruled out, including the confessions, there was nothing on Paille, but there was enough evidence in Thomas's fuzzy testimony to justify indicting August for murder—though the judge added, in a startling weighing of character rather than of evidence, "On the other hand, it is totally unlike defendant August."

The decision:

"Accordingly, the motion of the People is granted as to defendant August; it is denied as to defendant Paille.

"In view of the fact that in searching the record this Court found no reason to upset the judgment of one of the judges in setting bail, the bail as to defendant August is continued and that as to defendant Paille is cancelled."

13 | How Could It Be Self-Defense?

After the ruling, August's wife and mother sat sobbing at one of the tables. A picket line of plain-clothesmen formed across the front of the gallery to insulate the court from the crowd, which began to file out. Still in the courtroom, Mrs. Pollard started shouting at Judge DeMascio.

"It started," she told me, "with me yelling in the courtroom, when they was going to turn loose the police, and I say, 'How in the hell could it be self-defense? My boy didn't have no knife, didn't have no gun. And *he* had the gun. How could it be self-defense?' I just jumped up and told the truth. I couldn't take it no more. Turning them loose, and everybody was telling lies. I just told the judge, 'Don't turn them loose! Don't turn loose that son of a bitch, because I know damn well he's lying.' And I said, 'When he say he pulled the trigger one time and it didn't go off and pulled it another time he was lying. He done beat his damn face off before he started shooting him up. How in the hell could it be self-defense? He done beat him till he turned helpless. When he beat him, that was enough! I told the judge, I says, 'You know he's lying.' The judge didn't want to say anything. And I said to that prosecutor there, I say, 'You that's on his side, you know damn well he's lying. Because you all know you all beat his face off. Then you going to tell me it's self-defense! No way in hell it could be self-defense.' They started grabbing me and holding me and put me out of the courtroom. It was on television and on the radio. The man put the microphone out and said, 'Put it right here.' I want the world to know about it. I want everybody to know it. And I'm going to stay fighting and I'm going to hold up because I'm a damn good woman. It's not going to get me down. I might go down afterwards but I'm not going down before. I ain't planning on killing myself, and I'm not planning on hurting myself. But I'll tell you one thing, you'll see one thing: I'm going to fight this case as long as I got breath in me. I am. I'm telling you."

14 | A Mean Face

"Every time that I came out of court there," Paille told me, "I could see these people lining the hallways, and that there, and they could cry out in court and everything else. And there was one fellow there, he just stood there and he looked at me with a mean face and everything else, just like he was going to grab me, and I think that one time, one fellow was ready to grab August. And as I drove my car out from the underground portion of the building there, I could see these fellows with beards and everything else there, looked like Muslims, were waiting out there. So we didn't know what to expect."

35

The Law Was Made
by People

1 | Sickening, Man

It would be for other and eventually higher judges to sustain or overrule Judge DeMascio's decision on the constitutional issue in the murder hearing. But as to the perception of "justice" by the families of the Algiers victims, the response was immediate and virulent. The bare facts were known to all: The young men who had survived the incident had told them what Paille had done to them at the Algiers; Paille had been charged with killing Fred Temple, obviously for some reason; now he was scot-free, walking the streets of Detroit without bail. August, who had now been indicted but had tipped his hand that he would claim self-defense, was also at large, on bail, to be sure, but free.

"They told this other policeman," Omar Gill said to me, "that his statement couldn't be used in court that he made at the Police Department, stating that he killed Auburey Pollard, saying because he wasn't advised of his legal rights, and when a policeman picks you up he *tells* you of your legal rights, so he *knew* his legal rights. Why did he have to be advised of them? It was sickening, man, it was really sickening. If you could have seen it you would have just throwed up your hands."

2 | Over My Dead Body

"That judge," Mrs. Pollard said to me, "putting words in the police's mouth—that weren't nothing but a fishy trial. I even hate that damned judge. They ought to get his ass off the stand, so there can be justice. That's the way I feel about it. It hurts.

"Everybody got a temper to a certain extent. I got one. I got one. And I feel if those damned judges turn those policemen loose I feel I should start something in that damned courtroom, I feel that something should happen to them, and I feel if I was able I would do something to them, if I could do it. If I had something to do it with, I would. I been thinking about it. I just ain't got anything to worry me. I feel they got the dirtiest judge there is.

"And I'm like this man that came on television, I can't call his name, and he said, 'Let there be a white policeman and a colored policeman together when they go in these places.' And if they'd take the white polices out of the colored neighborhood I think he told the truth about it. Because one day two white policemen will be running in some of these colored neighborhoods, and some of these here places, and they going to have the same thing written on them that they did in the Algiers Motel. And it won't be no more than justice. Because you can't trust them in your house. And I feel right now, if the policeman came to my door and he was just a white police, I don't think I'd let him in. He could break down the door, that's the only way he could get in, but I don't think he could get in here. And I don't think as long as I live another one better set foot in my house. Now if a colored one come along, I'd open my door, but I'm not going to let another damned white police come in my house. That's the way I feel about it. If he do, he'll come over my dead body. That's the way I feel about it."

3 | What the Law Is For

"Those police," Mr. Pollard said to me, "was prejudiced in the first place. They was taught to be prejudiced in the first place. The average gray, you know for your own self, is brought up with the prejudice instinct within him. He don't want no black boy living over here. 'The black boy brings my property down.' We both know that, don't we, huh? Now you take it out at Birmingham, you think if I would move to Birmingham, by tomorrow afternoon—well, you know what I mean!

"You have to have enough common sense to know ignorance when you meet it. Because any time that a gentleman is over some thirty years old, and he's not a mental case, he's supposed to be broad-minded enough not to go out and slaughter a eighteen- or nineteen-year-old-kid. And I'll tell Judge DeMascio the same thing.

"The law is like this. The law was made by people, the people made the law. The community are the people, and the community made the law. The community did not make the law to be brutality. They made the law so they could have respect. The average Negro don't know that, he don't even know what the law is for. Now, you take the average Negro boy walking up and down the street, the police grabs him, hang his hands up side of the wall, go in his pockets, pull everything out he's got, kick him in the butt, turn him loose—he thinks he lucky because he's loose! Because he don't know no better. Now, send the same police out in Palmer Park, the same guys, and let them start kicking *those* young kids in the fanny, and see how long he'll do it. They'll put him so far out here in River Rouge walking around in a circle with nothing to hold him up and he'll have to stay till it's pitiful. Because the big shots that go up there aren't going for that, they're not going to go for that. But the Negro, he can talk loud but he doesn't have no help. He doesn't help himself."

4 | A Solution

"If those guys want to fight all that bad," Mr. Pollard said, "why in the hell don't they go over to Vietnam? All they got to do is take all those nuts that wants it bad, put them on a truck, drive them out, and say, 'Now, this is unknown territory, you can just fight and kill till you get your fill. When you come back we'll be sitting here waiting for you. And we'll give you a big Purple Heart.' "

5 | Too Young to Die

"I still say they're lying," Mr. Pollard said. "Every one of them is lying. Because somebody is covering up for somebody else. Each one of those kids was too young to die for nothing. Somebody's lying."

6 | A Letter

"Mrs. Temple sent me a letter in her own way there," Robert Paille told me. "She stated in so many words that if you did kill my son, which, you know, would be immoral, I hope you're getting everything that's coming to you. But she didn't say too much on the innocent side, you know. It was all illiterate, you know; *i*'s were small and all."

36

Law and Order for All?

1 | One Flame in a Nationwide Fire

On the second day of the murder hearing, as it happened, Mayor
Cavanagh and a team of men from his administration appeared
in Washington before the President's Commission on Civil Disorders.

There was an air of sadness and weariness in the Detroit dele-
gation. Before its riot Detroit had been one of our cities of hope,
and Mayor Cavanagh had been widely praised as one of the most
forward-looking urban leaders in the country. Now there were
ashes in his mouth as he began his presentation with a long cata-
logue of the warnings to all America that he had been uttering
for five years. He reviewed the history of race relations in Detroit, highlighting the race riot of 1943 and an incident in 1966
in the Kercheval district that might have flared into a mass disturbance but did not. The best he could manage was to relate
Detroit's great rebellion to a national condition.

"I think it should be emphasized from the beginning," he
said, "that both the incident last year in Detroit and this year's

tragedy are part of a national picture of deep discontent in American cities today.

"The explosion that ripped Detroit had many points of origin over a long, long period of time. It has its links with events of recent years in Washington, D.C.; in Birmingham and Tuscaloosa, Alabama; in Jackson, Mississippi; in Cambridge, Maryland; in Kansas City, Missouri; in the Watts district in Los Angeles; in Harlem and Bedford-Stuyvesant in New York City; on the South Side in Chicago; and in the cotton fields of Louisiana and Texas. . . .

"There has been no discernible relationship between the location or degree of violence in these disorders to social or economic or governmental factors. If there was a pattern, it was a crazy quilt. It is clear from our experience that you cannot extinguish a single flame in a general fire. You must extinguish the entire fire, and damp down all the sparks and ignition points.

"The explosion in Detroit was one flame in a nationwide fire. A spark fell in Detroit, and an ignition took place. Newark seemed to set the sparks flying, but the elements of combustion were there for many, many years.

"Every city has its individual aspects—its strengths and its weaknesses. We thought we were in a stronger position in terms of human relations than many other cities. Every outside observer agreed that we were. And I believe we were. But the difference wasn't deep or fundamental enough to forestall the catastrophe."

2 | The Fuse

After reviewing the specific short-range precautions his administration had taken "to forestall the catastrophe"—the Mayor's Summer Task Force, an Early Warning System, summertime activities at 589 recreation centers, the full range of anti-poverty programs ("funded at levels well below recognized needs in the city"), and a package of summer programs and summer-employment efforts which were all delayed by funding difficulties—he mentioned, for the only time specifically in his report, the Detroit Police Department, and then it was merely to point with pride to its "battle-tested" riot-control plan, from which we have seen some quotations, and to wonder whether the summer's labor troubles and the blue flu had affected police performance during the riot.

The Mayor then showed the commission some movies of the uprising, and after the lights went back on in the hearing room he said, "Look at the faces. You will see mostly young men. These young men are the fuse. For the most part they have no experience in real productive work. For the most part, they have no stake in the social arrangements of life. For the most part, they have no foreseeable future except among the hustlers and minor racketeers. For the most part, they are cynical, hostile, frustrated, and angry against a system they feel has included them out. At the same time, they are filled with the bravado of youth and a code of behavior which is hostile to authority."

3 | The Danger

"When a substantial number of people in a community come to feel that law and order is their enemy and their oppressor, that community is in danger. Such groups exist in most of our communities today."

4 | Molotov Cocktail

"As for those," the Mayor said later on, "who feel that the total answer to the situation—to the dangers whose manifestations we have seen—is simply more guns, clubs, and force, they are wrong, catastrophically wrong.

"Of course, the increased availability and more effective use of peace-keeping forces is vital and essential.

"But those who cherish the thought that the situation, nationwide, can be dealt with simply by sterner measures of force and repression are deluding themselves.

"Repression without channels of release is a Molotov cocktail. It takes only one match to set it off, and then its destructive effects can spread everywhere."

One must trust that the Mayor believed what he said, yet when, after many, many more words, he came to proposals for solutions, the very first of seventeen major recommendations was this:

"1. To restore law and order we must modernize our techniques for dealing with mob action, adopt the latest scientific devices, revamp our plans for dealing with civil disorder by planning for a more effective and fluid governmental response. I have requested planning assistance from the Secretary of the Army (letter attached) and support federal legislation which will grant aid directly to the cities in training, equipping, and paying police officers. There is the need for a federal riot police force to be located in our major cities and to be a part of the local police. I have asked Governor Romney to consider the formation of National Guard Riot Battalions located in the metropolitan areas to provide skilled and speedy response to civil disorders."

I do not mean to suggest by this ironic juxtaposition that our cities should abandon the principle that the business of life should be transacted in a setting of law and order. The point here is that the city of Detroit, in its presentation to the commission, failed to ask such questions as these:

In what relationship does the need for law and order stand to other pressing needs in our society? Or, to put it another way, whence stems widespread consent to law and order?

What kind of law and order must we have?

Is the law equally applied to all citizens?

Should law be used to support or to retard obviously needed changes in the fabric of society?

As things actually go in our cities and states, are not the performances of the agencies that enforce the law and keep the order—namely, the police, the irregular military, and the courts —heavily stacked against all who happen not to be white?

Is there time for gradual reform?

Do we not need—does not the Algiers Motel incident help us to see that we need—an urgent and thoroughgoing overhaul of our national system of policing and judging and penalizing, to the end that every United States citizen would truly be able to perceive law and order as benefits to himself?

5 | Not a Word

Not in all the several hundred pages of the report of Detroit's appearance before the commission, and not even in the sixty pages of tightly detailed summary of large and little occurrences in the uprising, entitled "Sequence of Events," is there a single word about the killings at the Algiers.

37

Under Indictment

1 | You Just Can't Sit

"After this happened I was home for a month," Ronald August told me. "I was suspended one week after the incident happened, then they issued a warrant for arrest two weeks after this incident happened. In the mail I had threats. My phone is unlisted. Haven't had one phone call that was a threat; had a few that offered help as far as assistance in attorney fees and so on and so forth, that came through the switchboard, Bell Telephone, that shouldn't even have got here, but they got through. Now if anyone wanted to make a threat, apparently they didn't get through, I don't know. I've just had mail. I'd give a guess at about six letters, which it came within a week after the incident. I stayed home for a month, just did nothing. My friends naturally came over and talked to me, and this was no good, either, because you just can't sit and do nothing. So I started working grounds maintenance. Our job was raking leaves and edging along the sidewalk and curb lines. It was a very good job if you like outdoor work, and which I do. But this is sort of a seasonal operation."

38

A Mother Speaks

1 | I Want Justice

The first time I talked to Mrs. Pollard, she told me her husband was still so upset that she was not living with him but had taken an apartment with her daughter, the youngest child, Thelma; her oldest son, Chaney, who had been brought back from Vietnam after the killing, was in a Naval hospital with a nervous breakdown; her second son, Auburey, was dead; her third son, Tanner, was in the Detroit House of Correction on a fifteen-day sentence for driving without a license; and her fourth son, Robert, was in prison for three years for stealing seven dollars from a newsboy.

"This broke up our whole house," she said. "Everything fell apart all at once. Including my girl that would stick by me and love me, I couldn't go nowhere, so nervous, so shocked. So the onlybody that's holding up is me and my daughter; we the only two living together. And she couldn't sleep at night without the lights on; she was scared in the other house, but she can sleep here with the lights off. Maybe my husband he might get well,

328

he might come to hisself; he come to hisself, we might be back together, but as long as he ain't hisself we can't be together. They'll wait till he do something out there, then they'll pull him in the hospital, or put him in jail, one. So it's just one of those things.

"My other boy, he's having a nervous breakdown; he needs psychiatric treatment. Both of them. *All three* of them. Since Auburey died, they don't have no good mind, they don't have no good spirits, they don't got no good mind about nothing.

"They got Tanner doing time. He's in the House of Correction right now. For driving without a license. And I swear I know they can give the police some time because they did a murder. Tanner's doing time, Robert's doing time. Robert couldn't even come home to the funeral. He didn't kill nobody, but still this policeman walks the streets. See, Robert robbed a paperboy. He's still doing time for that. They give him three years. Three years. And they ain't give that police not a day; that's what I can't understand. If they give Robert three years, they sure and hell ought to do something with them. That's the way I feel about it.

"I'm the onliest one, me and my daughter, that ain't went to pieces. Somebody's got to hold up. My husband, he's a Navy man, and he stayed in World War II from it started till it ended. And when he went to that morgue and identified Auburey, he ain't been right since.

"Mrs. Hudson, the Red Cross lady, I worried her so much she helped me to find Chaney. And I wrote his doctor a letter but I haven't got no answer from it. And I wrote his commanding officer; I didn't get no answer from it. Because he's supposed to go back to Vietnam, but I really don't want him to go back. In his state of mind he'd just as soon throw himself before a gun, one of them booby traps, or be nervous and blow up hisself and his crew with him. I don't want him back. She say he's in the best hospital out there in Oakland, California, but they haven't notified me; they haven't said *nothing*.

"The thing what hurt so bad, when we went to court, the

judge was telling the polices how to talk. He was telling them how to talk. And he was throwing out those cases just like that. He throwed out Fred Temple's killer, he throwed out Carl Cooper's killer." (No one was ever arrested for Cooper's death.) "And he was telling the polices how to talk to keep themselves from indicting they self. And the only reason they got Auburey's killer is because he made a confession of he killing Auburey. Then after he made the confession the old lawyer he had, he tried to say he shot Auburey one time because Auburey tried to kill him. So how could Auburey have been trying to kill him when he didn't even have a gun or knife, when he was begging and pleading for his life, and if Auburey was trying to kill the man—this is what hurt so bad—the man was beating him over the head and his face so that he tore off his face and half his eye was hanging out his head, and when he tore up his face like that, and he was still hollering, with life in his body, he didn't try to ease the pain none, and he was beating Auburey so bad and Auburey was trying to beg for his life, and Auburey said, 'Oh, I'm sorry I broke your gun.' He broke his own goddam gun on Auburey's head! That's a hurting feeling. And then after he broke his gun, he shot half his arm off. One of the detectives said that the shot was so close to that arm the powder burned. Till when he shot half his arm off it was enough to kill him, but he didn't die then, he was still hollering and begging. And when he finished killing him he shot him all in the chest; that's the way he killed him, and that's what hurts. Because he was pleading and begging. The man had no sympathy for him. He said he was a white-woman lover; it's not true. Those white girls say they never had nothing to do with Auburey. Them white girls said, 'You know, Mrs. Pollard, we had our clothes on.' They walked in there and called them nigger lovers, and they took their gun and cut the clothes off of them and beat their heads and called them nigger lovers and stripped them buck-naked before all them peoples up there to try to make them feel embarrassed.

"And then if it was on the level, you see, they could have

told me they killed him. Only way I knowed was through
Auburey's friends that didn't get killed, getting away, notified
me to tell me he was dead.

"And then when the police take this trial, he say, 'I only
killed him cause he was trying to kill me.' Wasn't no way in the
world somebody going to try to kill you, they ain't got nothing
in their arms and you got a machine gun and rifle and beating
his brains out. They beat him so they beat all his face off. I hope
that man have justice. I don't care how he get it, if he don't get
justice somebody ought to lynch him, too; that's the way I feel
about it. He needs to die, too. Just little bit by little bit. Like
Carl Cooper's mother, I feel—they shot her son's groins out down
there, that's how lowdown dirty they were. I guess they was
saying, 'All you old niggers done a little bit of time anyway,
we going to kill you off.' Here my son wasn't even looting,
wasn't even after curfew hours, he just was in his own place
what he was renting. And they walk in there and tear it up like
that.

"You know what hurt me so bad again? Because they never
was a white motel they could have, that the Negro police could
come in and shoot it up like they did that Negro hotel, that they
walk in out of the street and shoot a innocent guest like they
did, and get turned loose. Tell me what would have happened
if a Negro police had have walked into a all-white neighborhood
and shot it up, like they shot up the Algiers Motel. They could
not do it. Because I worked in private families all my life, and
I never seen a Negro cop walk into a white home and say, 'This
is a search, stick your hands up, throw your hands behind your
head.' That's the way they did. And this police is trying to say
it was self-defense. I don't want it to be self-defense! I can't see
it. I'm going to fight it. It can't be self-defense.

"When he tore off half his face and knocked one of his eyes
out he was blind-staggered then, he couldn't have killed the
police! Besides, then he had to put the bullets in him. I want to
know, I want to know why they killed him like that. He had
no feelings. He had no feelings! What kind of person is he?

How can he live with hisself? I couldn't do it. That's the truth. I couldn't do it.

"And all I want is justice done to this man. If they don't give him justice, I wish there was some kind of way I could kill him like he killed my son; that's the way I feel. And see what they would do to me if I killed him like he killed Auburey.

"I got a little boy, he got in some trouble out there, true enough. He went out there and robbed a paperboy. They didn't lose no time to send him up for three years. And here this man done murder my son—he's out on bond. He's out on bond. How can he be out on bond? He done worse than my son did, because Robert didn't cut this boy, he only got seven dollars off of him, he ain't killed nobody, but here they done murder Auburey and torture him to death, and they going to get out on bond for five thousand dollars? And when *we* go out and kill each other we got to pay ten thousand dollars and can't make no bond? And that—they call that justice?

"Only thing I wish I could do is kill him. I tell you how I feel. I'd like to see him have the same death he gave my son— only just a little worser. And see how they would like it. And see what they would do to me. If I went up there right in the courtroom while they was having the trial and started in on him, I'll be damned if they wouldn't kill me right there.

"And how do we know he put up bond? They could say he put up bond. We ain't seen him put up bond. All we know is he's walking the streets free. They might have turned him loose the next day, and they got burst laughing about it. Honest to God, they was laughing in the courtroom about them getting set free.

"Now you know how I feel. I tell you about me. I feel bad about it. If I had my way I'd kill me one. I'd do the same torture they did to my son—don't ask me to tell no lie—because every time I think about it, I be sick. That man beating him up so bad, here's a man breaking his own gun on Auburey head, tore off half his face, Auburey so excited, Auburey thought maybe he could get the man off him, he say, 'Oh, I'm so sorry, officer, I broke your gun.' The man beating him so bad he break his own goddam gun on Auburey's head, then have the nerve to shoot him and talk about self-defense. I want to know about that. If they turn him loose, they ought to turn every damn body in jail loose. Turn loose my son out there that did that little robbery. He didn't kill nobody. Turn loose the one that was driving without a driving license, and that judge didn't hesitate to send *him* away for fifteen days, put him in the House of Correction. And they didn't hesitate to come in with that policeman and say they got to put up bond. Can you *believe* that?

"And that ugly lawyer sitting up there with his puny face there, he was lying like a dog, and I told him, 'You lied, and you know you lied. Couldn't be no self-defense. How in hell you going to defend that man? You trying to prove that's self-defense and he done tore up his face and shot half his arm off before he killed him? It can't be like that.'

"I want justice done so bad I can taste it. And I ain't never had larceny in my heart, but I got it there now. I feel something should be done about it. And if I live, I'm going to stand up there and tell them about it. If they can send my baby off for robbery, robbed a paperboy of seven dollars, they had to give him three years, fifteen-thousand-dollar bond they had him on, he ain't hurt nobody or shot nobody—here a man talking about sudden death just because he was wearing a damned uniform and killing for nothing and he got no defense, and he can be put out free! Let's just talk about this thing. Let's turn them all loose. Let's turn them *all* loose! Then we won't have to worry about it. Turn them loose, that's the way I feel about it.

"So let's all have a break; that's the way I feel. Let something be done about it; that's the way I feel. I don't see how the son of a bitch can walk the goddam streets, and I don't see how he can sleep at night, from the way Auburey died screaming. Something ought to be on his conscience. Something ought to be on his goddam conscience. It would be on mine, if I'd killed somebody's child like that. Wouldn't you? It would be on my conscience. Every time I think about it I get madder than hell.

That's the way I feel. And I'm going to tell the goddam judge
how I feel, if you want to know the truth about it. I don't give
a damn. And I can say, 'You don't have to subpoena me to go
to court, because I'm going to tell it any damn way if they turn
that man loose.' I'm going to say, 'Don't turn that man loose,
because he ain't got no business being free!' If they let him get
away with that death, there'll be more death. There'll be more
kids killed that are innocent.

"To think that they shot that eighteen-year-old boy's groins
out before they killed him—the Cooper boy. Don't you think his
mother's a hurt mother? She's hurt! These things don't wear
off of us. They won't wear off.

"But it hurts more for all of us to know that they call this
justice. It can't be. I give it to you straight. Write the book!
Write it! Tell them how they killed them just because they seen
them two white girls in there in the room. God damn, if they'd
seen two Negro women up there with a white lover, they
wouldn't have said nothing, say, 'Well, so-and-so-and-so-and-
so.' They'd just *forget* about it; wouldn't have been nothing
done about it. But they wasn't even in the bed with them. I
can't see it. If they'd *been* in the bed with them, they're human
beings, you can't stop them from going out there and turning
tricks or doing what they want to do. The world wasn't made
in one day. They been doing it all the time. Any old rich ones
that got money, they can mix it up, they can marry white mens,
and colored mens are marrying white womens every day—if they
got money, it don't be at all. Look at Sammy Davis, Jr. He's
married to one. Look at Pearl Bailey. Look at there, they don't
say nothing about it. You can't stop them from making love. If
they want to love each other, that's their business; they're human
beings. One's better than the other one to them; everybody got
to be their own choice. I got one son, yeah, he's married to a
white girl; she's got babies for him. What do I care? They're
human beings. They can do what they want to do.

"Ever since the time he married that white girl and ever since
they kill Auburey, they were set to put Tanner's ass back in

jail. Every week I been having trouble with them. Ever since he been married to this white girl—she got babies for him, true enough—they been kicking his ass back in jail, keeping me getting a lawyer for him, for every little thing they got him on. Now why don't they get that policeman? He did a much bigger job. I'm going to tell that, too, in court. I'm going to tell it. I'm going to tell it if I have to drop dead and I have to pay a fine. I'm going to tell it! I'm going to see how they're going to cut me off—I'm going to tell it. I want the world to know."

39

The Net Is Thrown Again

1 | Illegal Manner

Robert Paille had slipped out of the Prosecutor's net; David Senak had never been in it. The reaction to the DeMascio decision, not only among the families of the young men who had been killed but in the black community at large, was open anger —distilled in Mrs. Pollard's tirade to me. Prosecutor Cahalan and his staff decided that they must try to bring Paille and Senak to trial somehow, and if not for murder, then—following the pattern of the federal backstopping of the failure of local justice in Mississippi after the murders of the three civil-rights workers in 1964—for a conspiracy. The description the Prosecutor chose in this case was "a conspiracy to commit a legal act in an illegal manner." In spite of the fact that Melvin Dismukes, the private guard, was already under indictment for Felonious Assault, the Prosecutor decided to throw the net over him, too; and it would be understood that Ronald August, though not charged here because he had been indicted for the more grievous crime of murder, had also been a co-conspirator.

On August 23, Dismukes, Paille, and Senak were arrested on this new charge.

2 | Crime Wherever It Occurs

"It is always distressing," Prosecutor Cahalan commented in a press release announcing the arrests, "to have to proceed against brethren in law enforcement. Not to do so, however, in the long run, damages its effectiveness. Unless we are able to show our willingness to proceed against crime wherever and whenever it occurs, we will not have the confidence of this community.

"I want to take this opportunity to stress very strongly that the action that I am taking against these few law enforcement officers cannot and should not be interpreted as detracting from the valiant, competent, and restrained action of the thousands of law enforcement officers who performed so well during the recent riot."

40

Snipers: The Myth

1 | Nationwide Plot?

Carl Cooper, Auburey Pollard, and Fred Temple were said by the police, in the first days after their deaths, to have been snipers killed in an open firefight. They died on what was long believed to have been the night of the Great Sniper Battle, involving 140 blocks in the heart of Detroit.

"Are Sniper Attacks Part of a Nationwide Plot?" a front-page banner headline in the Detroit *News* asked two days after that supposed battle. The *News* article began, "Police and military officials trying to unravel the vicious pattern of deadly sniping that prolonged Detroit's racial maelstrom say there already is strong evidence to suggest a national conspiracy." A nameless "top law enforcement officer" was quoted as having said, "We are convinced that this sniping is very well organized. . . . From the information we have now, this sniper activity is part of the network of the Black Power movement. It's divided into city groups that are called 'bays' and they roughly resemble

Communist cells. Indications are now that a 'lieutenant' is in charge of the Detroit operation and higher authorities are located elsewhere."

Police Commissioner Giradin told me some time after the uprising of the concern city officials had had during its course about possible purposive attacks on nerve centers of the city by RAM (Revolutionary Action Movement); and he catalogued other organizations, national and local, that had at one time or another been thought capable of mounting sniper and fire-bombing efforts: the Malcolm X Society, the Black Guard, the Northern Student Movement, the Blank Panthers, Uhuru, the Afro-American Youth Movement, and others.

By the time the Detroit team appeared before the Commission on Civil Disorders, Girardin and the Mayor were convinced that the Detroit riot was not, as Cavanagh said before the commission, "the work of revolutionaries who belong to the black extremist movements. . . . In fact, the discussions among the extremists were that 1968 was the year for Detroit."

But it remained for the Detroit *Free Press*, in a brilliant piece of team journalism published on September 3, to puncture once and for all the inflated myth of the black sniper in 1967.

2 | One of Forty-three

The article, "The 43 Who Died," prepared over five weeks by three reporters, Gene Goltz, William Serrin, and Barbara Stanton, was a careful analysis of the deaths that had been attributed to the riot; a full account was given of each one.

The horrifying conclusion of the team was this: "A majority of the riot victims need not have died. Their deaths could have been—and should have been—prevented."

At least six of the forty-three victims were killed by the National Guard, "five of them," according to the team, "innocent, the victims of what now seem to be tragic accidents." Five other deaths were caused by bullets that might have been fired by either police or National Guardsmen; four of these victims were clearly innocent. Two looters were shot by store owners; three others were killed by private citizens, two of whom were promptly charged with murder. Fire killed two looters; electric power lines killed a fireman and a civilian. We have witnessed the death of the only policeman killed, Jerome Olshove; a second fireman was killed, either by a sniper's bullet or, as seems more likely in the context, by a stray National Guard bullet; a nine-teen-year-old boy was killed accidentally by an Army para-trooper; a twenty-three-year-old white woman was shot by an unknown gunman; and Carl Cooper was killed by "an unknown assailant"—or, perhaps we can now say, by more than one.

Eighteen of the forty-three were killed by Detroit policemen. Fourteen of the eighteen were looters. One such was Joseph Chandler, who, as we have seen, was shot by Senak and another policeman as he vaulted a back-yard fence. (As we have seen, the other Senak killing outside the Algiers, that of Palmer Gray, Jr., was not considered riot-connected.) "The legal basis for shooting a looter," the team wrote, "is found in state law which permits officers to fire at fleeing felons after an order to halt is disregarded. Technically, most of those who were killed clearly fall in that category, though one is still left with a feeling that the thief who takes $5 worth of goods from a grocery store shelf and runs ought not to be required to pay with his life. Nonetheless, the question of whether looters will be shot is a matter of public policy. No decision was ever made and an-nounced publicly; as a result, the value of the law as a deter-rent was minimal."

The other four killed by the police were Auburey Pollard and Fred Temple; a suspected but unproved arsonist; and the one and only sniper killed in the uprising.

This sniper did not fit, by any means, the picture of the dedicated, educated, intellectually sharpened, politically aware, suicidally inclined black revolutionary zealot of the sort those who feared a national plot had been describing.

3 | Drunk and Dangerous

"His name," the team reported, "was Jack Sydnor, and on the afternoon of Tuesday, July 25, he was drunk and he was dangerous.

"For the riot's first two days, Sydnor, a Negro, had remained at home with his common-law wife, Zella Mallory, 37. On Tuesday, he went out, as Mrs. Mallory remembers it, 'to get a loaf of bread.' He returned with a companion, went out again, came back drunk.

"His wife found him fingering a pistol that had long been hidden in the apartment. 'I wonder if this thing will work,' he mused. It did. At 9:15 p.m., frightened tenants called police at the Livernois Station, reporting that Sydnor was shooting onto the street from the third-floor window of his apartment at 2753 Hazelwood.

"Thirty minutes later, Sydnor was dead. Wounded in the chest and abdomen by police gunfire, Sydnor jumped or fell three floors, then died, probably of gunshot wounds.

"Before he was killed, Sydnor had seriously wounded Patrolman Roger Poike, pinned down policemen in a two-block area, and terrified his wife and neighbors. A dozen more policemen risked their lives rushing Sydnor's apartment to silence his pistol fire. As Poike burst through the apartment door at the head of a group of officers, Sydnor fired, striking him in the abdomen. Police ripped the apartment with gunfire and hurled in tear gas."

4 | A Difference

"One major critical observation must be made," the team wrote. "Both city and Army authorities acted to try to keep the death toll at a minimum, though they did so in different ways. In both cases, their efforts were not successful and permitted unnecessary death.

"At 11:20 Monday night, within hours after the National

Guard had come under Federal control, Lt. General John Throckmorton, the commanding officer, issued a general order commanding all troops under his control to unload their weapons and to fire only on the command of an officer.

"Throckmorton's regular Army troops obeyed that order; only one person was killed in paratrooper territory"—Detroit east of Woodward Avenue, where order was quickly achieved —"in the five days that followed.

"The National Guard did not obey, in many cases because the order was improperly disseminated and was never made clear to the men on the street. As a result, the Guard was involved in a total of eleven deaths, in which nine innocent people died."

5 | Vastly Overstated

As to sniping, the team concluded, "Both the number of snipers active in the riot area and the danger that snipers presented were vastly overstated. Only one sniper is among the riot victims and only three of the victims may possibly have been killed by snipers, two of them doubtful. In all, some 31 persons were arrested and charged with sniping"—out of 7,231 arrested altogether.

6 | A Few

"These snipers, now," Ronald August said to me. "I don't believe there was a heck of a lot of them. I think there was a few, but I think they'd ring out one shot, these guys are no dummies, they're not going to stay there. By the time the police are called and get to the scene, this guy is six blocks away doing the same thing all over again. It was a merry chase. And he sure is not going to shoot one while you're down there. It can happen, but the average guy is not going to be that bold. Oh, we'd run and run and run; all night long. One end to the other. In fact, I got shot up, I mean I got shot *at*, coming home one night. Right about the Children's Hospital, as I was going to get on the Expressway. It was around two thirty in the morning. I seen all the National Guardsmen, and paratroopers, whoever they were, I don't know, but they seen me coming down the road, and they told me to halt, and I did step on the brakes, and I was halted. They didn't hit the car or anything, but the guy in front of me, they hit his car. He was a policeman, too. We both left the station and I was following him down Warren, and we got there by Beaubien and Warren, and *buhWOOM!*"

41

Fuel for the Fire
Next Time

1 | Sadness and Bitterness

"I viewed these deaths with great sadness and bitterness," Dan Aldridge, a young black nationalist, a Wayne State graduate student, wrote in an account of the People's Tribunal on the Algiers case which he helped to organize. "I realized that they had been executed, as have most of the deaths that occurred during the 'rebellion,' but the question was, Could it be proved?

"Then finally a break came. Dorothy Dewberry (SNCC) told me that she had spoken with Carl Cooper's family and was convinced that he and the others had been executed. At this point, a law student friend and I decided to go over to Carl Cooper's house and to take a statement from his stepfather, Omar Gill.

"Mr. Gill told us that his son had been executed and he wanted the guilty parties punished. He explained to us that early

Wednesday morning, July 26, 1967, while he was asleep, his wife received a call from Lee Forsythe and James Sortor telling her that Carl was dead. He further explained that he called the Motel and told someone in his son's room, who could have been either a policeman or a detective, that he was coming over to the Motel to see his stepson's body. A voice, apparently Caucasian, told him, 'You had better keep your black ass home. If you come over here, you'll get the same.' About this time Lee Forsythe and James Sortor stumbled into his (Gill's) living room covered with blood and telling how they were beaten and how Carl and Auburey were murdered. Mr. Gill told us that something had to be done.

"In possession of this information, Lonnie Peek, Curt Slaughter, and myself began to check all the witnesses involved and all of the evidence.

"Our first move was to check with the undertakers and parents in order to find out what the autopsy reports showed. We learned that while the parents were in the midst of their grief, the Detroit *Free Press* had taken autopsy pictures and had paid for the autopsy. An attempt was made by us to look at the pictures but the *Free Press* refused to let us see them.

"Finally, the week of the Preliminary Examination came for Patrolmen August and Paille. Curt Slaughter and I attended every day of the Examination. We noted that the Prosecuting Attorney Weiswasser's case was extremely weak. He decided not to call many of the witnesses who could have tied policemen Paille, Dismukes, Senak, Thomas, August, and the others all together. Although subpoenaed, Sortor and Forsythe were never summoned to testify. I became suspicious and decided to ask Weiswasser why he did not call the main Black witnesses involved. He retorted, 'Their testimony would be irrelevant.' Having spoken with Sortor and Forsythe and realizing the relevance of their testimony, I decided that this case must be taken to the Black community. During the Preliminary Examination, the police came into the court room before it opened and grabbed all of the prime seats. The 'white' press referred to this as moral support, but to the youths who were to testify, it amounted to intimidation—especially when some of the policemen who had abused them at the Motel were sitting on the front pews of the court."

2 | Black Jesus

In the third week in August a coalition of militant black leadership in Detroit was formed; it called itself the Citywide Citizens' Action Committee. The group chose as its chairman the pastor of the Central United Church of Christ, Rev. Albert Cleage, Jr.

Son of an Indianapolis surgeon, a Wayne State B.A. and an Oberlin B.D., Cleage had run unsuccessfully four times for public office—for Governor, for the Detroit Common Council, for the Detroit Board of Education, and for Congress.

In March 1967, issuing a "Call to a Black Ecumenical Movement," he promulgated a doctrine partly derived from the Negro nationalism of Marcus Garvey in the twenties and based upon the white North American categorization of any man who has a single drop of black blood in him as black—a doctrine of a black Jesus.

"For nearly five hundred years," Cleage wrote in his "Call," "the illusion that Jesus was white dominated the world only because white Europeans dominated the world. Now, with the emergence of the nationalist movements of the world's colored majority, the historic truth is finally beginning to emerge—that Jesus was the non-white leader of a non-white people struggling for national liberation against the rule of a white nation, Rome. The intermingling of the races in Africa and the Mediterranean area is an established fact. The Nation, Israel, was a mixture of the Chaldeans, the Egyptians, the Midionites, the Ethiopians, the Kushites, the Babylonians, and other dark peoples, all of whom were already mixed with the black peoples of Central Africa.

"That white Americans continue to insist upon a white Christ in the face of all historical evidence to the contrary and despite the hundreds of shrines to Black Madonnas all over the world, is the crowning demonstration of their white supremacist conviction that all things good and valuable must be white. On the other hand, until Black Christians are ready to challenge this lie they have not freed themselves from their spiritual bondage to the white man nor established in their own minds their right to first-class citizenship in Christ's kingdom on earth. Black people cannot build dignity on their knees worshipping a white Christ. We must put down this white Jesus which the white man gave us in slavery and which has been tearing us to pieces.

"Black Americans need to know that the historic Jesus was a leader who went about among the people of Israel, seeking to root out the individualism and the identification with their oppressor which had corrupted them, and to give them faith in their own power to rebuild the Nation. This was the real Jesus whose life is most accurately reported in the first three Gospels of the New Testament. On the other hand, there is the spiritualized Jesus, reconstructed many years later by the Apostle Paul who never knew Jesus and who modified his teachings to conform to the pagan philosophies of the white Gentiles. Considering himself an apostle to the Gentiles, Paul preached individual salvation and life after death. We, as Black Christians suffering oppression in the white man's land, do not need the individualistic and otherworldly doctrines of Paul and the white man. We need to recapture the faith in our power as a *people* and the concept of Nation, which are the foundation of the Old Testament and the Prophets, and upon which Jesus built all of his teachings two thousand years ago."

3 | Genocide

"I escorted Mr. & Mrs. Omar Gill, Carl Cooper's parents, and Mr. & Mrs. James Young, Carl's grandparents, to the first meeting of the City-wide Citizens' Action Committee," Aldridge wrote. "Mrs. Margaret Gill explained that she had lost her firstborn, and although she realized that she could never get him back, she wanted someone to do something so that other black mothers would not have to suffer as much as she had suffered.

"The meeting voted to send as many people into Judge De-Mascio's court the next day as possible to hear the verdict. The following day, one hundred sober Black faces heard Judge De-Mascio bind August over for trial on $5,000 bond and let Paille go free for lack of sufficient evidence. The credit for letting Paille go free belongs to Prosecuting Attorney Weiswasser, for he alone did not summon the witnesses and he alone only mentioned Paille's name once during the Preliminary Examination. Weiswasser made the statement, 'If they had only kept their mouths shut, they wouldn't be here now.'

"Having viewed these proceedings, we decided that we would hold a tribunal so that the people could evaluate the evidence for themselves. The Black community needs to see that the type of justice we receive in Recorder's Courts is the same kind that is meted out in Mississippi. That as long as you are south of Windsor, you may as well be in Mississippi. We wanted to show Black people that if this is the law, they had better be proud of their lawlessness because we must not respect a law which does not respect us. Our lawlessness may be the means for our survival, because one of the major downfalls of the Jews in Germany was that they were too damn law abiding. The Germans simply passed a law to march into camps.

"We invited the International Press because we wanted people all over the world to see what it means to be a Black so-called American. We wanted to inform Black people that the courts represent another subtle means of genocide that white America practices on us daily."

4 | Atrocities

"At the meeting last Wednesday," June Brown Garner wrote in a column in the *Chronicle*, "it was announced that the sex organs of the boys in the Algiers Motel had been shot off by police, and pictures of the bodies were shown. One boy's arm was shot off while he was still alive, and the undertaker had to piece his body back together and make him a face out of plastic. This case brought tears to the eyes of most of us, and it has increased our determination to rebuild the city so that things like the riot and the atrocities that followed it will never happen again."

5 | Our Brothers Have Been Brutally Slain

The tribunal was announced for Wednesday, August 30, at the Dexter Theater. The CCAC distributed leaflets that said, "Watch accurate justice administered by citizens of the community. Witness the unbiased, legal action of skilled black attorneys. Review and watch the evidence for yourself."

Three days before the meeting, Rap Brown spoke, urging that the black community "should hold a people's tribunal and give them a trial. If they are found guilty—and I don't see how they can be found anything else—the brothers should carry out an execution."

Shortly before the mock trial was to be held, Aldridge and Peek learned that the management of the Dexter Theater had gotten cold feet and that it would not be possible to hold the tribunal there. The executive board of Cleage's church met and announced that the affair would move to the church. "We love our church," the board statement said, "and the building in which we worship. But even if granting permission for the People's Tribunal to be held here means the destruction of our building, as churches have been destroyed in Birmingham and all over the South, we still have no choice. We serve the Black Messiah, Jesus of Nazareth, who came to unite and free an oppressed black nation. Our brothers have been brutally slain, and it is only right that the voice of truth, silent in the corrupt halls of justice, should ring out in the House of God."

6 | The Sheer Horror

Four men were named as defendants—August, Paille, Dismukes, and Thomas. The jury included the novelist John Killens and Rosa Parks, who started the transportation boycott in Montgomery, Alabama, in 1954, by refusing to yield her bus seat.

"The brothers and sisters don't know what fear is any more," Cleage wrote afterward in the *Chronicle*. "In spite of the last minute change of location, they began to arrive at Central Church at 5 p.m. to be sure of a seat. By 7 p.m. the sanctuary and Fellowship Hall were filled to capacity, and people were still coming from everywhere. More than two thousand people were in the building, and others were outside trying to get in. . . .

"There is no way to put down on paper the sheer horror of the recital of events by witness after witness. It is hard to believe that such bestiality could exist in the world, that a group of ordinary white men could so hate ordinary black men. . . .

"As the witnesses testified, the packed auditorium became more quiet than a courtroom. Each individual relived the horrible moments. . . ."

7 | People Were Interested

"I was there," Eddie Temple told me, "as a witness, actually as the person who identified my brother at the morgue. It had a tremendous value, in that it exposed to a large number of people what had happened there, what these people had had to go through, the beatings, the fear. If somebody tells you that they're going to blow your brains out and cock the rifle, cock the handle back, it gave them a chance to see what some people had to be subject to. It was a Negro audience, primarily middle-class. It was a large number of people, it was packed, and they had it outside, and they had another annex type of place where they had speakers. This place was really packed. People were interested in it."

8 | A Joke?

"This Tribunal," Aldridge wrote, "is the beginning of a new level of thinking in Black America. Black people are telling white judges, white juries, and white newspapers that we are 'hip' to your tricks. That Carl Cooper, Auburey Pollard, and Fred Temple have not died in vain. Their deaths have been the signal that flashes injustice in America.

"For Carl, Auburey, and Fred, 'no more water, but fire next time.' If I must die, better it be on Linwood than somewhere in Saigon; better Dexter than Da Nang.

"The Detroit *News* put it on page 1D next to the comics, and when I went up to ask the *News* about it, a Mr. Beck, a Re-write, said, 'We played it like the joke it was.'

"If it were such a joke, why was James Sortor picked up by police and charged with being a 'Peeping Tom' three days before the Tribunal and questioned not about said charge, but about the Algiers incident? He was released for several hours and picked up again—this time for felonious assault.

"If it were such a joke, why did detective Schlokman [Schlachter?], Assistant to the Prosecuting Attorney, Weiswasser, go by Lee Forsythe's home the night prior to the Tribunal and tell him not to appear?

"And why were certain types of pressure brought upon John Ashby when plans were made to hold the Tribunal at the Dexter Theater?

"If you think it was funny, we plan to keep you in stitches."

9 | No Solution

The following Sunday Albert Cleage preached a sermon entitled "Fear Is Gone."

"We had the People's Tribunal," he said, "to try the officers charged with the massacre of three black youth in the Algiers Motel during the July Rebellion. Right here, beneath the Black Madonna, witnesses testified. Everything possible had been done by the police to intimidate these black people, and yet they testified, they told the truth. Does that mean that as they sat there their hearts were not pounding? Of course not. They knew that 'the man' was going to brutalize them at the first opportunity, but that wasn't fear because they did what had to be done. A whole lot of you have guilty feelings about being afraid. You needn't have. It is not fear as long as you do what has to be done.

"America is set on a disaster course of conflict and violence. The black man cannot accept America as it is. The white man refuses to make the changes necessary for the black man to live in America with dignity and justice. These are two facts. We will not accept conditions as they are, and the white man will not accept the change. There is no solution to that except open conflict and violence. You don't have to feel guilty about that, either. It is his fault, not ours."

10 | Violence Breeds Violence

Rap Brown's injunction, that if the accused were found guilty "the brothers should carry out an execution," did not then prevail, but several weeks later there came an echo of it, and an example of the way in which violence copulates with violence and conceives bloody offspring. Late in the night of the assassination of Martin Luther King, Jr., a .45-caliber submachine gun, allegedly held by a black extremist named James Thomas Dawkins, who was standing in the shadows between two buildings on West Warren, stitched an arc across a police car cruising on that street and gravely injured, though it did not kill, Patrolmen Terrance Collins and Phillip Tuck of the Sixth Precinct. The worse-injured of the two, Tuck, was a son-in-law of Charles Schlachter, the detective in charge of the Algiers investigation. Policemen shot and killed two looters that night, one of them accidentally, the police said: "an eighteen-year-old named Robert Baughan, who, with his hands up, backed into a cop's gun and died of carelessness.

42

Harassment?

1 | What Happened Down There?

"Every time, seemed like, I wanted to walk somewhere," Sortor told me, "they'd pick me up. Each time they'd pull me in at the Fourteenth Precinct. They'd just pick me up out there on Grand River. I'd be going over to Allen's house, my friend Allen's house, to shoot some pool, and they'd pick me up over by his house. Been picked up four times.

"The first time they picked me up, they said I was peeping through somebody's window. I was walking down the street, it was on Meyers. The people said I was peeping through their windows. I said, 'What you talking about?' They say, 'Yeah, you's the one. Get in!' So I got in, you know, they took me down, they said they were holding me for an investigation of a B. and E. They can hold—investigation, they'll just *say*, you know—they can hold you in there for seventy-two hours. Stayed in there all night, and they let me out Sunday morning about eight o'clock.

"They picked me up one day, somebody say I had a gun,

353

they took me down to McGraw Station then, so they hold me in there. They were fighting in this here lady's house around here, you know, so she told me to break it up, so I pushed both of the ones who was fighting apart, you know. This guy run out the door and called the police, say I had a gun and I'd hit him, you know, so they put me on a year peace bond, and I ain't even did nothing.

"Each time I go down there, they keep talking about the Algiers. 'What happened down there?' So I say, 'I don't have to tell you.' And they keep coming back down there asking me to tell them, you know. And I say, 'I don't have to tell you nothing.'

"They kept me a couple of days, and then they let me go."

2 | Fifteen Dollars

Report on case investigated for warrant recommendation:
"Defendant: Karen Malloy, f/w/18

"On 9-7-67 at about 1:45 AM, Patr Samuel Stone assigned to the Vice Bureau was driving North on Woodward when at 3900 Woodward in front of the Astor Motel the officer pulled into the curb and observed the Def standing there. The Def motioned the officer to the rear of the Motel which he did. The officer parked in the rear and walked up to the Def. The Def then asked the officer how much he'd spend and he said $15.00. The Def said O'K and the officer asked what he'd get for his money and Def stated a Half & Half. At this time the officer identified himself and placed the Def under arrest for Accosting and Soliciting.

"Dispensation: 6 Months Probation."

3 | Have Some Fun

Report on case investigated for warrant recommendation:
"Defendant: Julie Hysell, W-18; Janet Wright, W-19.

"On Sept. 13, 1967 at approximately 11:45 AM the officer,

Patr. James Montgomery, was standing on Virginia Pk. west of Woodward in front of the Algiers Motel when the defendant, Julie Hyzell, walked out of the office of the Motel and walked toward the officer. The def. Hyzell said Hello to the officer and the officer returned the salutation. The def. Hyzell then asked the officer where he worked and the officer replied Intervale Steel Corp. The def. Hyzell then asked the Officer if he was a Police Officer and the officer replied no. The def. Hyzell then asked the officer if he would like to have some fun and the officer replied yes if it didn't cost too much. The def. Hyzell then asked the officer how much money he had to spend and the Officer replied $10.00. The def. then took the Officer to Rm. 17 of the Algiers Motel and the officer then asked the def. Hyzell what he would get for his money and the def. replied a 'Blow Job' or she would 'Fuck the Officer.' The Officer then asked the def what it would cost to have two girls and the def. Hyzell replied $30 to $40., the officer said he would like to try that but that the highest he could spend would be $30.00. The def. Hyzell then told the Officer to wait in the room and she then left the room and returned with the def. Janet Wright. The defs. then both entered the room and told the officer to make himself comfortable and take off his clothes. The Officer then asked the defs. what they would do, and the def. Hyzell replied that she would 'Blow' the officer and the def. Wright would 'Fuck' the officer. The def. Wright agreed to this and then both defs requested to be paid in advance. At this time the officer identified himself as a Police Officer and placed the defs. under arrest for Accosting and Soliciting.

"Disp. 6 months Probation and 75.00 Cost."

4 | You Got a Brother?

"One policeman," Tanner Pollard said, "stopped me out in the middle of the street, you know, Plymouth Street. I was going to get some groceries, corner of Fielding. He stopped me and he pulled me over, and he said, 'What your name?' He asked me

did I break in anything. He said, 'You done broke in around
here.' The other policeman ran around the other side. I gave him
my name and phone number and he searched me and everything.
He said, 'You got a brother named Auburey Pollard?' I say,
'Yes.' He say, 'He got killed, didn't he?' I said, 'Yeah, a policeman did it.' He said, 'That's what these pimps need to get.' I told
him, 'My brother never was a pimp.' I said, 'He had a job, working at Ford's.' And then he said, 'Well, that's what these pimps
get.' And they both started laughing."

5 | They Locked Me Up

"I had my car taken away," Tanner Pollard told me, "never got
that back, a '62 Cadillac. The police came and took it out the
driveway. I showed them all the papers on it and stuff. They told
me to come down to the station to take a report on it. I went
down to the station and then they took my fingerprints and
everything. I thought they was taking a report on my car. And
then they locked me up in jail and told me I can't go nowhere.
And I asked them, I say, 'Can I make a phone call?' 'No, you
can't make a phone call. Wait till you get down to the big jail.'
And so I waited and waited, and when I got down to the other
jail, they let me make a phone call, and come down to find the
car wasn't stolen, not by me, but they never did let me have
my car back. This was after Auburey got killed. This was when
the police kept on, you know, riding around the house. I was
washing—you see, my car had been sitting about a month and
had bird mess and all types of stuff all over it, and it was real,
real dirty, and I took and I scraped it and washed it and buffed
it and shined it all up. By the time I got it cleaned up the police
came and took it. They drove it until it ran out of gas, and
then the cars kept on bumping into it, pushing it and stuff, and
they dented the back trunk all up and everything. It was paid
for, too. I paid cash for it. And plus I had a new motor put in
it. Had the transmission worked on and everything. I asked the
guy that I bought it from and he said that the car was stolen,

and they sold it at an auction, and then he taken and sold it to me. The original owner had sunk about twenty-seven hundred dollars on it, something like that. They give it back to him. And I paid five ninety-five for the car. Plus one fifty for the motor.

"I had one policeman, this other time, he came out with a shotgun—I remember we was on Dunbar—and he asked me where—that was when the car was all dirty—they said, 'Whose piece of shit is this?' I told him that was my car. They said, 'Get it off the street.' He asked me for the title and registration, so I showed him the title, but I didn't have the registration for the car at that time, because I left it with the man at the station. He told me to get up against the tire, and he shoved me and stuff, you know, holding the shotgun up against me. He recognized my name from the title. He said, 'Is your name Tanner Pollard?' I said, 'Yeah.' He said, 'Was your brother killed over in the Algiers Hotel?' And I said, 'Yeah.' The policeman said, 'I should beat your head.' I said, 'Yeah, I'd like for you to do that.'"

6 | Read the Papers

"About a month later," Sortor told me, "then they came, and I was driving with this girl. She stopped, me and her and her brother, and we stopped on the street, on Cheyenne or one of those streets back over that way, so she say she was going over to her girl friend's house, and we were just fixing to get out the car, and the police pulled up, and so they started questioning us and everything, and they said, where were we going, and we said, 'We're going in this house right here.' This old lady, she came out and came over to the police car, from the house we were stopped right in front of. She was the one who said her house had been broken into. They told us to get out of the car and they searched us down. Held us there for about fifteen minutes, and they told us we could go. So we pulled off. And they caught up with us, you know. By the time we got to the corner, they come up there again, you know, and got us, and

put us under arrest. They let the girl and the other boy go.
Found out who I was and asked me, 'What happened over there
at the Algiers?'—you know, 'What happened over there?' I say,
'Well, I don't know what happened,' you know. I told them,
'Read the papers,' you know."

7 | Witnesses in Trouble

And so it went. On November 21, Tanner Pollard was sent to
the Detroit House of Correction for fifteen days (the police had
already held him two days) for driving without a license. In
mid-December, James Sortor was picked up again, and, evidently tired of being questioned about the Algiers, he gave the
name James Fry; then later at the police station thought better
of the deception and gave his own name; was held overnight;
was fined fifty dollars for giving false information to a police
officer. In January, Lee Forsythe was arrested on suspicion of
armed robbery in a furniture store and was held for several
weeks in Wayne County Jail on $7,500 bail, which he could not
raise, awaiting trial; on May 1, he was sentenced by Judge
Gerald W. Groat to seven and one half to twenty years for
Robbery Armed. On February 4, Charles Moore was stopped
for speeding by two policemen, who got out of their car and
said that Moore's automobile fitted the description of one that
had been used for a bank robbery. Moore objected. There was
an argument. The officers beat Moore up, took him downtown,
booked him for resisting arrest, and held him for investigation
of the bank robbery, on which, he told me, he had an airtight
alibi because of his time card at Rockwell-Standard, where he
worked. "It was," he said, "a fairy tale." On March 13, Michael
Clark was sentenced to ninety days for larceny. On April 26,
Karen Malloy was sentenced to forty-five days in the House of
Correction for violation of her probation.

43

The Paille Appeal

1 | Six Months

On September 16, Prosecutor Cahalan appealed DeMascio's freeing of Paille, arguing that the judge should have admitted the excluded statements in a pretrial examination; that only a trial judge could determine the admissibility of such evidence.

A strange quirk of local procedure required that first appeals should go not to a higher court but rather right back through Recorder's Court, so that another of the ten judges in Recorder's Court would have to pass judgment on the decision of a colleague. By chance the appeal fell to the lot of Judge Geraldine Bledsoe Ford, a woman and a Negro.

Elected to the bench less than a year before, four days after her fortieth birthday, Judge Ford was the first woman ever to sit in Recorder's Court. "Would you believe," she asked a *Free Press* reporter the day she was elected, "a man asked me what I would do if a rape case were brought before me? He seemed to think that women don't know anything about that sort of thing. I wanted to tell him it takes two to tango, but I didn't." Daughter of a prominent lawyer, she attended Howard University, the University of Michigan, and Wayne State Law School, and she married Len Ford, an all-American football player at Michigan who later became an all-pro lineman. As a judge she had a reputation, particularly among Detroit prostitutes, for dishing out tough sentences.

It took Judge Ford nearly six months to hand down a decision on the appeal.

2 | I've Always Led a Clean Life

"I just can't understand all this here, you know," Paille said to me, "because in the past I've always led a clean life here, I've always been responsible, I've done my job to the best of my ability, and I feel that I don't warrant this at all. I can't understand it to this day. And as far as I'm concerned there, I'd just as soon go back to work. And I've always treated these people with respect in the past. And even the whores there, you know, I've never really cussed them out like I've heard some fellows cuss them out. I've done my job. I just can't understand it.

"I feel this is going to affect all the policemen here, this case, to the sense that: What can they do for a few? You know? When they're separated from the many, you know? They take a few of us out of the ranks there, and they tried to put everything on us. And the city, they get out of the picture altogether. For instance the Mayor himself, in the past over here, he assaulted his sister-in-law, and nothing was done about that, it seems. It was in the paper one day, and the next day it was out. Nothing. And a man of his sophistication and all, you'd feel that they'd really try to make something out of this, but apparently he got out quick.

"But somebody like us, the policemen there, oh, that's beautiful when it gets in the news! They really build it up big."

44

A Numbness

1 | All the Hurt

One side of Roderick Davis's head remained numb for months. "They knocked all the hurt out of my head," he said to me.

2 | Bothering Him

"They've stood up well," Eddie Temple said of his brother's friends, "but I understand that Davis particularly was having terrible headaches, and I saw him one day—it had to be at least a month later—I just ran across him in a store, a department store. He wasn't looking well, and I talked to him, and he told me that his head had been bothering him tremendously, where he had been hit on the head. I tried to get him to let me take him to a doctor, but he insisted he didn't want one. I tried to get him to go see a doctor about this. Financially I don't think he had the money."

3 | If Something Really Bad Was Wrong

"There is a difference in him," Roderick's mother told me. "I took him to a neurologist, but he wouldn't go on with the treatment. The doctor wanted him to have a head X-ray, but he said he didn't want to do it unless there was something really bad wrong, and if something really bad was wrong, he didn't want to know what it was. He doesn't seem to reason properly. For a time he would get these headaches and suddenly run a temperature, and his limbs would give way under him, and he would go partially blind. He was quite edgy. He was quick to think my daughter and me were talking about him. He'd accuse my daughter and me of laughing at him. He was quite shaken up. He couldn't seem to reason; he was so much more childish. I took him twice to a neurologist, and he gave him an encephalogram. He said it showed a slowness of brain activity on the side that received the injury. He didn't feel it was permanent; it might last quite awhile, but it would probably clear up."

45

Conspiracy?

1 | The People Were Ready

On Wednesday, September 27, parenthesized on his elevated bench by two American flags, Judge Frank G. Schemanske of Recorder's Court, a man of sixty-eight years, wearing a black gown and metal-rimmed spectacles, said in a low voice, which, because of the profusion of acoustical tiles all up the walls above the courtroom's marble wainscotting and on the ceiling, too, could hardly be heard at the four rows of heavy oaken gallery benches at the back of the room, "All right, gentlemen, let's take our respective seats."

Louder, the court clerk cried, "Case of the People versus Robert Paille, David Senak, and Melvin Dismukes, Conspiracy to Commit a Legal Act in an Illegal Manner."

"People are ready," Mr. Weiswasser said.

2 | I'm Going to Be Tough

The bulk of Frank Schemanske's career up until his election to the Recorder's Court, eighteen years before this day, had been

spent as a prosecutor. "Terribly police-prone," one Detroit attorney said of him to me. The *Free Press* once accused him of
boasting of having sentenced 235 criminals in one day, and he
wrote the editor, affirming the sentences but denying he had
crowed about it. He has often made speeches about juvenile
delinquency, and in one of them he said, "We're not going to
allow any gangs of punks, hoodlums, and ruffians to run the
city. We won't let them go around insulting people and putting
them in fear for their lives. As long as I am on the bench, I am
going to be tough with these kids and get rid of this kind of
activity."

3 | Behave Like a Witness

The first witness was Michael Clark, and before he had left the
stand the case had gone completely out of Prosecutor Weiswasser's control. Michael, perhaps emboldened by the mood of
the tribunal, was insolent, inconsistent, and totally indifferent to
the purpose of the proceedings; and he was obviously enjoying
himself.

When asked where he had obtained money to pay for his
room at the Algiers, he replied, "From my mama . . . plus I had
some." Pressed to tell when he had changed rooms in the annex,
he said, "I said I don't know. If you want to know, go and ask
the people that own the place." "I don't write it down in a
diary where I go." How many blocks did his mother live from
the motel? "You count them: from Philadelphia to Oregon. Now
you can go count them." Did he recall where he ate on the
evening of the 25th? "Man, I don't even know what day the
25th was on!" Was an answer of his "Yes, sir"? "It wasn't 'sir,'
it was 'yes.' " "I don't know, I ain't got X-ray eyes." He didn't
remember a certain statement? "No, I don't. Uh-uh. See, when
the guy hit me on my head, I forget sometimes." "You don't
have to get mad at me." Maybe he would recover his memory
of a certain fact. "It ain't going to come back. I'm getting a
headache." Would he identify a certain gentleman (Dismukes)?
"There's a man sitting next to you. It ain't no gentleman."

On Thursday morning, having been instructed to appear at nine thirty because the lawyers were not through with his testimony, Michael moseyed in at 11:05 a.m., as Judge Schemanske angrily noted in the record. "Well," Michael said when the judge rebuked him, "I wrote my mother to call me and wake me up."

Though it took him ten weeks to hand down his decision, it was clear that Judge Schemanske had made up his mind by that second morning. At one point he openly lost his temper at Michael Clark:

THE COURT:　Now just a minute; just a minute. You are in a courtroom and you will behave the way you should behave in a courtroom. And I repeat again to you that this is an Examination and counsel have a right to ask questions, and if there are any objections to come, they must come from the Prosecuting Attorney. Now, I will not repeat it again.

THE WITNESS:　If he asked me a question—

THE COURT:　If you don't understand the question, you tell him that you don't understand the question.

THE WITNESS:　I understood the question.

THE COURT:　But I am not going to have you rule things in this courtroom, so get that in your mind. We will conduct this courtroom the way a courtroom should be conducted. And you are a witness, and you will act like a witness.

After the lunch break, Mr. Lippitt recalled Michael, and this exchange took place:

Q.　Mr. Clark, after the noon recess were you walking on St. Antoine towards Recorder's Court from Monroe with some other people?

A.　Yes, I was.

Q.　Who were you with?

A.　Lee Forsythe, Juli, and Karen. . . .

Q.　All right, and you saw me—you walked by me, didn't you, Mr. Clark?

A.　Yes, I did.

Q.　And did you tell me when I walked by you that I was going to be run over by a car?

A. No, I wasn't talking to you.
Q. You didn't say that?
THE COURT: What was that? . . .
Q. Did you say to me I was going to be run over by a car, Mr. Clark?
A. No, I was talking to James Sortor.
Q. Did you say that he was going to be run over by a car?
A. I said he's going to be run over by a car.
Q. Who were you referring to?
A. James Sortor. I was talking to him. . . . Me and James, we was—we was just talking. He was by the curb and I just happened to say it at the time he came by. . . .
THE COURT: (To Mr. Lippitt.) Well, I think you ought to further the matter to the prosecuting attorney's office. That's where the matter should be referred for proper investigation. All right. (To the witness.) You may leave.

4 | Goodness

Sortor was testifying:
A. Well, seemed like to me the ones that were doing all the hitting, like they was, you know, in a group, you know, like they had planned this or something, you know.
MR. LIPPITT [representing Paille]: Objection, Your Honor. My goodness!
THE COURT: Objection sustained.
MR. SMITH [representing Dismukes]: Thank you, Your Honor.

5 | Counsel Testifying

Warrant Officer Thomas was, to put it mildly, a malleable witness, and the defense lawyers were alert to the possibilities. Here he is under cross-examination by Mr. Kohl, who represented Senak:
Q. You were the one that reported the sniping incident to start with?

A. Yes, sir.

Q. As the result of which police and military personnel converged on the area?

A. That's right.

Q. And the report that was made was, in fact, there were snipers at the Algiers Motel when you were performing your duties there?

A. When I reported it, I reported where my location was and where I thought the fire was coming from.

Q. And you reported that again in the course of your job?

A. Yes, sir.

Q. That there was fire coming from the Algiers Motel?

A. Yes, sir, in that area.

Q. Gunfire coming from the Algiers Motel Annex?

A. Yes, sir. . . .

MR. WEISWASSER: I object to this line of questions. I can understand counsel has a right for cross-examination, but I do not think he can testify out of the mouth of this man which is all that he's doing. He's telling a story, testifying to it, and then he's asking this man, "Am I not right?" In fact, he's doing a ventriloquist's act. He's using this man as a dummy. . . .

THE COURT: I'll permit the answers to stand.

6 | Vacation

The hearing lasted three days. Judge Schemanske asked for briefs from the Prosecutor by October 9 and from the defense by October 23. He was planning an autumn vacation.

46

Padlocking

1 | Public Nuisance

On October 3, Prosecutor Cahalan filed suit in Wayne County
Circuit Court against the Algiers Motel, alleging that "said
premises, the buildings thereon, and the furniture, fixtures, and
contents therein are now and have been for a considerable period
of time prior hereto used, leased, conducted, and maintained as
a public nuisance." The complaint charged that the motel had
been used "for purposes of lewdness, assignation, and prostitution," and that between April 24 and September 6, sixteen persons had been arrested in its rooms on narcotics charges.

2 | From the Middle Ages

"This," Samuel J. Rhodes, a lawyer, one of the owners of the
motel named in the complaint, said to me, "is a proceeding *in
rem*, with very harsh penalties, reminiscent of the Middle Ages,
against an inanimate object. The extreme penalty would be padlocking of the doors, and removal and sale of the furniture. I

can't believe we're going to come to that. As for an injunction against these alleged practices, which would come after a hearing, that would be simply declarative of existing laws. What's to be gained by reaffirming laws that are already on the books? I'm hoping to be able to point out to the Prosecutor's Office, which surely doesn't want to hurt a man who has been practicing before the bar for over fifty years, that we should be given every opportunity for thoroughly effective supervision of the premises. We don't want that kind of traffic. Every hotel and motel in the country is plagued with illicit sexual practices."

3 | Informer #8814

The suit, known in the trade as a padlocking, could not possibly be construed as anything but a punishment of a locus of shame for the police force. About a month after the Algiers incident, the Police Department moved to discredit the motel. The Narcotic Bureau ordered an investigation of the Algiers, the Rio Gran, and the Alamo, three motels that were run by the managers of the Algiers, Sam Gant and McUrant Pye. Cursory paragraphs in the report of this investigation disposed of the Rio Gran and the Alamo. The heart of the report:

"On August 22, 1967, at about 6:00 p.m., our informer #8814 was conveyed to the vicinity of 8301 Woodward, where the informant was furnished with $30.00 in money from which the serial numbers had been noted. The informer then proceeded to the Algiers Motel at 8301 Woodward, where he rented Room #17 under the name of RAY HARRIS.

"A short time later, the informer met a Negro Male, 24, 5' 10", 150 lbs., who gave his name as 'James.' This subject invited the informer to his room, Unit #22, to meet a couple of girls. The informer was introduced to two white females, @ Gloria, W/F, 5' 4", 110 lbs., 18 to 20 years old, and @ Judy, W/F, 5', 100 lbs., 18 to 20 years old. James told the informer that if he wanted a girl or something to drink, all he had to do was call the office on the house phone. The informer then stated that he and James went back to Unit #17 where James called the office and ordered a pint of Teachers Scotch. The bottle was delivered to the informer by a Negro Female, who had previously checked the informer into the motel. The informer then paid this person $5.00 for the bottle. The contents of the bottle were then consumed by the informer and @ James. . . .

"On August 24, 1967 at about 9:00 p.m., the informer introduced himself to the person occupying Unit 18. The subject gave the informer his name as 'Fast Eddie.' The informer states that 'Fast Eddie' asked him if he would like to get 'high.' The informer said he would and was invited into Unit #18. Fast Eddie then told the informer he had some good cocaine he would sell for $5.00 a capsule. The informer then gave Fast Eddie $10.00 for two capsules. The informer used one capsule and attempted to leave with the remaining capsule, but was told by Fast Eddie, he had to use both capsules. The informer then used the remaining capsule and left the unit. Fast Eddie is described as Negro Male, 30, 6', 180 lbs., medium brown skin, long black hair. The informer stated that Eddie checked out of the motel sometime early on August 25, 1967.

"On August 26, 1967, at about 12:30 a.m., the informer met a man who introduced himself as 'Frank,' described as being Negro Male, 23, 5' 9", 145 lbs., medium complexion, occupying Unit #10. Frank asked the informer if he would like to buy some pills. The informer then went to Unit #10, where @ Frank gave the informer 12 capsules wrapped in toilet paper, 11 white capsules and one orange capsule, for which the informer paid $5.00. The informer then left #10 and returned to his unit and went to bed. At about 3:00 a.m., the informer was awakened by a knock at his door. When the informant opened the door, he was confronted by four uniformed officers who stated they had received a radio run to the motel, Unit 17, a report of a dead man in the room. The officers searched the room and left the premises. A check of the dispatcher's records disclosed that on August 26, 1967 at 2:47 a.m., Scout 13-11 and 13-70 received a run to the motel as described above. The informer then got dressed and left the motel for the remainder of the night.

"On August 26, 1967 at about 9:30 a.m., the informer appeared at the Narcotic Bureau where he turned over to Detective Conrad the 12 capsules purchased earlier from @ Frank. The capsules were placed in evidence folder #10682 and conveyed to the Scientific Bureau for analysis. The 11 capsules were found to be negative and the orange capsule, a derivative of barbituric acid.

"On August 26, 1967, at about 9:00 p.m., the informer was invited to Unit #8 by a Negro Male, 35, 5′ 10″, 140 lbs., who gave his name as 'Will.' Will asked the informer if he wanted to shoot dice. The informer states that 'Will' said he runs a game at the motel every Saturday night in one of the units. The informer stated that several persons, both male and female, were at the game. The informer further stated he purchased whisky at the dice game from @ Will.

"On August 27, 1967, the informer appeared at the Narcotic Bureau where he met Detective Conrad. At this time, it was deemed advisable to remove the informer from the motel in view of the fact that officers of the Thirteenth Precinct had received a radio run to his unit, indicating that the informer may have been recognized as such by one of the known narcotic dealers."

After the brief paragraphs on the other motels, the report said: "It is the conclusion of the reporting officers that there is no organized narcotic activity at the motels mentioned in this investigation at the present time. It would appear that most of the activity evolves around prostitution, liquor, and gambling."

4 | Three of Seven

In September the Police Department compiled a chronological list of all arrests made during 1967 in and around the Algiers. There were altogether fifty-seven arrests, of which sixteen were for Robbery Armed, sixteen were for Violation State Narcotics Law, and the rest were scattered over the whole range of human misery and mischief; there was no mention, however, of the arrests of two policemen for alleged murders on the premises on the night of July 25–6.

Seven of the cases were eventually chosen for use in the padlocking case. It could hardly have been a coincidence that three of the seven involved witness of the incident: Michael Clark, arrested, as we have seen, on a narcotics charge on July 10; Karen Malloy, Julie Hysell (under the alias Beverly Griffith, according to the police report), and Nancy Stallnaker (alias Janice McCoy), arrested along with seven others at an alleged marijuana party in room 35 of the Algiers on July 17; and Julie Hysell, arrested, as we have seen, for prostitution on September 13. The Department made the mistake of including one narcotics arrest of three people on July 12, which had to be thrown out of court; in red ink on the Narcotics Bureau disposition slip was written, "Illegal search!!!"

47

A Cutting

1 | Senak's Version

"The reason I got in trouble all over again," David Senak told me, "was because I was overzealous. It was my instinct of a police officer—even though I was suspended.

"It was about one thirty in the morning. I was leaving my girl friend's apartment downtown, took her to a show or something and I dropped her off, and I was leaving, had my car parked out in front of her place, and across the street I saw this red convertible parked at a flower shop. I noticed this fellow behind the driver's seat fiddling around down there. He couldn't find the key was what it actually was, but I thought he was hot-wiring the car. He started the car, and after that he opened the passenger door and two guys came running out of the shadows, and one guy got in the front seat and one guy got in the back seat.

"Well, to me this was a stolen car. Police officers tell you, you know, old-timers, they say, 'Don't get involved in that stuff,' and I've heard it a million times, and I said to myself that I wasn't going to get involved. I had my mind made up that the

first police car I came to I was going to give them the information, tell them what I saw, not tell them anything about who I
was or what I was, and just be on my way and let them take
care of it.

"Started following this car down Adams. Got to Grand
River. I followed them. Not a scout car in sight. Citizens tell me
this all the time: 'Whenever we need you, you're not there.'
But this particular time I needed a police car and I couldn't find
one, either. So I sympathize with them.

"We were going down Grand River, we passed the Olympia,
got to around West Grand Boulevard. I figured they were going
way out Grand River, and I was going the other way, I was supposed to be going out Gratiot, see, so I was just getting farther
and farther from my destination. So what I did was pull alongside of them and take a look at them, at the two fellows in front,
and tried to remember the face of the driver, and then I was
just going to fall back and start going my way, and as soon as
I saw a police car, tell them, have them radio it in and see if it
was a stolen car—be some help.

"So then I dropped back, and I was going to turn off, and
they turned in to the curb right next to a beer-and-wine store
that was still open. So it was still perfect; it was a perfect UDAA
[Unlawfully Driving Automobile Away]. So I passed them,
and I was watching them in the rear-view mirror, and I noticed
that their one headlight on the left was dim, and I could distinguish their car from the front, now. When they pulled into the
beer-and-wine place, I figured it backed my assumption, because
if they did steal the car they were going to stop for some booze,
get liquored up.

"So I was going down Grand River on the inside lane, and
I'm watching the headlights of this car, and I pass one light and
I'm coming to this other light, and it's green. So I slowed down
so that I could hit the light so they could catch up to me, because at that time I was almost convinced that I wanted to follow
and see where they go. Everything was pointing at their being
a stolen car.

"So the light finally changed red and I went up there and

stopped, and I was watching these two headlights, see, because there were other cars coming down Grand River at that time, and it was hard to distinguish the two; I wanted to keep them in my sight.

"Just at that time two prostitutes jumped in the car. Colored one and a white one. I had stopped for a paper downtown and I'd opened the door for the guy, so the stupid car door was unlocked; otherwise it would have been locked. The colored one did all the talking, she was the old pro, and the white one, she was real nervous, she was learning the trade.

"So they said, 'We'll give you anything you want for twenty-five bucks.'

"I said, you know, 'Get out of the car.' Because at this time, I'd been working with these girls for almost two years, and prostitutes don't really concern me, they're not something that really scares me now; I can look a prostitute in the face and not shiver. So I just halfheartedly pushed them out, and I was still trying to keep track of this stupid car. Told them to get out, pushed them. Looked up in the rear-view mirror and the next thing I knew the colored prostitute had a knife, a little thing; she had it right up to my throat. That wiped away all thought of the stolen car at that time.

"She said, 'Drive forward, make a left-hand turn at the next street.' So I waited till the traffic cleared, drove forward, made a left-hand turn. She seemed to know where she was going, so she said, 'Keep going.' It was getting darker and darker. So she says, 'Turn right on the next street.' It was all black down there, pitch black.

"After I turned down that street, she seemed to get a little lax, you know, she figured me as just an easy Murphy and dropped the knife from my throat down here"—pointing at his chest—"and as soon as she lowered the knife I had my chance. I slammed on the brakes, grabbed her hand, threw the gearshift in 'park.' I was wrestling with her in the car. I grabbed her hand that had the knife in it, and she grabbed me by this hand, started tearing my skin apart. She pressed so hard on my skin that I had a bruise for three weeks after that. I was down, I went into the well of the car with her, trying to knock the knife out of her hand, while her white partner was laying over her beating on my head.

"I had a knife in my pocket, so I pulled that knife out. I've got hundreds of knives I took off people, I just had one of the knives. Usually the people that carry these knives will work them so you can open them with one hand, they're so proficient at it they can open it faster than you can open a switchblade." Senak reached in his desk drawer as he talked and pulled out a clasp knife and opened it with his left hand. "So I more or less did what I'm doing now," he said, "and opened it. When she saw that thing of mine she let loose of her knife, and I closed it. I think this is where she got cut, I can't see anywhere else.

"And then we went into the back seat, we were halfway into the back seat. I knocked her knife out of her hand, and it fell down in the back seat. I figured, 'Beautiful!' You know, I had it made now. They were unarmed, I could get them out of the car. So, pulled her up, and I started pushing her toward the door, the other broad gets over the seat, starts picking up her knife and opening it. So I have to let go of the colored girl and grab the other one to stop her from opening the stupid knife. I knocked her back. I came back, I was getting the colored girl on the top of my back, and the white girl got scared, after I pushed her against the door, so she opened the door as she was getting out and I pushed the colored girl. Well, when I pushed her out, her wig and her shoe came off.

"And so, being the obstinate police officer that I am, I had no intention of giving them back to her, you know, shaking hands and leaving the scene. So I just left, and I threw the shoe and the wig out somewhere between there and my house.

"What happened was that they were walking back to the corner, see, down this street. A scout car happened to pass. She was really angry about losing her wig; those wigs cost quite a bit of money. And her shoe. So what she did was go to the police officer and say that she was having an argument with a guy and he cut her, and she wants to file charges. They gave the wrong names, wrong addresses. They said they were cut, and the wouldn't take any medical aid; the officers offered to take them to the station. But the only thing they said that was true was my license number. The only reason they gave my license number was that they wanted to get me in trouble because I took their wig. Working with prostitutes that was the last thing I thought they were going to do; I didn't think she was going to be so mad about her wig. Otherwise I would have given it to her.

"As it happened, they had my license number so they came over here and picked me up."

2 | The Female Negro Refusing to Leave

Oct. 13, 1967. To: Chief of Detectives.
Subject: FELONIOUS ASSAULT *of* DIANE TAYLOR *F/N/22 of 2740 W. Chicago, Apt. 104 and* PAT STAFFORD *F/W/21 of 2211 W. Grd. Blvd., Apt. 208 Rio Gran Motel phone 894-6200 and the Arrest of* DAVID SENAK *W/25. Held for F.A.*

"1) At 2:30 a.m. received a call from Patr. John Ronan who stated that at 1:55 a.m. while in company with his partner Patr. Gerald Boucher on scout 6-5 they received a radio run to 8924 Dailey Court 'A cutting.'

"2) Upon arrival at the run location they talked to the complainants who stated that at 1:40 a.m. they had just left the New Yorker Bar, 8985 Grand River. A lone white male in a late model gray-blue Chrysler AF7245 pulled up and called them to the car. They entered and he drove to Hillsboro and Dailey. An argument ensued over the female Negro refusing to leave the car. At this time he struck Taylor on the right eye, then produced a knife and cut both complainants about the hands and wrists. They got out of the car and the man escaped driving north on Dailey towards Grd. River. Both complainants refused medical attention.

"3) Vehicle is registered to the arrested subject, who at the time is a suspended Detroit Police Officer from the 13th precinct.

"4) At 2:50 a.m. Sgts. Henry Gizicki and Al Trafton arrested the subject at his home.

"5) Scout 6-5 was sent to 2740 W. Chicago to contact the complainant and she is unknown at this address, and also to the Rio Gran Motel Apt. 208 where it was found that Stafford lives there, but is registered under the name of Donna Crawford."

3 | Disposition

"Those girls," Assistant Prosecutor Garber said to me, "want to stay as far as possible from Beaubien Street, so they didn't press charges, though both were rather badly cut."

"They finally kicked the case," David Senak said.

48

A Winter of Waiting

1 | Surpassing Rage

On November 3, Chaney Pollard was released from the Naval Hospital in Oakland and was placed on guard duty at the Treasure Island station; later he was returned to full duty, and in the winter he was granted leave to visit his family at home.

Tanner Pollard managed to stay fairly broke. During the year he had worked part-time as a waiter and busboy at the Black Knight Supper Club, where, with tips, he averaged ten to fifteen dollars a night; that job had gone with the riot, during which the club had been burned down. He worked awhile as parking attendant at the Sir Loin Inn, where, with tips, he could make four or five dollars an hour. He also worked in passing as a salesman for Snow Maid foods and for places called Jimmy's and King's Arms. He had paid $595 for his car, $150 for its engine; a total loss. He had had a collision in the rain one night on the Expressway and had paid a lady $50 to fix her car; he had had to pay $45 in court costs on that case. On October 26 he had to pay a $5 fine for jaywalking. In November he paid $35 for a bondsman so as not to be held in Wayne County Jail while waiting for trial for driving without a license; that case cost him $70, plus a fine of $150 for foolishly trying to break away, while being boarded on a bus for Dehoco, to telephone his employer, because he was fearful of losing his job. On his release from Dehoco he found he had indeed lost it. He mostly stayed home after that taking care of the baby, Palarena. His wife Lucy earned $5 or $10 a night several nights a week go-going.

In January the family visited Robert at Ionia, and they found him in a surpassing rage. The source of his fury was the history of police beatings of Pollards—his own beating, the time the police told his mother he had tried to commit suicide; Tanner's beating, the night of the fight at the Twenty Grand; Auburey's beating, before he was killed. Mrs. Pollard told me that Robert had said he was a member of the "in crowd" at Ionia, and that when he got out he wanted to collect in person some of the debts of pain he felt the Detroit Police Department owed the Pollard family. Mr. Pollard was so upset by Robert's tirade that he got two tickets driving home from the prison. In February, Robert was moved to Cassidy Lake Technical School, at Chelsea, Michigan, where he would be able both to learn a trade and have some psychiatric therapy.

Mrs. Pollard waited.

49

Three Men at Work

1 | Everything on the Line

"It's a good thing I have something to back up on," Robert Paille said to me, "because I had operated machinery before. Construction equipment and that. And after this happened there, I went to the union, and I told them my previous experience, in that if I didn't have the experience I wouldn't never have got on, and I got a job, you know, as an equipment operator. I been working on cranes. I have been working at River Rouge here, where this other crane operator just went in. Most of the time I've been oiling, but I have operated machinery and that. It's the only thing I hadn't handled before was cranes, so the best way to get in as an operator is to oil; you see, you learn all the functions of the machinery and all, because it's too much responsibility, you know, you can kill somebody very easy with something like that. Getting much better pay than as a policeman, but I do like police work better. When I was working this other job here, this one at River Rouge there, I wasn't taking home anything less than $172 a week; I was getting only about $112 a week take-home as a police officer. I'm right between jobs now. I just got laid off this last Thursday, I was working over at the GM Tech Center.

"I was on one of the jobs over there, and this one fellow didn't recognize me, a white man, and right away he comes out of nowhere, and he says to me, he says, 'Remember that Algiers Motel last summer?' I says, 'Yeah, what about it?' He says, 'You know those policemen involved in that?' I says, 'Yeah.' He says, 'You know what they should do with them?' 'What?' He says, 'Hang them.' I says, 'Why?' He says, 'You and I both know what happened over there. These white policemen broke into the building over there, saw these white girls with these colored guys there and killed them.' I says, I says, 'You're all wet in that.' I says, 'How do you—' He says, 'What do you mean?' I says, 'First of all, the police is conditioned to that type of environment there. He's in contact with these whores all the time. You know, in fact, these colored guys are in bad company, as far as I'm concerned. And why should he put his life, his job, everything he has on the line just for one little single incident? There's no sense in it.' And I says, 'Were you there?' He says, 'No.' So I says, 'Well, don't make any hasty decisions about that.'

2 | Instead of Being a Peace Officer

"I am working now as a plant guard, security guard," Ronald August told me in midwinter. "I'm on midnights, which there's no sidearm or—all you do is make your fire patrols, it's strictly, instead of being a peace officer or police officer with the idea of law enforcement, you're strictly just like a fire patrol.

"I sleep practically most of the day—*she* says. I don't feel like it; seems like I get in there four hours, but my wife says it's all day. But we have a babysitter come in till two, and that way I can catch some sleep. She likes her nursing, she says she'll never quit. I believe I'd like to see her keep it up, but not so much, not so many days in a week. She's working now about four days a week. I'd like her to go back to three days. I guess she makes about eighty dollars, seventy-five dollars a week, depending on how many hours she puts in. When she was working full-time, she was making more than I was, when she worked down at Children's.

"I'm doing better. Before, I took home $122, after deductions, and now I'm taking home about $140 after deductions, weekly. Average, so to speak. If I work a Sunday, I make time and a half, where down there, you don't. Down there, you'll spend as much as three to five dollars a week on cleaning your clothes and buying shoe polish or something, but where I'm at now, you got your shoe kit and you shine your shoes; your clothes are dirty, you take them off and throw them in the basket and you get a lockerful of clean ones at their expense. So I mean this counts up a lot."

3 | A Broken Ankle

"When it got cold," David Senak told me, "I had a job with a friend's father for a while, scraping, bumping and scraping of machines. Worst work I ever did in my life.

"Well, for about a good three months there I think there were maybe four places I went to—here, two friends' houses, and driving around. Didn't go to a show, didn't go anywhere but those four places. Didn't see too many people because I was embarrassed that I got the Police Department into trouble. My close friends, like the police officer that was my partner for a year and a half, and him and his wife, you know, know me, and I know that they have confidence in me, but the general public and the Police Department, to them I let the Police Department down because I got them in trouble. I had a bad feeling about seeing people. I didn't want people to say, 'Aw, we know that you're all right,' you know, 'we know that you did good, and they won't do anything to you because you're innocent.' A lot of people just say it to say something, to be able to say something, and I don't particularly like it. You'd rather have them not say anything than to just compromise me, so I stayed away from people for a while.

"Then I got another job with a buddy in the Air National Guard helping him with delivering refrigerators, and fell off the outside of a house, about thirty or forty feet. Broke my ankle.

"This was before Christmas. I was helping him move refrigerators. This time we were installing air conditioners in Lansing, and their basements in Lansing are the type that are three quarters above the level, they're on a sloping hill; I fell from the second floor to the sublevel.

"What happened was that I was boosting this air conditioner up the stairs; the stairs were wooden, they were outside—and came to the last step on the second floor and lifted it up, and there was no guard rail in back of me, and the weight of the air conditioner pushed me back, and for a second there I was standing in midair for a long enough time for me to look down, see the concrete below me, and know that if I hit it I'd be in trouble. So as I was falling down I was facing the building, and I turned my body around so that I hit the grass, or all of me hit the grass but my ankle. My ankle caught the end of the concrete steps. The air conditioner stayed up, luckily; had it gone down there might have been a little more trouble.

"As I was falling, as I looked down, the first thing I thought of was the Road Runner cartoons. Did you ever see those? We got to a bar and they have Road Runner cartoons on Saturday, so we watch them, and you know how the Road Runner always out-maneuvers the fox, and the fox goes over the cliff, and for a couple of seconds he stands up there and runs in midair? That's the first thing I thought of, and I looked down and saw the concrete, so I spun around.

"They took me to the hospital in Lansing, fixed my leg up. I was there for a couple of days. They put it in a cast. I got out of the cast January 11.

"After that a friend of mine introduced me to the superintendent of the riggers' union, and I put my application in there. Took the physical and tests, passed those, and went into their apprentice program, and now I'm just waiting; it's a slack time of year, so I'm waiting for a job to open. All I can do is just sit around the union hall waiting.

"At the beginning I wasn't too logical about the thing, I figured there was no way of them firing me for what I did, but now you see all this bad publicity and stuff, and the Police Department can fire you for just about anything. So I'm looking toward the future. I was planning to get my education in police administration, even before the riots, but now it would be sort of ridiculous for me to go into police administration at this moment, because if I'm fired from the Police Department, obviously I can't go into that field.

"So what I'm doing is going into education. Liberal-arts education major. And plan on, if they fire me from the Department, go into teaching. I figure it will take me four years, four and a half years to get my bachelor's degree starting now, and it will take me two years to get my journeyman's card, so at the end of two years I'm going to go into gunsmithing, and this is a two-year course, nights. Hopefully I'll have my bachelor's degree and my journeyman's card as a rigger and a gunsmithing guild—this is more or less a hobby that I can do at night—so I'll teach nine months out of the year, and summer is the most productive time for a rigger, so I can go into rigging during the summer months, and have a well-rounded life there. I can still have the satisfaction of teaching and not be cramped by teacher's pay, because I'll have—riggers make $5.50 and $6 an hour."

50

The Legal Maze

1 | Get the Cops

Upon becoming senior judge in Recorder's Court at the beginning of the year, Judge Schemanske wrote, "No other court system in the nation has matched the Recorder's Court continuing record of prompt disposition of criminal cases. The 'law's delay' is not a problem in Recorder's Court."

On December 1, sixty-three days after the pretrial examination in the conspiracy case, and one hundred twenty-eight days after the killings at the Algiers, this same judge finally delivered himself of his opinion on the conspiracy warrants.

"All of these [black] witnesses were emphatic about repeated beatings and deliberately gave non-responsive answers in order to bring in further charges of violence against the various defendants and August, in an evident attempt to 'get the cops.' This was no doubt because of their resentment of what had happened to their friends, or it may have been instigated by relatives, such as Cooper's father who interested himself in seeing that these residents were witnesses at the 'mock trial.' The shooting of Cooper, possibly before the arrival of any officers, if the blood was congealed, may also have been a factor in their thinking. He *was* shot.

"However, in spite of their eagerness their incredible testimony could not possibly convince a disinterested arbiter of facts of their good faith or their truthfulness. Their calculated perverication to the point of perjury was so blatant as to defeat its object.

"That there *was* violence is evident and unfortunate but scarcely surprising when the emergency is considered. That the police may have been over-zealous to the point of violence because of 'the worst incident of the rioting' is apparent. The testimony establishes that two men were killed and there is reference to a third not identified. Whether or not the person shot and still bleeding when the Troopers arrived was shot while resisting an officer is a question; the testimony could well support a verdict of justifiable homicide if that were the issue here, which it is *not* here. As to the man who lay dead in the first room entered by the Troopers, it is even probable that he was shot before any officers entered the building since his blood was already congealed and perhaps even coagulated. . . .

"After careful review of the notes taken during the trial and of the testimony from the transcript, the Court is unable to find any credible testimony supporting the theory of a conspiracy. . . ."

Prosecutor Cahalan promptly appealed.

2 | Padlock Withheld

On January 8, the padlocking case was heard in the State Circuit Court by Judge George E. Bowles. Judge Bowles did not order the premises shut down and the furniture removed, nor did he, for the time being, even issue an injunction against continuance of the alleged public nuisances in the Algiers. He asked both prosecution and defense to prepare further briefs, which were a long time coming.

3 | Pain and Mental Anguish

On January 9, 1968, Fred Temple's mother brought in United States District Court for the Eastern District of Michigan a civil suit against August, Paille, Dismukes, Thomas, Senak, Fonger, and four John Does, alleging that the defendants had conspired to deny her son his civil rights and "the equal protection of the laws because of his race or color," and "that as a direct and proximate result of the aforesaid acts of the defendants, the plaintiff's decedent, Fred Temple, prior to his death suffered great bodily harm, pain, injury, and mental anguish and was greatly humiliated."

4 | The Issue

On February 20, Recorder's Court Judge Gerald W. Groat, the man who later sent Lee Forsythe to prison for seven and a half to twenty years, denied the People's motion for reinstatement of the conspiracy warrants.

"It is evident," he wrote, "that the People were indeed hampered by the type of *res gestae* witnesses on whom they had to rely. The handicap of the Defense was the undisputed fact that some officers may have been overzealous to the point of violence, although these officers were not well identified. Furthermore, another handicap has been the tendency of public communications media to inject the idea of police brutality and to see racism where that is not the issue. It was not the issue here. . . .

"One element of the crime alleged, conspiracy, was sustained by no credible evidence direct or inferable. That was the element of concerted action. In the Court's opinion the action of the Examining Magistrate was correct.

"The motion to reinstate is denied."

5 | Back to the Confessions

On March 28, Judge Ford, acting on the Prosecutor's appeal of Judge DeMascio's decision to free Paille of the murder indictment, ordered Judge DeMascio to reopen the case and examine Lieutenant Hallmark, the man to whom August and Paille confessed. Such an examination would probably have the effect of causing Paille to be indicted for murder after all. Attorney Lippitt at once appealed on Paille's behalf, questioning the legality of one Recorder's Court judge's reviewing a decision of another Recorder's Court judge—a procedure to which Mr. Lippitt had naturally not objected when Groat had reviewed Schemanske and agreed with him.

6 | A Federal Case

On May 3, the United States Attorney for the Eastern District of Michigan, Lawrence Gubow, announced that a federal grand jury, held secretly in Detroit in the preceding days, had indicted August, Dismukes, Paille, and Senak on a charge of conspiring to deny civil rights to Auburey Pollard, Fred Temple, Lee Forsythe, Cleveland Reed, Roderick Davis, James Sortor, Robert Lee Greene, Julia Ann Hysell, Karen Malloy, and Michael Clark. That Carl Cooper was not among those alleged to have been deprived of their rights indicated that the grand jury had not unraveled the mystery of Cooper's death.

Apparently the United States Justice Department thought there was reasonable doubt of the position taken as to a conspiracy by Detroit's Judges Schemanske and Groat. At any rate, the sorry linkage of Michigan with Mississippi was at last complete, for this was precisely the federal charge brought in the deaths of Chaney, Goodman, and Schwerner in Philadelphia, Mississippi, in 1964.

7 | Distance

The first actual trial of a human being in this maze of legal actions was that of the only accused black man, Melvin Dismukes, charged with Felonious Assault. The trial, before Recorder's Court Judge Robert J. Colombo and an all-white jury, began on May 7.

The demeanor of the witnesses for the People in this trial was quite different from what it had been in the pretrial examinations. Juli Hysell appeared first. She had been living with her family back in Columbus, working; she took the stand in a tasteful yellow-orange suit and low-heeled shoes, with her hair pinned up, her complexion flawless, makeup at a minimum. She answered hard questions with poise—candidly admitting a short period of prostitution beginning after the incident and ending with her arrest in September, and giving the impression that all that was far behind her—but she did not add much to her previous testimony on the incident itself. Sortor casually admitted he had done some looting—said he'd been caught with looted clothes in the car of a friend but hadn't been prosecuted; this cast some backlight on his story to me of the cashmere coat that had been, he had told me, his all along. Michael Clark seemed transformed; he was cool and cooperative, hostile to no man. He confirmed Carl Cooper's having fired the starter pistol, and when Defense Attorney Smith noted that this was the first time he had admitted the presence of the pistol in the annex, Clark at once said that it was not the first time; he had given the same testimony to the federal grand jury. This was a clue to the change in the tenor of the People's testimony: The Justice Department had given the witnesses some sense of what was at stake in all these trials.

But the vile events were now at nearly ten months' distance; the passions of the accusers were not deeply engaged against this black man. The evidence against Melvin Dismukes began to seem somewhat thin, and Attorney Smith, eliciting from the witnesses a picture of confused mayhem in the annex, succeeded in making it appear that his client was a not-too-active participant in the affair.

The verdict, agreed upon by the jury in thirteen minutes: not guilty.

8 | New Hint

Unobtrusively, while these moves and countermoves were taking place in courtrooms in Detroit, presaging months and perhaps years of trials and appeals to come, workmen scaled the gaudy sign at 8301 Woodward, took down certain metal letters and put up others, and when they left, the neon palm tree drooped over a new name for the motel, a new hint of romance and sun-heat: THE DESERT INN. The Algiers Motel was no more.

51

Last Words

MRS. GILL: "It really turns a family around, it turns you around, it really does."

MAYOR CAVANAGH: "Victimized by rumors, the citizens of Detroit—both Negro and white—are arming themselves in unprecedented numbers. And in the suburbs surrounding Detroit gun sales have also soared. This arms race must be stopped. We must return to sanity."

JAMES SORTOR: "I want to buy me a house and a nice television and just set back and watch."

DAVID SENAK: "I'm just a patrolman. I don't know, I can have a view on police matters, I don't know if I have a view on race relations. I like to follow orders. If I have to risk my life for the Police Department and go into a place with criminals and arrest criminals, why that's one matter. I think if the prosecutors would go as wholeheartedly toward the general laws and prosecute as they're trying to prosecute

392

myself and my partners, I don't think they'd have any trouble at all. Because they're doing things that are unprecedented in our case simply because it's a civil-rights case."

MRS. TEMPLE: "They're trying to cover up a little too much down there. There's too much to try to hide. It's a little too much to sweep all this under the rug."

TANNER POLLARD: "I know some guys want to go down and burn down that police station."

PRESIDENT LYNDON B. JOHNSON: "We will not let violence or lawlessness take over our country. Crime that haunts the streets of our cities today is a major disgrace."

PRESIDENT JOHNSON'S COMMISSION ON CIVIL DISORDERS: "The policeman in the ghetto is a symbol not only of law, but of the entire system of law enforcement and criminal justice. As such, he becomes the tangible target for grievances against shortcomings throughout the system: Against assembly-line justice in teeming lower courts; against wide disparities in sentences; against antiquated correctional facilities; against the basic inequities imposed by the system on the poor—to whom, for example, the option of bail means only jail. The policeman in the ghetto is a symbol of increasingly bitter social debate over law enforcement."

RONALD AUGUST: "I wish I could be more verbal. One never knows what something like this is until he gets involved in it. I don't classify myself as a murderer, like a few people have. I feel like I'm free in the wind, like I feel like a balloon on a string. Who's going to pull the string for me?"

DONALD LOBSINGER, head of a white Detroit suburban organization called Breakthrough: "If another riot comes, we will protect our property. . . . We will protect our homes. . . .

And we will fire! . . . If any blood is shed, it is going to be their blood and not the blood of our families or of our children. . . . Thank God."

AUBUREY POLLARD, SR.: "I don't hate anyone."

ROBERT PAILLE: "I think the best is yet to come."

THE NEW DETROIT COMMITTEE, a coalition of business, education, labor, and civil-rights leaders, formed after the riot as "a great healing source" for the city: "The issue raised by the Algiers Motel case is fundamental, beyond any particular case or participant. It is no less than the credibility of our system of justice as embodied in our criminal courts. Any case which fails or appears to fail to achieve justice contributes to decline in respect for the rule of law and to the impulse to resort to alternative, extralegal, or illegal recourse. The New Detroit Committee believes full and fair examination of the Algiers Motel case is essential to arresting this trend in Detroit."

MRS. POLLARD: "I'm going to fight this case as long as I got breath in me."

52

What Is Wrong
With the Country?

1 | A Tremendous Emotional Effect

On June 5, 1968, there took place a jointure of American tragedies, vastly different in kind and force yet fitting together like
mortises and tenons cut to be glued.

In May, Prosecutor Weiswasser, foreseeing that Robert Paille
might, after all, be indicted for murder and urging that he and
Ronald August should be brought to the bar together, had moved
to have August's trial for the murder of Auburey Pollard post-
poned until autumn. But Attorney Lippitt had vigorously argued
on August's behalf against putting the trial off, and Recorder's
Court Judge Vincent Brennan, ruling for the defendant, had set
June 5 as the trial date.

Early on that very morning, in the kitchen of a hotel in Los
Angeles, Robert F. Kennedy was shot down—the only pursuer of
the Presidency in either party who had won a widespread affirma-
tive response from the black community and who might have

helped to narrow the racial gulf in our country. Heavy on that morning's air, as we pondered the streak in America that had already taken another Kennedy, was the memory of the recent assassination of Martin Luther King, Jr., shot by a racist.

At half past eleven in Detroit, when the Recorder's Court of Judge Robert J. Colombo was gaveled to order, Attorney Lippitt stood before the bench:

MR. LIPPITT: If the Court please, I have been in conference with Mr. Weiswasser since early this morning about the matter of this trial; this particular matter was to commence today, and I told him in my conference with him that I was extremely troubled over the fact of the assassination attempt in California last night, and it's my earnest belief, your Honor, that there is a very good possibility that this could have a tremendous emotional effect on any jury one way or the other that were drawn. For that reason I have asked Mr. Weiswasser if he would be kind enough to consent to an adjournment of this matter. . . .

THE COURT: Mr. Weiswasser?

MR. WEISWASSER: The People cannot have any objection under the circumstances as it now exists.

THE COURT: I concur in that, too, and let the record indicate that we've had a long and lengthy discussion on this matter in chambers. . . . It raises a very definite question of whether or not, on this day, certainly, any defendant in a jury trial could receive a fair and impartial trial, free from any inflammatory feelings that there are in not only this community but throughout the country. . . . Nobody could foresee yesterday the tragedy that occurred last night. The very reports on the radio and television are indicative of the feeling of the people in general about what has happened; very inflammatory statements about what is wrong with the country. I do think that this would have an adverse effect on this trial, possibly almost any trial which would be tried on this date. And I accept the stipulation of counsel for both the prosecution and the defense, recognizing that Mr. Lippitt is the moving party, and I do adjourn this matter until . . .

This trial and all the others growing like weeds around the late Algiers Motel would doubtless be reconvened and repostponed and heard and appealed and retried and finally brought to the weary end of the road of judgment, if not of justice. But surely there could not be, in any of these trials, another coming together like this one, demanding by its conjunctions answers to the "inflammatory" query: What is wrong?